Petticoats and Pinstripes

Petticoats and Pinstripes

Portraits of Women in Wall Street's History

Sheri J. Caplan

AN IMPRINT OF ABC-CLIO, LLC
Santa Barbara, California • Denver, Colorado • Oxford, England

Library of Congress Cataloging-in-Publication Data

Caplan, Sheri J.
    Petticoats and pinstripes: portraits of women in Wall Street's history / Sheri J. Caplan.
        pages cm.
    Includes bibliographical references and index.
    ISBN 978-1-4408-0265-2 (hbk. : alk. paper) — ISBN 978-1-4408-0266-9
(ebook)   1. Women capitalists and financiers—United States—Biography.
2. Securities industry—United States—History.   I. Title.
    HG2463.A2C3697   2013
    332.64'27309252—dc23   2013000213

ISBN: 978-1-4408-0265-2
EISBN: 978-1-4408-0266-9

17   16   15   14   13   1   2   3   4   5

This book is also available on the World Wide Web as an eBook.
Visit www.abc-clio.com for details.

Praeger
An Imprint of ABC-CLIO, LLC

ABC-CLIO, LLC
130 Cremona Drive, P.O. Box 1911
Santa Barbara, California 93116-1911

This book is printed on acid-free paper ∞

Manufactured in the United States of America

*In memory of my father, Harry B. Caplan,
and grandmother, Lillian Kaliner;*

in honor of my mother, Helen Kaliner Caplan;

and with love to Ken, Clarisa, and Samuel.

In a word, Wall Street is not the place for a lady to find fortune or character.

—Henry Clews, *Fifty Years in Wall Street*

Contents

Preface

More than six years ago, after reading several financial histories of the United States, I looked for information about the particular history of women on Wall Street. Although I found some books featuring contemporary women in finance, I was surprised not to find any text on the library shelves devoted to this subject, and only scant references to a few individuals in the general histories.

Could there really have been no female presence in this country's financial history that has spanned more than two centuries? Doubtful, I thought. I contemplated undertaking this project then, but was overwhelmed by its seemingly daunting nature. When I returned to it several years later, I was surprised that the subject appeared to be still unexamined.

If there truly is no cure for curiosity, then I was ailing. I began to cautiously investigate the topic, still not knowing exactly the nature of my approach or whether, indeed, sufficient material existed to make it promising for a book project. Armed with a few names of individuals, I began to search for more, and for both greater detail and broader scope. Scouring newspaper articles from various different eras to glean data and to absorb the cultural milieu, I began to discover a wider breadth of female accomplishments in the financial realm. Little by little, I began to cobble together a rudimentary outline by which to frame my research. As I learned more about these women, both individually and collectively, I became more convinced that their place in history merited study and that their stories should be told.

Undoubtedly, my personal interest in the topic draws from my own professional experience. I had worked for several prominent investment banks on Wall Street, first in the late 1980s as a financial analyst and later during the 1990s as internal legal counsel. Even in this relatively small expanse of time, the attitudinal changes I observed toward women were remarkable.

During my first stint, a time when now defunct retailer Alcott & Andrews catered to upscale yuppie women by selling tailored suits inlaid with large shoulder pads and festooned with even larger bows, one could occasionally find female strippers visiting firm trading floors for employee birthday celebrations or stumble on workstations adorned with pornographic images. While human resource departments may have cried that these acts violated corporate codes of conduct, these rules seemed to largely go unenforced.

Upon my return nearly a decade later, I could see that the environment had shifted. While every firm fosters its own unique culture, the changed atmosphere owed more to evolving times than institutional idiosyncrasies. The prevalence of corporate clone couture for women had waned and more individualized styles of dress were now in vogue. More importantly, gone were the celebratory strip-o-grams and openly lewd behavior and language. But a general informal bias against providing an equal career platform for women persisted. Amid an exclusionary social undercurrent that fostered all-male golf outings, poker games, and drinking sessions, few women reached the highest professional ranks. Those that did faced issues of balancing work and family that their male peers often did not confront to such a degree in an industry in which it was not atypical to log many frequent flier miles or to move abroad at a firm's behest. For those farther down the ladder, even scarcer options existed to address workplace flexibility.

Wall Street attracts ambitious individuals but can nevertheless wear out its suitors, both male and female, without remorse. The considerable stress and long hours make a combustible mix that readily chews up and spits out many talented individuals. At both its best and its worst, it is a dynamic place, one with few peers in terms of its power, energy, and hubris. Throughout its existence, colorful characters have made it their professional home. It is now time to tell the stories of some of these women and write them into this country's financial history.

Acknowledgments

Over the course of this project, I have been fortunate to have had the support and assistance of various individuals and institutions. My editor, Michael Millman, believed in this project from the outset and I thank him for his confidence in me and his expertise. Credit is also due to Ethan P. Bullard, Curator at the Maggie L. Walker National Historic Site; Nancy Egloff, Historian, at the Jamestown-Yorktown Foundation; Kristin Aguilera, Deputy Director, and Alexis M. Sandler, General Counsel, of the Museum of American Finance; Janet Linde, Archivist at the New York Stock Exchange; and Sue Cartnick and the rest of the helpful staff of the Farmington, Connecticut Library.

I have been particularly privileged to have been in touch with all of the contemporary women profiled in this book. I thank Muriel Siebert, Elaine Garzarelli, Abby Joseph Cohen, and Amy Domini for sharing their thoughts and time with me, as well as their respective assistants and colleagues, Yesenia Berdugo, Elisa Korman, Leslie Shribman, and Colleen Berlo. Likewise, I thank Mark Montgomery and Peggy Walsh Cornog, children of Julia Montgomery Walsh, for their enthusiastic cooperation. Roberta Karmel, the first female SEC commissioner, was also very accommodating and I am only sorry that her full story could not be included here due to my decision to restrict the focus on present-day women to those whose careers primarily emanated from within the financial industry.

Family and friends have been most important in providing encouragement from the outset. In particular, both my grandmother and my mother served as inspirations and role models of strong women. They taught me not only the importance of financial literacy and autonomy, but that the greatest dividends are not the pecuniary kind but the sort that come from investing in family and community. My parents, sister, and in-laws have urged me on, and I regret that my father could not see this book published. To Ken, Clarisa, Samuel, Socrates, and Palma, my deepest gratitude for your patience and understanding while laundry has gone unfolded, board games unfinished, and walks cut short.

Finally, special recognition is due my husband, Dr. Kenneth A. Merkatz. He has served from the beginning to end as unofficial co-author and editor and has spent countless hours polishing this manuscript. To him, this book owes any of its merits and none of its faults. He improved this book in many ways, just as he makes me a better person and the world a better place.

Thank you all.

Introduction

If asked to name the first woman on Wall Street, most people would likely identify Muriel Siebert, owner of her own firm who, in 1967, became the first woman to purchase a seat on the New York Stock Exchange. Scholars of presidential politics might conjure up nineteenth- century spiritualist Victoria Woodhull, who together with her sister opened the first female-run stock brokerage, and then leveraged the publicity and wealth gleaned from that venture to launch the first U.S. presidential bid by a woman. A few prescient aficionados of Wall Street lore might recall Hetty Green, popularly known during the Gilded Age as "the witch of Wall Street." Apart from those few individuals, most would draw blanks.

Meanwhile, if asked to name the first man on Wall Street, those same people would likely proffer a slew of names, such as J.P. Morgan, Jay Cooke, and those of other robber barons. Although not the very first financiers, these men were great movers and shakers to be sure. If one wanted to trace their forebears, one could read any of several good anthologies on the making of Wall Street. Even if one could not name names, the personalities envisioned would be male. If one wants to pursue research into the contributions to finance of Jewish or African Americans, published works also exist. Collectively, however, these works contain little, if any, mention of any female players in the "great game."[1]

In fact, women have helped shape the financial affairs of the United States. Dating from times even preceding the founding of the nation, they conducted commerce and traded securities. They did so even when the law denied them property rights or suffrage. Most women's histories, many of which ably survey female contributions to this country's development, rarely delve into the specialized area of finance. When they do, seldom do names other than those of Woodhull, Green, or Siebert appear. The fact that most people may not have heard of other female financiers or have been aware of their accomplishments, gained individually or *en masse*, reflects the scant attention paid to this subject by leading histories of Wall Street and of women alike.

Both the fields of financial history and of women's history are relatively nascent. That a richer inquiry into the intersection of women and finance has not yet been set forth is neither conspiracy nor negligence. Women simply did not number among the two dozen men who formalized their business dealings beneath a buttonwood tree in 1792, the date ascribed as the "official" beginnings of Wall Street. Nor do their names appear atop the most prominent financial firms centuries later. One must search beyond the most well-known figures and more broadly into history to explore the topic.

As far back as the seventeenth century, women participated in European capital markets. Indeed, they speculated alongside men in both the Dutch tulip frenzy of 1637 and the South Sea bubble nearly 100 years later. The rudimentary economic underpinnings of America also included the participation of both men and women. Despite a popular view that early colonial women played little part in household management other than cooking, cleaning, and caring for the children, this misconception obscures the fact that they often played an important role in determining and allocating the family budget. The early settlers primarily tilled the soil for their sustenance and visions of comfort. Once the financial evolution of the colonial economy began to take shape, early capital markets emulated the market structure of Europe, and American women also took part.

One of the great scholars of Wall Street, Charles R. Geisst, asserts that its history is comprised of four distinct periods. The first, from 1790 to the beginning of the Civil War, traces the rudimentary beginnings of trading and the first fortunes made. The second, from the Civil War to 1929, is epitomized by the rise of railroads and trusts and ushered in the robber baron era. The third, between 1929 and 1954, was marked by the rise of regulation as depression and war squeezed the country's financial system, and the fourth, beginning in the late 1950s, heralded the great bull market and the rise of the small investor.[2]

In each of these periods, women also played varying roles. But a history of women on Wall Street is better described by a different paradigm, one that accounts for their gender since that immutable characteristic so often barred them from full participation. Uniquely informed by a frequently discounted legal and political status, the female financial experience is reflective of societal norms to a far greater extent than its male counterpart. It is no fluke that while a few individual women became involved in finance early on, it is not until later, once the collective engagement of women made their presence felt, that personalities then emerged who made more headway and achieved greater respect.

This book will explore the roles of women in finance from colonial times to the present era by setting forth a brief overview of the status of American women and the development of Wall Street within a particular period, followed by essays that profile selected women. The individual stories reflect various catalysts that throughout the years intertwine and gradually produce conditions that broaden advancement: financial literacy, wartime urgency, personal necessity, technological change, legal and political empowerment, and cultural acceptance. Above all, the nation's intermittent wartime needs provided the greatest impetus to female financial engagement, whether due to the need for soliciting public funds or filling absentee male positions in households and workplaces. Female contributions supported and sustained the very foundation of this country's beginnings and ensuing turbulent times. Even so, the history of woman in finance is not a continuum of ever increasing advances on Wall Street or elsewhere. Women often appeared as a temporary palliative to the nation's ills only to be cast aside when conditions improved.

The years spanning the World Wars proved the most decisive in ushering women to Wall Street. Echoing the fund-raising efforts undertaken by women during the Revolution, the involvement of women in the Liberty Bond drives of World War I gave rise to the most enduring changes in the female financial experience by broadening their knowledge and influence. Between the conflicts, women continued to advance in commercial banking, and some of the first respected female leaders in finance emerged in this field. World War II cemented the changed landscape for women. While male labor shortages opened additional doors for women, some of which proved temporary, the conflict and concurrent technological advances transformed Wall Street into the global epicenter of money and power. An increased need for talent was created that offered more employment possibilities and career paths.

By no means did the post-World War II years usher in equal opportunities for women on Wall Street. Women now had greater access to professions in finance than ever before and certain individuals achieved great success. However, certain inequities, such as overt or subconscious discrimination, still restricted gains. Some may say that these same limiting conditions persist. Depending on one's point of view, change can be seen as coming quickly, in terms of the increasing numbers of women in financial careers or quite reluctantly, when viewed through the prism of discrimination lawsuits and the stalled entree of women into the top echelon of executive suites.

If one bemoans the paucity of equal opportunities afforded women and the lack of a genuine meritocracy, then it should be asked whether it makes sense to segment a history into groups based on immutable characteristics. Is it perpetuating separatism to reference gender rather than to assess significance with regard only to individual accomplishments? The answer is probably yes in a utopian world. In that setting, all would have welcoming opportunities for advancement. Unfortunately, reality renders that assumption moot.

Women have been restrained from financial endeavors over the years by formal laws, societal norms, varying degrees of discrimination, and even their own personal inhibitions. Yet, female accomplishments within the realm of finance have also gone unnoticed, an oversight that can unwittingly reinforce ill-conceived notions of women's "inherent" inability to competently compete in this sphere. When a group as a whole is largely shunted aside, then those within that class who strive to transcend those barriers, either consciously or in spite of such, bear dramatic testimony to the strength of individual and collective will. Theirs are the stories that will be told in these biographical essays.

By its very nature, this book is a highly subjective work, further marked by limitations imposed by resources and scope. Relying largely on available primary documents and supplementing those with secondary resources, the subjects chosen reflect my personal bias as to their significance and interest, as well as the accessibility of source material. Quite likely, I omitted more than a few individuals who merit discussion and would stand in good stead next to their peers.

Defining "Wall Street" also entails subjectivity, as the term no longer strictly defines an address in lower Manhattan but connotes the vast financial world interconnected through technology and unfettered by physical boundaries. This book covers developments at the national stock exchanges more thoroughly than those at the regional and futures exchanges, though the appendices note significant milestones achieved in these venues. Perhaps more guided by capriciousness than consistency, I have chosen to focus predominantly on those individuals engaged in investment services provided through banks and brokerages rather than those, for example, conducting financial affairs as corporate treasurers or insurance trust officers. Academic economists also escape this study, as do financial journalists and securities attorneys.

Time itself is a defining factor. I have chosen to begin this survey not only prior to the formal beginnings of Wall Street, but before the formal birth of the United States. The unique colonial experience created an early opportunity for some women to venture beyond the hearth and home. Native American society at the time also evidences women in leadership roles, but I did not feel sufficiently knowledgeable about this topic to discuss it in these pages. On the flip side, I have chosen to end this discussion at the conclusion of the twentieth century for two reasons. First, more attention to and media coverage of the careers of leading women financial professionals has arisen in recent years. Second, the passage of approximately two decades affords the luxury of stepping back to assess significant change over time and seems reasonable by which to mark an unofficial boundary between history and current affairs.

That many of these women represent "firsts" in their field begs the question of whether the earliest merits special recognition, whereas the second, third, or even thirtieth might display greater skill or other special attributes. Even the designation of "first" in certain instances may be scrutinized given the paucity of comprehensive authoritative accounts. No claim is made that these women necessarily represent the "best," but surely in this environment historically hostile to females, breaking barriers counts for something. Collective contributions of groups of women whose work proved significant are also included. Without the organized efforts of women, many individual advances would have been more difficult to attain.

Every project has its inherent limitations and these were mine. I do not purport to call this work the definitive reference and all encompassing tome on the subject. Not at all. In fact, I hope that these essays and related information contained in the appendices spur additional research and that more neglected legacies are celebrated. As the field of women's history continues to evolve, we will likely uncover more primary materials that may supplement or alter what we now know. That would be a rich and welcome issue to encounter.

Further contemplation of women's progress on Wall Street is enhanced by reading Melissa S. Fisher's ethnography, *Wall Street Women*, that follows the career paths of women who entered finance in the 1960s, as well as Susan Antilla's book, *Tales from the Boom-Boom Room: Women vs. Wall Street*, that chronicles the sexual harassment lawsuits brought against major brokerages in the 1990s, and Louise Marie Roth's study, *Selling Women Short: Gender and Money on Wall Street*, that examines gender inequality with particular focus on the prevalent bonus compensation structure. In addition, Anne B. Fisher's *Wall Street Women: Women in Power on Wall Street Today* and Sue Herera's *Women of the Street: Making It on Wall Street—The World's Toughest Business*, both published in the 1990s, feature profiles of selected women then working in the finance industry, including several of those appearing in these pages.

It is my belief that women are no more or less inherently suited to finance than are the members of any other demographic group. Women on Wall Street display similar traits found in their male peers: intellect, creativity, determination, ambition, and on occasion, greed. Whether we celebrate their success, lament their shortcomings, or simply marvel at their tenacity, do let us take note.

Abbreviations

ABA	American Bankers Association
ABW	Association of Bank Women
Amex	American Stock Exchange
CBOT	Chicago Board of Trade
CFTC	Commodity Futures Trading Commission
DJIA	Dow Jones Industrial Average
EEOC	Equal Employment Opportunity Commission
ERA	Equal Rights Amendment
FWA	Financial Women's Association
NASD	National Association of Securities Dealers, Inc.
NOW	National Organization for Women
NYSE	New York Stock Exchange
SEC	Securities and Exchange Commission
SIF	Social Investment Forum
SRI	socially responsible investing
Title VII	Title VII of the Civil Rights Act of 1964
WBC	Women's Bond Club
WLLC	Women's Liberty Loan Committee

PART I

Revolutionaries

Financial historians often begin telling Wall Street's past with reference to its early beginnings in the late eighteenth century. Not surprisingly, women remain largely absent from these accounts. The historians are not wrong; no evidence yet discovered documents female leadership in the structuring of formal capital markets in the United States.

But women did participate in the rudimentary American capitalist system that predated and gave rise to Wall Street. Just as existing historical precedents and contemporary colonial society shaped the mercantile and investment experience of its male citizens, so, too, did they influence that of its females. While women remained primarily ensconced in activities relating to the hearth and home, some engaged in a wider role in the colonial economy.

Long before the American foray into capital markets, the Europeans held sway in capital formation and investment creation. Exchanges have flourished since the *courtiers de change* managed agricultural debts in eleventh-century France. In the thirteenth century, commodities trading took place in Bruges, Ghent, and Amsterdam, while government securities trading occurred in Italy. The trading of corporate shares originated in Amsterdam at the dawn of the seventeenth century. The first large-scale corporate equity offering occurred with the issuance of shares of the Dutch East India Company on the Amsterdam Stock Exchange in 1602. Eighty years later, the British began trading equities on a London exchange.

Growing financial sophistication did not obviate accompanying greed. In fact, it may have encouraged it. Excessive speculation cropped up from time to time, as witnessed in such market frenzies as the Dutch tulip mania that hit its zenith in 1637 and the British South Sea bubble that burst in 1720. While it is not surprising that a yearning for high returns affected both sexes, it may be unexpected to learn that "even chimney sweeps and old-clothes women dabbled in tulips"[1] and "Persons of distinction, of both sexes, were deeply engaged"[2] in trading shares of the South Sea Company. Popular culture reflected the latter event through various forms, including the ballad *Stock Jobbing Ladies* that describes the widespread inclusion of women among the participants.[3]

Joint stock companies formed abroad financed the first American settlements. Although these ventures were predominantly comprised of men, a small number of upper-class women, most of whom had family ties to the male investors, numbered among the investors in the Virginia Company which was the British venture chartered in 1606 that financed Jamestown.[4] Early Americans of both genders, however, had neither time nor resources available to reflect upon the European investment experience. With no uniform colonial currency or established banks, the nascent economy depended upon business transactions carried out through differing means, whether involving the use of limited specie, private lending, bills of exchange, bank debt, or promissory notes. By the early eighteenth century, colonies began issuing public bills to finance military needs and commercial expansion, even while their citizens remained wary of paper money.

Land served as the primary vehicle for economic production and provoked aspirations for current and future prosperity. Within the agrarian economy, colonists concentrated on maintaining their farms, raising their families, and building communities. Women toiled alongside men in providing for the household and their chores encompassed "candle making, soap making, butter and cheese making, spinning, weaving, dyeing and of course all the knitting and sewing and dressmaking and tailoring and probably the shoe making and millinery. . . ."[5] They developed informal barter networks where they could exchange their homemade goods for other needed items, and some maintained customer accounts with certain merchants.

Yet even if a married woman's contributions were esteemed by her spouse, the law did not accord her the same respect: she held no legal rights to property. In accordance with the Anglo patriarchal tradition of coverture that dominated an otherwise fragmented colonial legal system and body of law, a woman relinquished any assets in her name to her husband, and remained unable to transact business independently. The husband exerted sole control over family finances. The majority of wives did not object. As much as the wife may have shared burdens and contributed to the household economy, money management remained apart from the typical woman's responsibilities.

Only *femmes soles,* women single either due to widowhood or spinsterhood, enjoyed the same legal rights as men regarding property ownership, business transactions, and access to the legal system. While society looked askance at spinsters, many of these unmarried women operated small businesses in traditionally feminine endeavors such as nursing, midwifery, sewing, and teaching. Widows found themselves running small enterprises left by their deceased husbands, including taverns, dry goods stores, and print shops. They often contended with residual debts and creditors who sought to profit from their lack of business familiarity.

Limited exceptions to the law existed. Married women in certain jurisdictions could manage their own businesses if their husbands so approved, as evidenced by written documents or tacit consent.[6] These rights were not clearly defined, but generally permitted such *femme sole* traders to execute contracts in their own name and gain access to the courts for redress of grievances. The common law also provided some assistance to women permanently abandoned or to those whose husbands left temporarily.

Once these early American businesswomen, so-called "she-merchants," hastened to understand accounting, a subject surprisingly sometimes found along with basic financial principles in school textbooks written for girls, they often conducted business at the cutting edge of colonial finance. Many extended credit to customers, themselves having received British financing, though often on stricter terms than that offered to men. Participating in a small yet developing market for private loans, women entered into promissory notes, made assignments of debtors' notes, and sometimes sought redress for unpaid debts through dunning.[7]

While many of their names and stories are forgotten, a few enterprising colonial women left enduring legacies. Among the most prominent, Margaret Brent's business activities in Maryland merit attention. Together with her sister, she obtained a 70-acre plot in Maryland, managed the property, and lent sums to newly arrived settlers. Unafraid to seek legal redress for unpaid obligations, she was a plaintiff in 134 suits between 1642 and 1650 and often served as her own counsel. Her chief notoriety, however, stems from her appointment by Maryland's governor as executor of his estate in 1647. Amid political unrest, she quelled a local uprising by selling estate assets to pay disgruntled soldiers. In January 1648, Brent appeared before the Maryland Assembly and requested two rights to vote, one for herself and the other in connection with her role as executor of the deceased governor's estate. Although it denied her motions, the Maryland Assembly nonetheless wrote the governor's brother, "We do Verily Believe . . . that [your estate] was better for the Collonys safety at that time in her hands than in any mans else . . . ."[8]

The rise of colonial mercantilism and consumerism provided other women with economic opportunities. Unmarried Elizabeth Poole purchased Massachusetts property in 1637 and became a major stockholder in a local ironworks.[9] Twenty-two-year-old Dutch immigrant Margaret Hardenbroeck arrived in New Amsterdam in 1659 and ultimately built a shipping and real estate empire. Widower Martha Turnstall Smith founded a whaling business with her inheritance in 1705. Wealthy New York City merchant Mary Alexander conducted a thriving dry goods trade between the 1720s and 1760s. Left in charge of her family's South Carolina plantation in her father's absence, teen Eliza Pinckney began cultivating and championing indigo, leading the crop to account for more than a third of the colonies' exports prior to the war.

Many other women, not all of whose names are well known, also worked outside the home. During the 60 years preceding the Revolution, no less than 90 women in Boston engaged in commerce.[10] Throughout the colonies, female businesses spanned the spectrum of colonial enterprise, including such endeavors as inn keeping, printing, importing, tailoring, baking and brewing, teaching, and health care.[11] Mary Peck Butterworth even found her calling in allegedly operating a large counterfeiting ring in New England between 1716 and 1723.

In addition to operating businesses, some women interacted with the early financial market. Professor Robert E. Wright has found that women actively bought and sold colonial government securities for their personal accounts and as family agent. Women even comprised the majority of investors when they accounted for nearly 61 percent of the subscribers to Pennsylvania's Indian Commissioner Loan of 1759–60. During the Revolution, women continued to number among investors in colonial government securities.[12]

Female empowerment during the colonial era reached its zenith in the struggle for independence from Britain. While combating their political enemy, women also struck blows at societal norms. Among them, Deborah Sampson and Margaret Corbin fought in the war, 16-year-old

Sybil Ludington staged a heroic nighttime ride to warn colonial forces of encroaching enemy troops, and Prudence Wright led women to defend their Massachusetts town.

Off the battlefield but no less revolutionary, in homes and in teashops, the war also gave rise to heightened female forays into finance and money management. Women, some prominent citizens and others not, helped to supply the economic lifeblood that fortified the military struggle. Through a wider lens, one can see that their engagement in the stirrings of a young nation foreshadow and underscore a recurring theme in the historical relationship of American women to finance: necessity may breed female financial empowerment, but it is not always warmly welcomed, easily endured, ultimately appreciated, or long lasting.

ONE

The Philadelphia Ladies

Who, amongst us, will not renounce with the highest pleasure, those vain ornaments, when she shall consider that the valiant defenders of America will be able to draw some advantage from the money . . . when they will have it in their power to say: This is the offering of the Ladies.[1]

—*The Sentiments of an American Woman*

In late August 1780, while the Revolutionary War waged on, a prominent Philadelphia wife wrote her husband, complaining of an army officer who "still continues his opinion that the money in my hands should be laid out in linen."[2] That odd comment becomes stranger still given that the officer in question was General George Washington. His bickering with a civilian woman over her spending preferences would seem an unproductive use of his time, were it not that this matter related to the considerable influence that she and her collaborators held in enabling the ultimate Continental Army victory over the British.

The particular woman who wrote that note was the very same one who two months earlier had used the anonymous pen name "An American Woman" to sign a broadside that rallied colonial women into action for war relief efforts. That Esther de Berdt Reed, a dynamic and effective leader, chose not to sign her name underscores her political savvy and implies the willing spirit of a broad coalition of women who contributed economically to the revolutionary cause.

While the identity of this particular American woman is known, the names of many others are not. Despite their relative obscurity in the pages of history books, their efforts not only significantly improved the condition of the troops, but empowered themselves as well. Political in nature, their activities broadened the participation and impact of women in the economic sphere, and demonstrated the importance of financial engagement.

For many of these women, the fight against the British provided a myriad of opportunities, welcomed or otherwise, in which they used their talents outside of their insular domestic sphere. As men joined the Continental Army, women stepped in to assume more of the unfulfilled chores and responsibilities left behind. In addition to maintaining the home front, some women even accompanied the troops, tending to their cooking, laundry, wounds, and even physical desires.

Other women answered the call to liberty from within their realm of relative comfort. Many female groups had joined in support of the cause prior to the outbreak of hostilities. In Lancaster, Pennsylvania, ladies who joined the Whig Association of the Unmarried Ladies of America pledged not to "give their hand in marriage to any gentleman until he had first proved himself a patriot."[3]

Beginning in 1766, women in various colonies began to organize, and these so-called Daughters of Liberty often held spinning bees by which they made their own yarn and linen for clothing in an effort to boycott British goods. Tea, that icon of colonial revolt symbolized by the Boston Tea Party, provided a rallying call for women. They readily embraced and organized tea boycotts. Just 10 months after the dumping in Boston Harbor, women in Edenton, North Carolina, organized one of the better known acts of female defiance. Forty-six-year-old Penelope Barker, one of North Carolina's wealthiest women, issued a public call for a boycott of tea and other banned British imports when she hosted a meeting of 51 women in October 1774 at the home of Elizabeth King. Barker urged the guests to endorse the statement, exhorting that "Maybe it has only been men who have protested the king up to now. That only means we women have taken too long to let our voices be heard. We are signing our names to a document, not hiding ourselves behind costumes like the men in Boston did at their tea party. The British will know who we are."[4]

Barker then sent the proclamation that was signed by the attendees to a London newspaper that published it, referring to the gathering disparagingly as the "Edenton Tea Party." One Englishman remarked drily in a letter to his brother living in North Carolina, "The only security on our side . . . is the probability that there are but few places in America which possess so much female artillery as Edenton."[5]

He was wrong. Female embracement of their boycott power continued to spill over their teacups and across the colonies. In spring 1775, women in Wilmington burned their tea. Even when it came to mourning, women showed their contempt for the British and upheld the Continental Congress ban on British imports by joining with the men in dressing in colorful garb instead of donning the customary imported black attire.[6]

By far the most significant women's wartime efforts were those undertaken by the Ladies Association of Philadelphia. Just a month after giving birth to her sixth child, 33-year-old British-born Reed swung into action. Spurred on by the fall of Charleston on May 12, 1780, and General George Washington's lament to her husband, Pennsylvania's governor, concerning the public's indifference to the inadequate military conditions, she wrote a broadside entitled *The Sentiments of an American Woman*, that called on women "to contribute as much as could depend on them, to the deliverance of their country."[7]

Published on June 10, 1780 by a local printer, Reed's manifesto spawned the establishment of the Philadelphia Ladies, the first widespread women's organization. The document itself represented a significant step toward the breach of conventional norms of female activity. Expressly eschewing "barren wishes," Reed urged supporters to be "really useful," similar to heroines of the past.[8] Her invocation of provocative women such as Joan of Arc and Catherine the Great dispelled any notions of the formation of another quaint spinning bee. She artfully chose language that simultaneously roused patriotic fervor while quelling potential disapproval by declaring that anyone critical of such female activity "cannot be a good citizen."[9] By staging boycotts and refraining from indulging in "vain ornaments," she called upon the implicit economic power of "the Women of America . . . to contribute as much as could depend on them, to the deliverance of their country."[10] Collectively, these donations would constitute "the offering of the Ladies."[11]

Three days following the publication of the *Sentiments*, three dozen women met to plan their activities, including Sarah Franklin Bache, the daughter of Benjamin Franklin. Instead of focusing solely on the Philadelphia environs, the group sought a nationwide initiative to engage all women in the fundraising effort. Their ambitious plans were detailed in an appendix to the *Sentiments*, entitled *Ideas, relative to the manner of forwarding the American Soldiers, the Presents of the American Women*, and published in the *Pennsylvania Gazette* on June 21, 1780.[12]

Within weeks, newspapers across the land reprinted the *Sentiments* and *Ideas*. Women in other states soon followed Philadelphia's lead, with groups in Maryland, New Jersey, and Virginia taking particularly active roles.[13] Organization was critical, a matter already recognized and addressed by the women in the *Ideas*. Each local group appointed a "Treasuress" to oversee

The SENTIMENTS of an
AMERICAN WOMAN.

ON the commencement of actual war, the Women of America manifested a firm resolution to contribute as much as could depend on them, to the deliverance of their country. Animated by the purest patriotism, they are sensible of sorrow at this day, in not offering more than barren wishes for the success of so glorious a Revolution. They aspire to ten-
der themselves more really useful; and this sentiment is universal from the north to the south
of the Thirteen United States. Our ambition is kindled by the fame of those heroines of antiquity, who have rendered their sex illustrious, and have proved to the universe, that, if
the weakness of our Constitution, if opinion and manners did not forbid us to march to glory by the same paths as the Men, we should at least equal, and sometimes surpass them in our
love for the public good. I glory in all that which my sex has done great and commendable.
I call to mind with enthusiasm and with admiration, all those acts of courage, of constancy and patriotism, which history has transmitted to us: The people favoured by Heaven,
preserved from destruction by the virtues, the zeal and the resolution of Deborah, of Judith,
of Esther! The fortitude of the mother of the Macchabees, in giving up her sons to die before her eyes: Rome saved from the fury of a victorious enemy by the efforts of Volumnia,
and other Roman Ladies: So many famous sieges where the Women have been seen forget-
ing the weakness of their sex, building new walls, digging trenches with their feeble hands;
furnishing arms to their defenders, they themselves darting the missile weapons on the enemy, resigning the ornaments of their apparel, and their fortune, to fill the public treasury;
and to hasten the deliverance of their country; burying themselves under its ruins; throwing
themselves into the flames rather than submit to the disgrace of humiliation before a proud
enemy.

Born for liberty, disdaining to bear the irons of a tyrannic Government, we associate ourselves to the grandeur of those Sovereigns, cherished and revered, who have held with so much
splendour the scepter of the greatest States, The Batildas, the Elizabeths, the Maries, the Ca-
tharines, who have extended the empire of liberty, and contented to reign by sweetness and
justice, have broken the chains of slavery, forged by tyrants in the times of ignorance and
barbarity. The Spanish Women, do they not make, at this moment, the most patriotic sacrifices,
to encrease the means of victory in the hands of their Sovereign. He is a friend to the French
Nation. They are our allies. We call to mind, doubly interested, that it was a French Maid
who kindled up amongst her fellow-citizens, the flame of patriotism buried under long mis-
fortunes: It was the Maid of Orleans who drove from the kingdom of France the ancestors
of those same British, whose odious yoke we have just shaken off; and whom it is necessary
that we drive from this Continent.

But I must limit myself to the recollection of this small number of achievements. Who
knows if persons disposed to censure, and sometimes too severely with regard to us, may not
disapprove our appearing acquainted even with the actions of which our sex boasts? We are
at least certain, that he cannot be a good citizen who will not applaud our efforts for the relief
of the armies which defend our lives, our possessions, our liberty? The situation of our soldiery
has been represented to me; the evils inseparable from war, and the firm and generous spirit
which has enabled them to support these. But it has been said, that they may apprehend, that,
in the course of a long war, the view of their distresses may be lost, and their services be forgotten. Forgotten! never; I can answer in the name of all my sex. Brave Americans, your
disinterestedness, your courage, and your constancy will always be dear to America, as long
as she shall preserve her virtue.

We know that at a distance from the theatre of war, if we enjoy any tranquility, it is the
fruit of your watchings, your labours, your dangers. If I live happy in the midst of my family;
if my husband cultivates his field, and reaps his harvest in peace; if, surrounded with my
children, I myself nourish the youngest, and press it to my bosom, without being affraid
of seeing myself separated from it, by a ferocious enemy; if the house in which we dwell; if
our barns, our orchards are safe at the present time from the hands of those incendiaries, it is
to you that we owe it. And shall we hesitate to evidence to you our gratitude? Shall we hesitate
to wear a cloathing more simple; hair dressed less elegant, while at the price of this small priva-
tion, we shall deserve your benedictions. Who, amongst us, will not renounce with the highest
pleasure, those vain ornaments, when she shall consider that the valiant defenders of America will be able to draw some advantage from the money which she may have laid out in these;
that they will be better defended from the rigours of the seasons, that after their painful toils,
they will receive some extraordinary and unexpected relief; that these presents will perhaps
be valued by them at a greater price, when they will have it in their power to say: *This is*
the offering of the Ladies. The time is arrived to display the same sentiments which animated
us at the beginning of the Revolution, when we renounced the use of teas, however agree-
able to our taste, rather than receive them from our persecutors; when we made it appear to
them that we placed former necessaries in the rank of superfluities, when our liberty was interested; when our republican and laborious hands spun the flax, prepared the linen intended
for the use of our soldiers; when exiles and fugitives we supported with courage all the evils
which are the concomitants of war. Let us not lose a moment; let us be engaged to offer the ho-
mage of our gratitude at the altar of military valour, and you, our brave deliverers, while mer-
cenary slaves combat to cause you to share with them, the irons with which they are loaded, receive with a free hand our offering, the purest which can be presented to your virtue,

By An AMERICAN WOMAN.

The Sentiments of an American Woman, Philadelphia, 1780. (Library of
Congress, Rare Book and Special Collections Division).

and record the collection of funds. These members answered to a "Treasuress-General," the wife of each state's governor, who then in turn forwarded funds to Martha Washington. Later, General Washington effectively solidified Philadelphia as the central point for organizational matters by requesting that all money originating from the various state groups be sent to Reed.

Ultimately, General Washington could use the funds at his discretion, provided that "The American Women desire only that it may not be considered as to be employed to procure to the army the objects of subsistence, arms or clothing, which are due them by the Continent."[14] According to the *Ideas*, the money represented "an extraordinary bounty intended to render the condition of the soldier more pleasant, and not to hold place of the things which they ought to receive from the Congress, or from the States."[15] Through this restriction, the women simultaneously stated their political views and asserted their influence over the use of any capital they might raise.[16] The power of the purse already figured largely in their minds, even before the purse was filled.

Few citizens were overlooked in their vigorous fundraising efforts. On city streets, pairs of women canvassed the Philadelphia neighborhoods. In homes, they undertook letter campaigns directed toward outlying areas. One participant wrote how "They have not omitted one house," as even the poorest contributed what they could.[17] Another wrote a friend on July 6, 1780, "It will suffice to inform you, that we have been witnesses of scenes of patriotism extremely affecting, and capable of inflaming the coldest minds with love of the public good; I have learned more than ever to respect my countrywomen, and there is no title in which I shall hereafter more glory than in that of an American woman."[18] Soliciting former Loyalists, the Philadelphia Ladies offered them absolution by "relinquishing former errors and of avowing a change of sentiments by their contributions to the general cause of liberty and their country."[19] Nor did the women hesitate to enlist their "feminine charms" in support of the cause.[20] According to loyalist Anna Rawle Clifford, they

> . . . paraded down the streets . . . some carrying ink stands; nor did they let the meanest ale house escape. The gentleman were also honoured with their visits. Bob Wharton declares he was never so teased in his life. They reminded him of the extreme rudeness of refusing anything to the fair sex; but he was inexorable and pleaded want of money, and the heavy taxes, so at length they left him, after threatening to hand his name down to posterity with infamy.[21]

Clifford cynically ascribed the fundraising success to the imposing social stature and relenting persistence of some participants: "But of all absurdities the Ladies going about for money exceeded everything. . . . [They were] so extremely importunate that people were obliged to give them something to get rid of them."[22] Perhaps so. In any case, the coffers flowed regardless of solicitation method or source of inspiration. Contributions ranged in form and in size. Some women sold their jewelry or other cherished items to raise cash; one even contributed a pair of leather breeches.[23] Sums collected included 8 Continental dollars given by "Widow Fox," 5 from "Polly Frits, a little girl," 8 gold dollars from "Miss Somebody," 150 Continental dollars from "Miss Nobody," and 10,000 Continental dollars from the wife of wealthy merchant Robert Morris.[24]

Capital flowed in from other states as well as from abroad. One Pennsylvania editor wrote that "the women of every part of the globe are under obligations to those of America, for having shown that females are capable of the highest political virtue."[25] General Marquis de La Fayette sent 100 guineas on behalf of his wife, writing in an accompanying letter dated July 25, 1780, "In Admiring the New Resolution in which the fair ones of Philadelphia have taken the Lead, I am induced to feel for those American ladies who Being out of the Continent cannot participate in this patriotic measure . . . May I most humbly present myself as her Ambassador to the Confederate ladies, and solicit in her Name that Mrs. President Be pleased to accept of her offering."[26] Even the wealthy women of Cuba pitched in, donating jewels and more than one million pounds sterling.[27]

By early July, the Ladies had collected over $300,000 Continental dollars, just a few hundred dollars shy of the figure raised by the city's male citizens in their drive to establish a bank, and equivalent to approximately $7,500 in specie. Reed wrote to General Washington, ". . . although it has answered our expectations, it does not equal our wishes, but I am persuaded the money will be received as a proof of our zeal for the great cause of America and our esteem and gratitude for those who so bravely defend it."[28]

After transferring the funds, Reed held fast to the stipulation that the sums raised not be used for necessities. General Washington had never been in favor of this condition. He wrote to Reed:

> If I am happy in having the concurrence of the Ladies, I would propose the purchasing of course Linnen, to be made into Shirts, with the whole amount of their subscription. A Shirt extraordinary to the Soldier will be of more service, and do more to preserve his health than any other thing that could be procured him; while it is not intended, nor shall exclude him, from the usual supply which he draws from the public. This appears to me, to be the best mode for its application, and provided it is approved of by the Ladies.[29]

During an exchange of letters over the next several weeks, Reed and General Washington considered the best use of the money. The two staged a cordial dance with respect to each other's sensibilities. She told him of her reasons opposing the use of funds for shirts, including the difficulties in obtaining linen and the news of imminent shipments of clothing from Pennsylvania and France. Instead, she preferred giving each soldier 2 dollars to use at their own discretion. She wrote "This method I hint only, but would not be any means wish to adopt that or any other without your full approbation."[30] He, in turn, reiterated his desire for shirts and wrote of his concerns that the soldiers would spend the money on alcohol. He had even suggested the money be deposited in the new bank, reasoning "I should imagine the ladies will have no objection to a union with the gentlemen."[31] His imagination proved incorrect. Reed did object, not wanting the Ladies' efforts to be diluted.

Finally, Reed acquiesced to General Washington's emphasis on the army's dire need for shirts. In an August 22, 1780, letter to her husband, she recounts "I received this morning a letter from the General, and he still continues his opinion that the money in my hands should be laid out in linen; he says no supplies he has at present, or has a prospect of, are any way adequate to the wants of the army."[32] Perhaps she detected a growing impatience reflected in General Washington's last note, ". . . his letter is, I think, a little formal, as if he was hurt by our asking his Opinion a second time, and our not following his Directions, after desiring to give them."[33] Her husband agreed, advising her that "The General is so decided that you have no Choice left so that the sooner you finish the Business the better. [I]t will be necessary for you to render a publick Account of your stewardship in this Business & tho you will receive no thanks if you do it well, you will bear much Blame should it be otherwise."[34]

Reed then organized the women to manufacture the shirts, no small task. Just two weeks after production of the shirts commenced, she died from dysentery in September 1780. An obituary praised her, while speculating whether her fate occurred because she had "imposed on herself too great a part of the task."[35] Bache assumed leadership and the manufacturing of over 2,000 shirts, each bearing the name of the woman who had sewn it. The entire order was delivered to General Washington before Christmas.

General Washington thanked the ladies, writing that the Army need not "fear its interests will be neglected, while espoused by advocates as powerful as they are amiable."[36] He acknowledged that they had "exceeded what could have been expected, and . . . entitles them to an equal place with any who have preceded them in the walk of female patriotism."[37]

The Ladies' demonstration of female patriotism embodied "the love of country . . . blended with those softer domestic virtues."[38] To General Washington, civic duty could not still wholly transcend gender boundaries and he wrapped the Ladies' contributions in pink, white, and blue.[39]

Some male praise came coupled with condescension.[40] John Adams offered sardonic tribute, writing to Benjamin Rush, "[that] The Ladies having undertaken to support American Independence, settles the point."[41] His wife saw things differently. Abigail Adams believed the Ladies' achievement proved that "virtue exists, and publick spirit lives—lives in the Bosoms of the Far Daughters of America" and that "America will not wear chains while her daughters are virtuous."[42] Other women echoed similar satisfaction, with one noting, "I am prouder than ever of my charming countrywomen."[43]

The Philadelphia Ladies surely deserve more acclaim than peremptory dismissal as "General Washington's Sewing Circle."[44] At their own initiative, they organized the first national women's political advocacy group, and did so through a highly effective structure. In carrying out their tasks, they astutely cloaked their unorthodox activities in acceptable patriotic rhetoric. Reed's leadership from the start demonstrated a concern over the current social norm. She realized that the group's activities and foray into a traditional male sphere might threaten male sensibilities, and so she creatively articulated their mission in an appealing way. Yet, for all her artful prose, she did not abstain from voicing her opinion in direct opposition to the most powerful male figure of the day.

Through their offerings of time, energy, talent, and trinkets, the Philadelphia Ladies mobilized support and raised capital on an unprecedented scale. In doing so, they created public roles for themselves in which they articulated their political views and demonstrated that women could effectively organize, raise, and account for money. More philanthropists than financiers, these ladies nonetheless revolutionized the idea of female participation in monetary matters. The women did not undertake the capital campaign to forge ahead in finance but to support the war of independence. Despite providing funds sorely needed for the country's liberty, they ultimately did not achieve long lasting freedom from convention for themselves. That had not been their goal. Still, they raised more than sorely needed dollars. They also amplified awareness of their abilities, and possibly of their own expectations, even if society showed a deaf ear toward considering any larger ramifications of their efforts.

The endeavors of the Philadelphia Ladies mark the first time a widespread group of women organized and involved themselves in money matters. Setting their spinning wheels aside, their collective patriotic ambitions raised essential moneys for the country's defense. This would not be the last instance of women breaching convention and stepping into financial affairs to help a nation in crisis. Nor would it be the last when they would be ushered aside and led back to the sewing room once normalcy returned.

TWO

She-Merchants and Deputy Husbands

With this money which I call mine I wish you to purchase the most advantageous Bills and keep them by themselves.[1]

—*Abigail Adams*

Amidst the tumult of both preparing to send son John Quincy Adams home from England to complete his education at Harvard and readying husband John for his imminent commission to the Court of Saint James, Abigail Adams made time to write her uncle in Massachusetts and instruct him to invest 50 pounds in bonds on her behalf.[2]

Far better known as a proponent for women's rights than she is for her financial savvy, Adams showed that the two actually go hand in hand. Like so many women of her era, she rose to the demands imposed by the Revolution by expanding her grasp of business and monetary matters.

Adams voiced her opposition to the restricted rights accorded women under existing laws when she admonished husband John in March 1776 that when drafting the nation's new laws he should ". . . remember the Ladies, and be more generous and favorable to them than your ancestors. Do not put such unlimited power into the hands of the Husbands. Remember all Men would be tyrants if they could. If particular care and attention is not paid to the Ladies we are determined to foment a Rebellion, and will not hold ourselves bound by any Laws in which we have no voice, or Representation."[3]

Mr. Adams dismissed this advice. He replied, "As to your extraordinary Code of Laws, I cannot but laugh."[4] Given the strength of her convictions, it is quite likely that she was not at all joking.[5] Adams reproached him, writing, "I can not say that I think you are very generous to the Ladies, for whilst you are proclaiming peace and good will to Men, Emancipating all Nations, you insist upon retaining an absolute power over Wives. But you must remember that Arbitrary power is like most other things which are very hard, very liable to be broken. . . ."[6]

Adams knew firsthand that female subjugation weakened during times of crisis. For most of 1774 through 1784, while her spouse was away serving the country, she had continually undertaken greater responsibilities managing the personal and business affairs of her family.[7] In fact, Adams had become a "deputy husband,"[8] entrusted by her spouse with management of the family farm during his absence. Writing Mr. Adams in September 1776, she boasted, "We are no ways dispiritted here. We possess a Spirit that will not be conquerd. If our Men are all drawn of and we should be attacked, you would find a Race of Amazons in America."[9] Her tone belied concerns that surfaced from time to time when she worried that she might be "uneaquil to the cares which fall upon me."[10] Despite anxieties, she remained resolute in her purpose.

Adams was not the only Founding Father's spouse thrust into such a role. Among them, Benjamin Franklin's wife Deborah assumed many of her husband's responsibilities. Throughout most of her married life, she helped run the print shop and postal service while managing the family's finances.[11] In 1765, she even branched into real estate speculation when she purchased land in Nova Scotia while Mr. Franklin was abroad. She wrote, "So you see I am a real Land Jobber. . . . I hope I have done as you would have me or as you would if you had been at home yourself."[12] Likewise, Sarah Livingston Jay, wife of colonial statesman John Jay, took on the role of household financial manager during the absences of her husband.[13]

These prominent wives numbered among the many women who were affected by wartime needs causing them to broaden their scope of responsibilities. As military conflict always does, the Revolution wreaked havoc beyond the frontlines. Women of all socio-economic strata were forced to expand their domestic duties. Namely, this meant dealing with family finances, over which few married females had exercised authority prior to the conflict. Most wives previously had remained uninformed about fundamental transactions, and contentedly so.[14] Now, with their husbands gone to wage war, wives were left to stage their own battles in order to provide for their children and to hold on to their family homes, farms, and businesses. As William Hooper, a signer of the Declaration of Independence from North Carolina put it, "A Soldier made is a farmer lost."[15]

Countless husbands never returned from battle. Approximately 10 percent of white American women at the second half of the eighteenth century were widows. Many of these women became executors of their husbands' estates, and often found their financial inexperience compounded with the burden of debts of which they had no prior knowledge. But necessity breeds opportunity and innovation, and they soon joined the ranks of their single sisters who had already assumed financial control of their lives. Many of these women had taken up commerce as "she-merchants," and their immersion in business affairs led to familiarity with fiscal management and financial instruments.[16]

"Temporary widows" were no different in terms of having to quickly come up to speed on pecuniary matters. What differs is that for them, their spouses remained in the picture to some degree. Professor Mary Beth Norton points out a typical pattern affecting these women. At first, a husband might tell his wife to seek guidance from male friends and relatives. As his absence lingered and she became more immersed in his affairs, her confidence grew. So did his. Directives became less specific and more vague, such as these instructions: "I Can't give any Other Directions About Home more than what I have Done but must Leave all to your good Management" or "Apply [the money] to such as you think proper."[17]

Sally Logan Fisher's story illustrates this paradigm. After her husband was arrested and exiled to Virginia in September 1777, she confided in her diary nine days later, "I feel forlorn & desolate, & the World appears like a dreary Desart, almost without any visible protecting Hand to guard us from the ravenous Wolves & Lions that prowl about for prey."[18] Who could fault her misgivings, as her plight appeared all the more dire given that she was eight months pregnant. Her despair continued the next month: "[N]o future Days however calm & tranquil they may prove, can ever make me forget my misery at this time."[19]

But by November, practical exigencies demanded her attention, such that "I have to think & provide everything for my Family, at a time when it is so difficult to provide anything, at almost any price, & cares of many kinds to engage my attention."[20] Six days following the birth of her daughter, she exalted "[I have] been enabled to bear up thro' every triall & difficulty far beyond what I could have expected."[21] She continued to miss her husband, but no longer feared any inability to manage during his incarceration. Once he returned, her diary reveals that she and her husband discussed financial concerns from time to time, a topic not broached prior to his absence.[22]

Overall, increased responsibilities over managing family finances let to a growing self-confidence of wives and the attendant respect of their husbands. Some women expressed their desire for even more autonomy by no longer desiring or acquiescing to the former status quo.[23] Lucy Flucker Knox, for example, directly challenged her husband when she disapproved of his sale price for horses as she considered herself "quite a woman of business."[24] In August 1777, she wrote to him, "I hope you will not consider yourself as commander in chief of your own house—but be convinced . . . that there is such a thing as equal command."[25]

Adams knew a thing or two about equal command. For years, she counseled her husband on familial and political concerns as he was drawn further into public life. Mr. Adams held her in high esteem, proclaiming "I think you shine as a Stateswoman, of late as well as a Farmeress."[26] However, Adams recognized the subservient role of a wife in American society, evident even within her own family.[27] Mr. Adams, himself schooled in the classics, found it "scarcely reputable" for his daughter to be similarly educated.[28] Adams herself embodied a certain ambivalence to challenging the status quo and acknowledged a feminine tendency toward dependency.[29] An advocate of female property rights and educational opportunities, she nonetheless wrote, "I believe nature has assigned each sex its particular duties and sphere of action, and to act well your part, 'there all the honor lies.'"[30]

Yet Adams encroached upon traditional boundaries in her relationship with her husband. While she may have professed certain respect for a gender-based division of labor, she did not always follow her husband's directives in that most masculine zone of authority—fiscal matters. When Mr. Adams did not acquiesce to her suggestion to purchase a carriage, she went ahead and did so by using the profits she had earned from the import trade she carried on during the war.[31]

She again sidestepped her husband's authority in 1782. Despite her acknowledgement that "I think you would not advise me to do it," she wrote her husband in April of her pursuit of Vermont real estate.[32] Three months later, without consent from Mr. Adams, she purchased 1,650 acres, subdivided into parcels for her husband and each of her children.[33] Mr. Adams did not approve. "Make the best of all—but don't meddle any more with Vermont," he replied.[34]

Most interesting of all was her indulgence in the cutting edge of finance, securities speculation. Scholar Woody Holton has researched

A. Adams, from an original painting by Gilbert Stuart. (Library of Congress, Prints and Photographs Division)

Adams's investing activities in detail and points out that her speculation was the very object of her husband's contempt. Adams first dabbled in bonds in 1777. Wary of inflation, she wrote to her husband that June, "A Dollor now is not eaquel to what one Quarter was two years ago, and their is no sort of property which is not held in higher estimation than money."[35] She sought his approbation, concerned that "If I do not explain the matter I fear you will suspect me of being concerned with the Hampshire money makers."[36] This initial 100-pound investment in a federal Loan Office certificate proved enormously rewarding. Not long after her purchase, sagging prices in paper money led Congress to pay interest with bills of exchange drawn on the government of France that were valued on par with precious metals. Although predicated initially as more an inflationary hedge than as a speculation, Adams earned a 24 percent annual return for four-and-a-half years.[37]

Adam's success emboldened her.[38] When Mr. Adams requested in the autumn of 1783 that she investigate the selling prices of neighboring farms, she agreed, but replied:

> There is a method of laying out money to more advantage than by the purchase of land's, which a Friend of mine advised me to, for it is now become a regular merchandize. Dr. T[uft]s has sold a Farm with a design of vesting it in this manner, viz in State Notes. Provision is now made for the anual payment of Interest, and the Notes have all been consolidated. Foreigners and monied Men have, and are purchaseing them at 7 shillings upon the pound, 6 and 8 pence they have been sold at. I have mentiond to you that I have a hundred pounds sterling in the hands of a Friend, I was thinking of adding the 50 you sent me, and purchaseing 600 pounds L M [the official Massachusetts currency] in state Notes provided I can get them at 7 shillings or 6 and 8 pence. This would yeald me an anual interest of 36 pounds subject to no taxes: and be some thing to leave in the hand of a Friend for the support of our Sons.[39]

The following year, he wished to purchase a neighboring farm, but she intervened by asking her uncle, Cotton Tufts, who served as the family's agent now that both were abroad, to refrain from doing so, ". . . Veseys place is poverty, and I think we have enough of that already."[40] Seven months later, Mr. Adams wrote to Tufts, "Shewing what I had written to Madam she has made me sick of purchasing Veseys Place. Instead of that therefore you may draw upon me, for two hundred Pounds at as good an Exchange as you can obtain and lay it out in such Notes as you judge most for my Interest. . . ."[41]

Bonds appealed to Adams both for their lucrative potential and ease of ownership, as they were "less troublesome to take charge of then Land."[42] She found her differences with her husband's perspective on securities frustrating, confiding later in a letter to her sister that "in these Ideas I have always been so unfortunate as to differ from my partner."[43] In that same letter, Holton notes that she complained that had she and her uncle "been left to the sole management of our affairs, they would have been upon a more profitable footing. In the first place I never desired so much Land unless we could have lived upon it. The Money paid for useless land I would have purchased publick Securities with."[44] While Mr. Adams distrusted speculation on ideological grounds, she viewed bonds as a "much more productive investment" even while sharing some distaste for the label of speculator and criticizing her son-in-law's investing activities.[45]

That difference with her husband did not stop Adams from continuing to purchase bonds. Whether as a means to ultimately improve the family's personal wealth or to provide for charity, she embraced securities investment. Eight years after her first foray into bonds, while abroad in Europe, she directed her uncle in May 1785 to invest on her own behalf. Her decision was particularly remarkable given the degree to which she knew her husband opposed such activity and in the circumspect manner in which she went about it.[46]

As a married woman, Adams's property was subject to her husband's discretion in accordance with the common law of coverture. Adams not only found this notion appalling, she essentially subverted it for years.[47] Massachusetts did not recognize the status of *femme sole* trader at the time, but she numbered among other women who did not always heed the coverture restrictions.[48] In that same April 1782 letter in which she told her husband about the Vermont property, she wrote that "About six months ago I placed a hundred pounds Sterling in the hands of a Friend. . . ."[49] This sum may have provided the source of funds by which she attempted to purchase a farm the following year as an inducement for Mr. Adams to return home.[50] She offered:

> If my dear Friend you will promise to come home, take the Farm into your own hands and improve it, let me turn dairy woman, and assist you in getting our living this way; instead of running away to foreign courts and leaving me half my Life to mourn in widowhood, then I will run you in debt for this Farm; I have a hundred pounds sterling which I could command upon such an occasion, but which upon all others is a deposit I do not chuse to touch.[51]

Adams clearly understood the importance of financial independence and the subtleties of economic power. By 1785, she had become well versed in financial analysis. When Mr. Adams had agreed that she ask her uncle to invest a certain sum, she could not refrain from adding her own advice,

> With regard to our family affairs Mr. Adams has written you upon them, he has however directed me to enlarge to you upon the subject of Bills, and to

request you to invest 3 or four hundred pounds sterling in them, and in that kind which you shall judge most for his advantage. I should think it might not be amiss to invest one hundred pounds in the Army certificates which tho not so valuable at present, will become so in time.[52]

In a closely following letter, she again segregated some money as her own when she sent her son home with 50 pounds and the directive to her uncle that he purchase additional bonds for her.[53]

Adams's investments, not all of which were profitable, did more than enrich the family's wealth. She augmented her own influence and authority over family affairs through her growing financial acumen. The letter of the law limited her rights and the dynamics of her marriage informed her ways, but she understood that the power of the purse nonetheless gave her sway to accomplish her intended goals. Nor did she let the law stand in her way. For years she used her uncle to both conduct and conceal her hand in personal investments.[54]

Alongside her undertakings as both a she-merchant and deputy husband, Adams had grafted the role of investor and speculator. She may have been particularly prescient about the growth potential of investments, but she was not the only such woman. Through the trove of correspondence she produced, however, her activities are more easily known. Likewise, letters sent between Sarah Livingston Jay and her husband also evidence the financial actions Jay undertook on their behalf during his absences. Between 1794 and 1795, those activities included collecting sums due on debt instruments as well as investing in bank shares.[55] More reticent than Adams to embrace these responsibilities, Jay preferred to receive counsel from her husband or nephew, but nonetheless stepped up to the task. With respect to certain bank shares she purchased, she wrote:

> Had I not been diffident of acting without yr. advice I shd. already have cleard 12 pr. Cent. But I shd. not now have done what you when here, disapproved, had I not been of opinion that were you here at present, you would have altered your sentiments with the times. I shall however respect yr. sentiments more than my own, & will therefore probably sell out again in a month's time, perhaps les. . . . I sincerely hope that what I've done will receive yr. approbation, as my Conduct has not been the effect of a Gambling disposition, but the result of mature reflection aided by the Advice of those in whose judgment I had reason to confide.[56]

In that same letter, after recounting various social matters, she returns to the subject in a postscript, noting, "I fear you'll think my mind wholly occupied with pecuniary matters. The fact is, that your being removed at such a distance from your family & affairs, I think it my duty to turn my attention more to those subjects than would otherwise be either proper or necessary."[57]

Mrs. John Jay, from an engraving of a painting by Robert Edge Pine. (National Archives and Records Administration)

Whether or not proper or necessary, scores of women purchased securities during this era.[58] In the 1790s, women comprised approximately 10 percent of federal bondholders in South Carolina, 13 percent in New York, and 60 percent in New Hampshire.[59] While these women, single, married, and widowed, may have had more readily available financial resources than others, the war transformed the daily lives and experiences of many more. Women of all economic strata and domestic status had endured hardship and recognized that understanding fiscal affairs was central to survival.

The experience of mid- to late-eighteenth-century American women, that of being called upon to expand their economic and financial activity in times of crisis, whether public or private, is an example of a familiar pattern to be seen throughout ensuing decades. The cataclysmic event of the Revolution exacerbated and magnified this archetype. Still, at the root of all the upheaval, lay a personal story for each woman. When calmer times returned, their heightened sense of empowerment led some women to increased independence and a truer partnership with their spouses. For others, even if their more assertive roles did not endure, new perspectives informed their choices. The participation of women in varied facets of the early economy had certainly broadened their sphere of comfort in spite of their legal rights remaining at bay. Given their new frame of reference and now more proactive inclination, financial affairs might no longer remain solely the masculine domain—even if society was not disposed to readily grant them such access.

PART II

Pioneers

Following the Revolution, the role of women in the domestic sphere received greater focus and heightened import. The infant nation had attained independence, and its fathers looked to women to further nurture its growth through the home and family. During these nation-building years, the notion of "Republican Motherhood"[1] took root. Political theorists believed that the country's future depended on the public and private morality of its citizens, and that mothers bore primary responsibility for fostering development of patriotic values. Praised as the sources of virtue in society, female domestic duties thereby became associated with significance for the national agenda.

Otherwise, little had changed legally to alter the balance of power between the sexes. No new rights were articulated for women amid the conservative underpinning of early American jurisprudence. Instead, women saw some privileges actually eviscerate, as when the New Jersey legislature in 1807 repealed a law in place for 24 years that had given female property owners the right to vote. Not until the mid-nineteenth century did states again begin to pass married women's property rights acts.

The glorified perception of women reflected more than just empty rhetoric, however. Though lacking both suffrage and legal safeguards relevant to their own economic independence, the female domestic realm, now infused with notions of patriotism, had attained new political meaning. Women became exalted as providers of the "civic backbone."[2] In spite of even the most liberal societal perceptions that might equate women and men in terms of their intellectual levels and their political and cultural contributions, women nevertheless remained apart, relegated to their domains of wives and mothers. The growth of manufacturing and male employment outside the home during the half-century following the Revolution only underscored this acceptance of a separation of spheres. Unlike the more home-based economy of the colonial era, men and women's work now became more strikingly segregated. With their domestic responsibilities deemed critical to the destiny of the country, most women did not consider questioning traditional roles.

Few voices called for greater egalitarianism. One who did, writer Judith Sargent Murray, advocated for educational reform in her 1790 essay "On the Equality of the Sexes." Within several years, Murray refined her views to seek even more radical changes. She admonished that daughters should be taught not to seek marriage as their goal but to be "qualified to administer by their own efforts to their own wants."[3] Even as educational opportunities began to expand with more public elementary and private academies offering educational opportunities for females in the final decades of the eighteenth century, the few women who did seek outside employment found few career paths open to them other than teaching prior to marriage.

While women were entrenched with their domestic duties, the country's economy began to evolve from its agrarian foundation. A merchant class began to take root despite parochial jealousies between the states and the absence of a formal stock exchange. Even a federal Treasury did not exist until 1789. One year later, the issuance by the federal government of $80 million of bonds to raise funds to satisfy the country's immense war debt effectively gave birth to the early American capital markets. These government bonds, together with corporate securities, were sold primarily on the streets of New York. Transactions, modeled roughly on European practices, occurred between auctioneers and dealers at several local sites. Due to rampant scandals and price rigging, two dozen men comprising 21 individual brokers and three firms met beneath a buttonwood tree on Wall Street in May 1792. There, they signed the Buttonwood Agreement that established a new market for a more orderly system of buying and selling of securities.

Other institutional developments significant to the nation's economic progress took place during these first several decades of the nineteenth century. Not all went according to plan. The Bank of the United States had been founded in 1791, only to be dissolved 20 years later amidst ideological conflict over the limits of federal power. Congress established the Second Bank of the United States in 1816. The Supreme Court's landmark ruling in *McCullough v. Maryland* in 1819 legitimized the bank, but it too met dissolution when President Andrew Jackson vetoed the renewal of its charter in 1832. This action spawned a banking collapse. Without a permanent and dependable regulated banking structure, the nation's economy became prone to frequent gyrations. The capital markets grew, however, as underwriting and trading strategies developed. In 1817, the signatories to the Buttonwood Agreement established the New York Stock and Exchange Board, the nation's first organized stock exchange. Even so, a gaming atmosphere persisted for decades as manipulative selling techniques and widespread securities speculation proliferated.

As Wall Street strained for solid footing, other events transpired that soon transformed the financial industry. Corporations arose to furnish roadways, canals, and railroads for the growing country. Their capital-intensive projects required financing. Issuance of railroad securities alone encompassed one-third of the market by the start of the Civil War. The advances in transportation provided routes to lowered manufacturing costs and made further industrialization more feasible. As the demand for financing increased, the communications revolution heralded by the invention of the telegraph in 1844 and its widespread use in the ensuing years allowed for quicker price dissemination. New York City, the country's largest securities market, quickly seized the power of the telegraph to cement its position as the chief financial hub.

While the Civil War wreaked havoc on the battlefields, it lavished riches on Wall Street, propelling the country's securities market to the second largest in the world. The war itself required prodigious federal financing, and demand for supplies heated up the manufacturing and transportation sectors. A soaring national debt prompted the government to market war bonds to the public. This innovation proved a success and attracted new investors in droves.

The notion of "Wall Street" as symbolic of the nation's securities market became entrenched as the economy continued to grow following the war.[4] The New York Stock Exchange (NYSE), having changed its name from The New York Stock & Exchange Board two years earlier, moved in 1865 to its permanent location in lower Manhattan. This move further cemented the city's association with the capital markets. Pretentious displays of wealth became *de rigueur* for the privileged and prompted the era's dubbing as the Gilded Age. The business and social affairs of industrialists and financiers such as Andrew Carnegie, John D. Rockefeller, Jay Gould, Cornelius Vanderbilt, and J. P. Morgan populated the press and titillated the public. That these individuals were among those alluded to as "robber barons" attests to their dominant power in an investment banking industry largely unregulated.

Industrialism powered the capital markets and communications advances including the introduction of the Atlantic cable in 1866 and the stock ticker one year later further accelerated growth. As stocks became more popular than bonds, the number of shares traded on the NYSE doubled in the decade beginning in 1875. The meteoric rise in trading was punctuated by the first million share day recorded in 1886. The *Wall Street Journal* was born as the nation's first newspaper dedicated to financial reporting in 1889. Seven years later, the newspaper began publishing the Dow Jones Industrial Average (DJIA). By the turn of the century, the term "Wall Street" connoted American economic strength and the great power of its financial and industrial complex.[5] The stock market made for front page news and attracted both male and female investors.

For all its luxuries, the Gilded Age was not without its blights. Industrialization led to increased urbanization and immigration, and polarization between the rich and the rest of society became greater. Progressivism sought to address some of these disparities through an amalgam of citizens and politicians who advocated a wide range of reforms intended to improve social, political, and economic matters.

Women comprised a large percentage of advocates of these reform movements. Some continued their decades-long crusades for abolition and others supported the early women's rights movement ushered in by the Seneca Falls Convention in 1848. By this time, women had become a more significant component of the workplace. Increasing numbers of middle- and upper-class women obtained degrees from women's colleges, and to a lesser degree, coeducational institutions.

Industrialization brought more job opportunities for women, but also continued segregation within the labor pool. Following the Civil War, single women numbered among the rising urban population and found employment mainly as teachers, nurses, and office workers.[6] The United States Census of 1870, the first to document women working outside the home, reveals that women accounted for 15 percent of the 12.5 million workforce. While two-thirds of teachers were women, they could also be found working in factories, mines, the medical and legal professions, and a surprising few even toiled as ship riggers, stock-herders, and trappers.[7]

Financial affairs also beckoned in several ways to women. Most auspicious was the addition of female employees to the staff of the U.S. Treasury beginning in 1862. When Treasurer Francis Spinner hired the first woman, Jennie Douglas, to cut and trim paper for currency, he believed that "the first day Miss Douglas spent on the job settled the matter in her behalf and in woman's favor."[8] Despite external criticism from those who doubted female abilities to withstand workplace pressures and function efficiently, Spinner hired more women and maintained that his female employees were "hardworking, efficient, had excellent work habits and integrity."[9] To be sure, these women did not play a role in policy matters, but their very proximity to the heart of federal fiscal authority commanded attention.

Less controversial were the women with access to funds who for decades purchased bank and corporate securities as attractive vehicles for passive income. Nor did women prove immune to the speculative fever that animated the times. Out West, they speculated in mining stocks and several even established their own mining stock exchange.[10] The lure of quick riches even prompted one notorious lady to operate beyond the bounds of the law. Forty years before the term "Ponzi scheme" became coined as a result of the illicit schemes of Charles Ponzi, Sarah Howe preyed on female investors in Boston in the 1880s. Through her Ladies Deposit Bank that promised high rates of interest but made no investments, she attracted half a million dollars from more than a thousand women, using some of the funds to pay off other investors and pocketing the rest prior to her arrest.[11]

By 1890, nearly four million women worked outside the home. Most were single and needed the income. Those who did not work, including many newly college-educated women, advanced the nascent women's club movement that now boasted over 200 women's groups. Initially predicated on literacy and cultural activities, many soon focused on improving social conditions. The female volunteer and organizer actively advanced a reformist agenda, embracing such causes as alleviating conditions affecting the urban poor, promoting temperance, and building suffrage support.[12]

While the image of an independent woman gained strength through expanding educational opportunities, employment, and civic ventures, the gender differentiation and income gap between traditionally male fields and pink collar jobs continued. In addition to teaching, nursing, and librarian work, women were beginning to make inroads in the arts, as well as in medicine and journalism; the legal and ministry professions offered fewer opportunities. In her 1898 book, *Women and Economics*, Charlotte Perkins Gilman promotes the cultivation of economically independent women. Unconventional and unpopular, her ideas went unheeded. For many women, the very concept of balancing family and career proved an obstacle.

In 1910, a Radcliffe alumna lamented 10 years after her graduation, "I hang in a void midway between two spheres. A professional career puts me beyond reach of the average woman's duties and pleasures, but the conventional limitations of the female lot put me beyond reach of the average man's duties and pleasures."[13] There was nothing conventional about the first women who pursued financial paths. They pushed their way into the male-dominated world that had captured their imagination for various reasons and shattered traditional notions of a female's proper place. If not each a financial genius, all exhibited extreme determination and pluck as they sought their share of the Gilded Age's riches on their individual terms.

THREE

Tennessee Claflin and Victoria Woodhull

I think a woman is just as capable of making a living as a man. . . . I don't care what society thinks . . .[1]

—*Tennessee Claflin*

[We wanted] to know the secrets of money that had heretofore been a male preserve.[2]

—*Victoria Woodhull*

When Tennessee Claflin and Victoria Woodhull knocked on the office door of Commodore Cornelius Vanderbilt in 1868, the two young women were about not only to visit the workplace of one of this country's leading industrialists, but to begin a relationship that would secure their own place in financial history. The professional trajectories of the financial magnate, whose shipping and railroad empire evolved from the ferry business he had built during his youth, and those of the two sisters could not have been more different. Gender was not the only distinguishing factor.

Victoria and Tennessee Claflin's family life in Homer, Ohio did not give rise to any conventional Horatio Alger tale. Two of ten children, Victoria was born in 1838, followed seven years later by Tennessee. Their entrepreneurial father gravitated from one business pursuit to another, often without success and consumed by alcoholic rages. Their mother, a woman lacking any formal education, passed her time memorizing Biblical passages and cultivating her family's introduction to spiritualism, a growing American religious movement.

When Victoria began school at age eight in 1846, her intelligence became quickly noticed. Her mother ascribed her intellect to supernatural powers, a belief that Victoria came to share. Due to the unavailability of teachers, her schooling totaled less than three years. She then resumed her spiritualist life with her mother and was convinced that her psychic abilities controlled her destiny. Meanwhile, her father squandered any money he had accumulated. A notion of lost wealth was fostered that endured with Victoria and Tennessee throughout their adult lives.[3]

A flair for showmanship ran in the family. Starting in her teenage years, Tennessee traveled as a fortune-teller under her father's auspices. Whether she offered other less reputable services as well is ambiguous; Victoria once demanded that Tennessee "had no right to prostitute her powers."[4] Victoria's penchant for the dramatic involved an early marriage that perhaps stemmed more from a 15-year-old's desire to escape the circumstances of her home life rather than the pursuit of an idealistic love. In 1853 she married a seemingly wealthy doctor, Canning Woodhull. Any thoughts of an easier life soon dissipated. Her husband had few patients but many personal bouts with alcohol and adultery. The birth of a mentally handicapped son the following year amidst her husband's continuing philandering convinced her that the family should move to San Francisco to get a fresh start. Once there, Victoria landed a theatrical role, but sensed that she was "meant for some other fate."[5] While performing one night, she claimed that she saw a vision of her sister, Tennessee, calling her to come home. The next morning, Victoria packed up her family and boarded a train bound east.[6]

Nothing about the sisters' personal lives was placid. Upon Woodhull giving birth to a daughter in 1861, her drunken husband cut the umbilical cord so clumsily that he endangered the infant, and then left home without returning for three days.[7] They divorced in 1865, after Woodhull had already met Colonel James Harvey Blood, a married Union officer, who had solicited her spiritualist services. The two began an affair and soon wed, although the dates of his divorce and their own marriage are unclear. Claflin, too, harbored a secretive history. Once charged with manslaughter relating to her healing practice, she had also been briefly married to a man named John Bortel, from whom she later claimed that she had quickly divorced.

The sisters' bond had meanwhile strengthened. The two shared a belief in an unnatural superiority and a desire to "regain what should have been our own."[8] They became known as spiritualism's leading personalities as the movement enjoyed its zenith in popularity. In 1868, they ramped up their business plan for the New York City spiritualist salon that they now operated together. With the input of their father, they set their sights on the richest man in America, who was known as much for his wealth as for his predilections for both women and clairvoyants.

Like many details of their lives, specific accounts of their first meeting with Vanderbilt and the ensuing relationship vary and may very well have been embellished by the sisters over time to serve their needs.[9] According to a popularized anecdote, upon arriving at Vanderbilt's office, Woodhull and Claflin introduced themselves with business cards advertising their clairvoyant services.[10] They regaled him with a tale of how a spirit had directed them to New York and specifically to his "fatherly care and kindness."[11] Their use of spiritualist rhetoric rife with references to his personal history may not have fooled Vanderbilt, who is said to have immediately ascertained that the sisters were "ladies of resource."[12] Nevertheless, they charmed him. He basked in their attention and the three soon became frequent companions. The women offered Vanderbilt insight and guidance to a metaphysical world, while he provided the sisters with more earthly and profitable advice.

Claflin turned into more than Vanderbilt's spiritualist confidante. The two became lovers, even though he remained married. According to Claflin, "Commodore Vanderbilt knows my power."[13] Indeed, he did, as she was often allegedly spotted by his servants, "rosy and tousled, in the Commodore's bed in the morning."[14] Once his wife passed away, Vanderbilt proposed to the unsuspecting Claflin. Concerned that her own marriage, of which Vanderbilt had not known, had not been legally dissolved, she demurred. Vanderbilt's attraction only increased.

Vanderbilt's adult son William did not approve of the liaison between his father and Claflin. Possibly at William's behest, while away from the city in July 1869, Vanderbilt married a cousin. The sisters, though shocked at the news, remained friends with the financier, whose world of wealth provided a greater attraction to them than did his personal affections. In fact, they had specific personal and political motivations to desire access to capital.

Inspired by her attendance at the first national convention of the women's suffrage movement earlier that year, Woodhull entertained thoughts of future political office. She also witnessed the social snobberies exhibited by some of the leaders, for many came from privileged backgrounds. Recognizing that her spiritualist career could detract from her newfound quest for political prominence among the suffragists, she discontinued practicing medical clairvoyance. Instead of immediately directing her energies squarely on politics, Woodhull focused on Wall Street. There, the sisters might secure their financial security and lay the foundation for a future public role.[15]

Against the backdrop of the gold panic, Woodhull made her mark. Two of the most well-known speculators, Jay Gould and James Fisk Jr., had nearly cornered the gold market during the summer of 1869. Issued to finance the Civil War, greenbacks remained backed by only the government's pledge, and had spawned an increase in gold trading. Gould and Fisk lobbied the Grant administration to curtail gold sales and any greenback contraction. After President Grant caught on to their planned market manipulation, he ordered the sale of $4 million of the country's gold reserve. When news broke on September 24 of the government's action, troops stood guard as panic selling engulfed the inflated gold market.[16]

That same day, while many firms and individuals faced financial ruin, Woodhull made a fortune while sitting in her carriage and observing the scene outside the Gold Exchange. Whether her profits were achieved solely through her own prescient trading or through an arrangement with Vanderbilt is unclear.[17] Woodhull claimed, "I came out a winner,"[18] proudly noting that Vanderbilt, who had pumped $1 million into the stock market to stem the selling from spreading to equities, had called her a "bold operator."[19]

Despite Vanderbilt's remarriage, the sisters continued to cultivate their relationship with him and the threesome remained close. Their relationship continued to anger both his wife and son. When William tried to get rid of the sisters by sending them on a lengthy European trip, his offer backfired. By shrewdly transforming William's scheme into a spiritualist tale for Vanderbilt, Woodhull related how a spirit had told her to abandon travel plans and to instead establish an office on Wall Street. Not fooled but intrigued by the underlying subterfuge, Vanderbilt wrote them a check for $7,000. He thereby underwrote the sisters' professional financial career.

The idea for a Wall Street brokerage may have emanated from Woodhull's husband, Colonel Blood, as a way for her to garner publicity for her political ambitions. Although Claflin claimed that they had decided to enter Wall Street for "The necessity of earning a living . . . and unfitness for the slow, dreary methods by which women usually earn a living,"[20] Woodhull clearly had an agenda. She saw her Wall Street career as a way to gain political prominence and later acknowledged her "female invasion of the masculine precincts of finance"[21] as a way to secure notoriety and aid her advancement within the upper echelons of the suffragists. In a letter written in 1873 to the *Pittsburgh Leader*, she surmised, "There could have been nothing else in a legitimate business that could have attracted the public notice or called forth the comments of the Press more fully than the establishment of a banking house by two women among the 'bulls' and 'bears' of Wall Street."[22]

The sisters adroitly managed their entree into the financial world. By depositing Vanderbilt's check with well-known banker Henry Clews, they encouraged perceptions of respected community support even though Clews regarded his position as initial creditor as a "rather doubtful distinction."[23] Capitalized and now effectively carrying the business endorsement of a prominent Wall Street figure, the first Wall Street brokerage owned by women now set up shop. On January 20, 1870, the *New York Herald* reported, "The general routine of business in Wall Street was somewhat varied today by the mingling in its scenes of two fashionably dressed ladies as speculators. . . . After investing to the extent of several thousand shares in some of our principal stocks and selling others, and announcing their intentions to become regular habitués of Wall Street, they departed, the observed of all observers."[24]

Following publication of the article, the sisters sent the new business card of Woodhull, Claflin & Co. to the newspaper.[25] During a subsequent interview with the reporter, Claflin alluded to Vanderbilt without specifically stating his name.[26] On January 22, a new article noted, "The firm looked contented and happy and seeming to do well. It would seem as though the mantle of the genial old Commodore had descended on their shoulders, his photograph on the wall seems to indicate that his spirit was there—and they are not prepared to deny that they know a thing or two about the Commodore's notions of the rise and fall of stocks."[27] A concurrent editorial commended them, "We congratulate the brokers that their labors are to be shared by the fair sex. How refreshing the time when the halls of the Stock Exchange shall exhibit a variety of costume as diverse as the floors of a ballroom,"[28] concluding "*Vive la frou frou.*"[29]

Once the newly crowned "Queens of Finance" opened their downtown office at 44 Broad Street in February, they immediately drew throngs of visitors, including poet Walt Whitman who called it "a prophecy of the future"[30] and famed trader Jay Cooke.[31] Crowded with customers, the office boasted a parlor with a portrait of Vanderbilt and provided a large back room accessible through a rear door only to women, who came from all walks of life to deposit sums both small and large.[32] From the beginning, women "fresh and fair as pippins . . . bewitched by curiosity and afterwards delighted with all they saw and heard, left the premises bethinking themselves that there were other things to live for besides cosmetics, the toilet, fashion, and vanity."[33] Woodhull recalled that "when we entered the precincts of Wall and Broad Streets they were blocked with crowds of people until the novelty wore away."[34]

More press attention ensued, carrying with it mixed opinions. "Petticoats Among The Bovine and Ursine Animals" warned the *New York Sun* on its front page.[35] Instead of universally castigating them, some reporters praised the sisters as "straightforward, well-bred American women who were perfectly capable of taking care of themselves in the dangerous byways of Wall Street."[36] The *New York Times*' headline announced "Wall-Street Aroused," reporting negativism toward them not because they were women but because of their past psychic exploits: "Insulting remarks and shameful allusions were carried to the ears of the women (who pretended to be very busy in the transaction of their business) by the throng that curiously examined everything in the offices, and who sang and whistled after the fashion of the Bowery pit. A short, speedy winding up of the firm Woodhull Claflin & Co. is predicted."[37] While many traders mocked them and gentlemen's magazines depicted them in bawdy cartoons, Susan B. Anthony trumpeted their feat in her suffrage newspaper. She declared, "These two ladies (for they are ladies) are determined to use their brains, energy, and their knowledge of business to earn them a livelihood. . . . The advent of this woman firm in Wall Street marks a new era."[38]

Vanderbilt remained silent about the new firm. However, both he and rival Gould used it to stage speculative contests with each other. Gould commented that

> I picked the ladies' firm myself—without them realizing it—because, you see, the Street when Woodhull & Claflin sold would just naturally jump to the conclusion that the principal was Cornelius Vanderbilt. . . . Rather neat finesse I thought that was. . . . When the Stock Exchange was surest we were squeezing Vanderbilt. . . . I was supplying them with all the stock their unkind suspicions would bid for . . . [and] paid Victoria and Sister Tennie $1,000 a day commission through quite a . . . spell.[39]

The firm attracted clients due to the sisters' proximity to Vanderbilt, to whom they increasingly alluded, their own notoriety, and their allure to women. Female investors, many of them novices, sought out the firm. Despite their potential as role models for women, however, Woodhull and Claflin did not lavish attention on their clients or even always supply them with suitable investments; they pushed many into gold speculation.[40]

Instead of pursuing serious financial analysis, they excelled at crafting public personalities for themselves.[41] Business meetings took the form of posh affairs at the Astor House Hotel where they courted the press, and Claflin easily supplied memorable lines. Declaring that "Wall Street was tabooed to petticoats," she allowed that ". . . we did not intend to let our petticoats interfere with anybody, or take up anymore room in the street that the other brokers' trousers . . ."[42]

They swept their petticoats aside, however, to begin wearing men's banking suits to attract more attention.[43] More surreptitiously, on the other hand, they quickly and quietly allowed Blood to take control of the firm's daily operations. In March 1870, the sisters quietly signed a contract with him by which he managed the firm in return for a monthly salary and share of profits. Blood's name did not appear in the press in connection with the brokerage, and the sisters retained ownership and remained the firm's public faces.[44]

Claflin particularly basked in the limelight. In addition to attention focused on her close personal relationship with Vanderbilt, she gained further acclaim for her apparent business sense on account of establishing the firm's initial credit with Clews and for avoiding a fraudulent check scam.[45] She displayed her savvy again when she violated the ban in place at the popular Wall Street restaurant Delmonico's that barred females from dining there without escorts. By pulling a coachman off the street to dine with her and Woodhull, they enjoyed both tomato soup and more favorable press attention.[46] Claflin noted that "If I had engaged a little fancy store upon Broadway and sold ribbon and thread, it would have been perfectly proper . . . . No one would have remarked it. But because I have brains sufficient to carry on a banking house people are astonished."[47]

Woodhull next indulged her political ambitions. In April 1870, amid strife between abolitionists and suffragists, she announced her candidacy for president in a letter to the *New York Herald*.[48] Her self-described qualifications centered on her independence, and she asserted that "while others argued the equality of woman with man, I proved it by successfully engaging in business."[49] She penned position papers and announced that she would "spend a fortune" to promote her political ideas.[50]

That fortune funded *Woodhull and Claflin's Weekly*, a newspaper that the sisters launched in May 1870. Dedicated to promoting Woodhull's candidacy and suffrage, the paper covered a gamut of topics, including financial news. Initially under Woodhull's editorial leadership and Claflin's advertising management, Blood soon assumed daily management of the

Tennessee Claflin/J. Gurney & Son, Fifth Ave., N.Y. (Library of Congress, Prints and Photographs Division)

paper while the sisters retained financial ownership and ultimate authority. Half of the 16-page paper's initial $35,000 budget was rumored to have come from Vanderbilt, whose business dealings received laudatory coverage.[51]

When Woodhull and Blood recognized that the paper could gain more readership in a bear market by exposing corruption than by trying to lure additional customers, the paper shifted to a muckraking mentality, one that could also bolster Woodhull's popular appeal. In a September 1870 opening salvo against fraud, the *Weekly* declared:

> We entered upon the walks of money "change" to do a legitimate business in American securities. That business has been of vast extent and profitable to our clients. It opened to us unusual facilities and sources for correct information. The natural, the hereditary keen intelligence of our race and sex was brought with all its force upon the subject, and soon revealed the startling fact that frauds existed in many of the securities deemed first class and current upon the market. We were enabled to save many of our clients from serious losses. In doing this we discovered that larger, bolder and deeper frauds were contemplated by petroleum and shoddy bankers, who, like scum, had risen to the surface in boilings of the dishonest caldrons of war.[52]

Railroads, insurance companies, securities frauds, and real estate speculators numbered among the targets of the paper's ire.[53]

The relationship between Vanderbilt and the sisters had meanwhile grown strained due to Claflin's indiscretion in publicly alluding to their intimacy. In May 1871, she hinted at her personal relationship with Vanderbilt during a Claflin family courtroom battle in which she admitted to "humbug[ing]" people in order to provide for her kin.[54] An embarrassed Vanderbilt severed ties to Woodhull and Claflin and they never again saw him.

In the meantime, Woodhull also burnished her political credentials. She became the first woman to address a congressional committee when she spoke before the House and Senate Judiciary Committees on the topic of constitutional equality in January 1871. Seven months later, she showcased her economic acumen by addressing labor reformers on "The Principles of Finance" at Cooper Institute in New York City. She espoused nationalizing banks, opposing the gold standard, and returning greenbacks to circulation. Despite apparent insincerities between her words and her business dealings, the speech augmented her reputation as a serious reformer who understood money matters.[55]

Fanning the flames of Progressivism sweeping the country, Woodhull threw Vanderbilt to the fire. On February 20, 1872, she fingered him along with other aristocrats in a speech attacking the inequitable distribution of

Engraving of Victoria Woodhull addressing Judiciary Committee of the House of Representatives. (Library of Congress, Prints and Photographs Division)

wealth: "A Vanderbilt may sit in his office and manipulate stocks, or make dividends, by which, in a few years, he amasses $50 million from the industries of the country, and he is one of the remarkable men of the age."[56]

While the paper flourished, the brokerage floundered. The firm had engaged in gold speculation since it opened.[57] As Europe teetered on the brink of war, fluctuations in the gold market left Woodhull, Claflin & Co. with losses. Customers, many of whom were relatively inexperienced investors, sued.[58] The firm's dissociation with Vanderbilt had further eroded any business base, hastening the ultimate demise of the overextended brokerage during the ensuing recession and Panic of 1873. The sisters' Wall Street days were over.

They faced financial woes with their money depleted due to political endeavors, unsuccessful speculation, and frivolous spending habits. Woodhull's broader political appeal also waned as she drew fire from different constituencies for her unorthodox views on marriage and free love, her associations with communists, and her radical economic positions. She received the nomination of her contrived Equal Rights Party, an amalgam of disaffected splinter groups, as its presidential candidate in 1872, and Claflin ran for Congress on the ticket. The party did not garner any electoral votes. The sisters themselves spent election night in jail, part of their four-week confinement due to obscenity charges stemming from their paper's salacious coverage of the alleged extramarital affair of the renowned minister, Reverend Henry Ward Beecher. After months of legal battle, they were found not guilty.

Over the next several years, the sisters continued to espouse controversial views on sexuality and to remain politically active even while their public appeal further dwindled. Vanderbilt offered no salvation, both ignoring their plea for him to subsidize their now struggling newspaper and declaring in an 1875 investor suit, "I think I have not had business relations with them as bankers or brokers."[59] *The Weekly,* which had earned praise from the journalistic community in its early years, ceased printing in 1876, the same year that Woodhull divorced Blood.[60] Following Vanderbilt's death in 1877, more details of the intimate business and personal relationship between Claflin and Vanderbilt became exposed. Claflin unsuccessfully staked a claim against the magnate's will for over $100,000 allegedly owed her from a $10,000 investment that she had deposited with him six years earlier.[61]

Amid rumors that William Vanderbilt had provided the funding, the sisters left for England later that year. There, they married wealthy men and engaged in various philanthropic pursuits. Woodhull staged a trip to the United States in 1892 to test the waters for another presidential run but was met with a hostile reception. Claflin too visited several times while maintaining her life in England, where she even established a bank, Lady Cook & Company, that survived only briefly. She died in 1923, followed four years later by Woodhull.[62]

The Wall Street experience of Claflin and Woodhull is often regarded as little more than a joke perpetrated by women of questionable morals. But their time spent as brokers was not an empty prank lacking significance. Although not serious about pursuing long-term financial careers, they used their abilities most effectively. Endowed with acuity, business sense, beauty, charm, and showmanship, they recognized that their valuable skills and assets could galvanize the public's attention and be used to harness Wall Street's moneymaking potential for their own ends. To that end, they acted not unlike many of their male counterparts of yesterday and today.

Hypocrisy characterizes the way in which history looks upon the sisters, and also marks their own roles in making financial history. Their dealings as speculators and financial entrepreneurs attracted women as investors, yet they offered this constituency on whom they based their political support little, if any, sound advice. Their journalistic writings promoted financial literacy and their political speeches rallied for increased economic opportunity, but one finds little evidence of direct assistance to other women. In fact, one female type compositor turned down from working for *The Weekly* claimed that Woodhull told her "We can't have our paper spoiled by women."[63]

Their legacy, though tarnished, has import. They did not just talk of equality and opportunity, they seized it. By recognizing the powerful symbol of a woman upending conventional norms, they made both Wall Street and Main Street take note that a woman could do battle in the financial world. That their early banker, Clews, later opined in his memoir that women did not belong as speculators and called the firm a failure illustrates the prominence that the firm had achieved.[64] Woodhull and Claflin had transformed the unimagined notion of a woman on Wall Street into a reality.

FOUR

Hetty Green

I am able to manage my affairs better than any man can manage
them; and, what man has done, woman can do.[1]

—Hetty Green

The heavily veiled woman entering J.P. Morgan's library on an early November evening in 1907 to attend an emergency meeting of New York
City's most prominent bankers was rumored to be Hetty Green.[2] That all-
night conference, aimed at staving off a run on banks, led to an ultimately
successful plan to inject liquidity into the market. At the time, no central bank existed to shore up support for the nation's troubled financial
institutions, and President Theodore Roosevelt looked to J.P. Morgan to
engineer a financial solution. Morgan, in response, turned to his peers to
devise a strategy.

   As significant as was that success, which immediately halted the Panic
of 1907 and paved the way for the introduction of the Federal Reserve
banking system six years later, so too was the reported inclusion of Green.
While no confirmed evidence of her attendance exists, reporters could not
fathom any other woman who might have been included among those 30
leading bankers and industrialists—or who would have been so attired.[3]
Green's predilection for dressing in a long shabby black dress and veiled
hat, together with her miserly ways, earned her the unfavorable title of
"The Witch of Wall Street" by her detractors,[4] a sobriquet still often
invoked. Yet, it was her financial astuteness and independent spirit that
should have been celebrated.

Hetty Howland Robinson, the girl who later became Wall Street's first female financier, was born into a prominent New Bedford, Massachusetts family in 1834. Her family's wealth from the whaling industry had made them the town's richest residents, but their Quaker sensibilities helped them maintain a life unencumbered by the opulent excesses enjoyed by many of the Gilded Age's well-to-do. Growing up as an only child after a younger brother died in infancy, Green learned the rudiments of finance at a young age. Her father suffered from poor vision, so he relied on his daughter to read him the financial news. This early immersion in trade news, statistics, and investments led Green to confidently allow that by her teenage years, her accumulated financial knowledge already surpassed that of most professionals. She later remarked that "I came to know what stocks and bonds were, how the markets fluctuated, and the meaning of bulls and bears."[5] This knowledge may have also cultivated an early love of money. A family acquaintance later recalled how young Green behaved properly during a visit to the dentist only upon being given a silver half-dollar. Perhaps she deposited that coin, together with her $1.50 per week allowance, into the bank account she first opened at age 8.[6]

Instead of following the standard debutante path and entrenching herself in the ways of the upper crust, Green chose to return to New Bedford after spending a month as a society belle in New York. During that time, she seemingly indulged in the privileges afforded a wealthy young woman when she appeared in a fancy filigree dress and pink slippers at a function with the Prince of Wales. Apparently this outfit must not have set her back too much. Among her first self-appointed tasks once home was to deposit the $1,000 remaining from the original $1,200 given by her father for a clothing allowance.[7] Another mission was to frequently visit with her mother's spinster sister, Sylvia Ann Howland, the heir to the bulk of the family's fortune.

One year later, in 1861, Green's father recognized that the whaling industry was entering its decline. He decided to shut down his business and move to New York City. Green accompanied him, but often went back to visit Aunt Sylvia. As her aunt posed the final barrier to her anticipated inheritance, it remains debatable as to whether Green's attentiveness stemmed more from affection or from avarice.[8]

Another explanation is possible. Green's interest in Sylvia's money can be characterized as not one motivated solely by personal greed, but more as one emanating from her own self-appointed role as steward of the family's wealth.[9] Believing that only she could protect the assets, Green displayed a keen eye for expenses. The two quarreled over items ranging from modest party expenses to a planned addition to her aunt's house, as well as over Green's unattractive wardrobe.

Their most acrimonious disagreement regarded Green's request that Sylvia prepare a will that would bequeath her the inheritance directly and not held in trust, as did the existing document. Finally, and with great chagrin, Sylvia signed a will which left Green everything in her own name. Green remained fearful that Sylvia might revise the will, and her misgivings proved correct. A new will provided for various disbursements and gave Green only half of what she had anticipated, with the principal to be held in trust.[10]

While preoccupied with worries over her aunt's affairs, the unexpected death of her father in 1865 left Green with an estate worth approximately $5.7 million. To her dismay, most of that fortune was kept in a trust for her, which was managed by two of her father's aides. Still, Green was now a very rich woman, with her inheritance income estimated at $300,000 a year during a time when just three percent of that sum would provide a secure upper-middle class lifestyle.[11]

Green's wealth increased several weeks later upon Sylvia's death. Once again, the terms of the bequest did not suit her. Under the terms of the later will, Green received approximately $65,000 a year in interest, instead of the $2 million estate outright. Angered by the bequest, she contested the will over the course of a lengthy litigious fight spanning seven years during which Green argued that the earlier document included a second page that invalidated any subsequent wills. Eventually, although that second page was ruled a forgery, she and the trustees reached a settlement that added to her coffers $1.3 million in cash and bonds whose face value totaled $600,000.[12]

By now, several of the central themes of Green's life had been established: obsessions with both wealth and frugality, an appetite for litigation yet a disdain for lawyers, a distrust of financial intermediaries, and a disregard for fashion. The stage was now set for her to assume the role for which she had long prepared and most coveted—that of money manager.

Green would soon prove her skills but she also had other more domestic interests. During her legal battle over the will, she had met one of her father's business associates, Edward Henry Green. A successful self-made businessman, he had favored her legal position and indeed was her lone supporter during her fight. Although onlookers might have surmised that he was more interested in her money than anything else, her thriftiness stood at odds with his free spending disposition. If she harbored any mis-givings about his intentions, she resolved them by making sure that she kept her money segregated from his. This was surely an atypical arrange-ment for her era. The pair married in 1867 and relocated to London. While he focused on his business, she tried to escape the intense public scrutiny stemming from the trial and her possible indictment for alleged forgery concerning Sylvia's will. She began a family, giving birth to a boy in 1868, and a girl two-and-a-half years later.

During their years abroad, Green continued to purchase U.S. "green-backs," the bonds sold by the government after the Civil War, which she had begun purchasing in 1865 upon receiving her first distribution from her father's estate. Greenbacks had dropped significantly in value, to as low as 40 cents on the dollar of gold, as the public remained wary of the country's post-war prospects. To Green, however, the recovery seemed assured. In fact, her affinity for bonds and her steady approach toward the market epitomized her investment strategy. As she once commented, "Before deciding on an investment I seek out every kind of informa-tion about it. There is no great secret in fortune making. All you have to do is buy cheap and sell dear, act with thrift and shrewdness and be persistent."[13]

Amid Green's claims of making $1.25 million in just one year from her fixed income holdings, her financial success grew. She expanded into railroad bonds and her wealth increased exponentially. The fattened port-folio helped lead to the family's decision in 1874 to return to the United States, where it would be easier to stay abreast of financial developments as railroad securities flooded the market.

The family's settlement in Mr. Green's hometown of Bellows Falls, Vermont caused a stir. The eagerly awaited arrival of a woman of such great wealth quickly gave way to disappointment and gossip over her odd and penny-pinching ways. Stories abounded of her haggling with local merchants and obsessively searching for a postage stamp. A false but widely transmitted rumor persisted that she had even denied her son medical treatment for his chronic limp. But if the Vermonters had been in for a shock, that didn't come close to the ruckus soon created by Green on Wall Street.

Most of Green's portfolio, consisting of over $500,000 in cash and $26 million in securities, as well as her husband's investments, were held in the New York office of John J. Cisco and Son. When the firm teetered on financial collapse in January 1885, and that news reached Green, she immediately requested a withdrawal of her assets. What

Green did not know was that while she was the bank's largest depositor, her husband had racked up over $700,000 in debts and became its largest debtor. When Cisco announced suspension of its operations, Green jumped into action. She thundered into the bank's offices and demanded, "I've come to get what's mine."[14] Over the next several days, press accounts covered her ranting and raving, while the bank agreed to release her securities only if she repaid her husband's debt. Finally, she acquiesced and then promptly hauled away her holdings to Chemical National Bank.

The Cisco failure produced several repercussions. While catapulting Green more fully into the public spotlight, it also led her to wage another legal battle, this one predicated on claims that the bank had defrauded creditors. According to her, she brought the fight because "I come of good old Quaker blood. All I care for is to do right. Then I am sure to go to heaven."[15] Ultimately, she lost the legal battle, but won her quest for personal freedom.[16] Her fury over her husband's financial mismanagement had led to the practical end of their marriage, although they were never legally divorced.

The once "Mrs. E.H. Green" became referred to as "Hetty Green" in the press, and she embraced her greater independence. She and her children moved to a modest apartment in Brooklyn, and she continued to direct her investments and take part in some of the largest financial deals of the time. Green's holdings proved central to the outcome of the unsuccessful takeover attempt of the Georgia Central Railroad in which she profited handsomely. She also waged a lengthy fight over her rights as a significant bondholder of the Houston and Texas Central Railroad. Her maneuvering during this latter battle accentuated a focus on her gender, with the *New York World* observing that "Wall Street men, usually very gallant where women are concerned, have no very great liking for Mrs. Green and her close business methods."[17] Green herself did nothing to disavow stereotypes when, following a reversal of her presumed stance at one point amid negotiations, she asserted that it was a woman's prerogative to change her mind.[18]

As Green adhered to her strategy of focusing on intrinsic value while buying low and never speculating or buying on margin, her wealth increased. According to her, the general secret of success was to "buy when things are low and no one wants them. I keep them, just as I keep a considerable number of diamonds on hand, until they go up and people are anxious to buy."[19] Able to finance her own purchases by acquiring real property primarily through foreclosures from collateral underlying her bond investments, she expanded her real estate portfolio to encompass

Hetty Green, c. 1897. (Library of Congress, Prints and Photographs Division)

holdings in New York, Boston, Chicago, and Saint Louis. In keeping with her frugal nature, instead of improving these properties, she held onto them for long-term gains.[20]

Financially strapped businessmen and even municipalities came knocking, looking for assistance from Green who began operating essentially as a private bank. Years before she heeded Morgan's call to help avert a banking crisis, she had lent funds to New York City several times. She offered fair terms often well below the current rates. Despite her ability to dictate terms, she could not abide usury, telling a reporter that "no one knows it better than the wealthy men who have had business dealings with me."[21]

After moving to Hoboken, New Jersey, in 1895 where her apartment door read "C. Dewey" for the Skye terrier she loved, Green maintained her daily routine of taking the ferry to Manhattan and sitting at her allotted desk at Chemical National Bank, clipping bond coupons while keeping astride of developments in her portfolio. She continued to covet complete control of her affairs. In 1902, at age 68, she even obtained a pistol, telling police that although only lightning and "religious lawyers" frightened her, "Because I am a rich woman some people want to kill me. I have often been threatened."[22] Not until well into her seventies did she begin to relinquish managerial control over her assets, asking her son for his assistance in looking after her interests. She remained involved in her business affairs until within 10 days of her death, despite suffering a series of incapacitating strokes over the preceding three months. When she died at age 81 on July 3, 1916, her estimated wealth of $100 million made her the wealthiest woman in the country.[23]

Green's wealth had set her apart from the many "idle rich women"[24] of the times. But she wasn't the only woman trying to make money on Wall Street in the Gilded Age, just the most successful and prominent. Castigated as naïve, emotional, and poor losers, many brokers shunned women as clients, and women typically transacted trades over the telephone or by visiting uptown brokerage offices rather than going downtown.[25] In the rare instance that women's financial acuity was noted, it was most often in a negative instance, with references to schemers and "get-rich quick" promoters.[26] Although banker Henry Clews grudgingly admitted to her prowess in managing one of her railroad holdings, he remained dubious of her abilities.[27] In contrast, the newspapers of the time lauded Green's financial acumen, opining that she exemplified a rare female specimen of such savvy by having "a masculine instinct for finance."[28]

Despite Green's acumen, her shortcomings were often magnified both then and now. Most people have never heard of her, and the few that have may know her only through her *Guinness Book of World Records* title as the "greatest miser."[29] Her dowdy dress and stingy ways certainly did not help cultivate a favorable image, nor did her dour expression frequently seen staring back from photographs. Her litigious disposition, however, owed more to a desire to protect her principles as she saw them, rather than a need to meaninglessly increase her wealth. In her words, she didn't want to be known as an "easy mark" and simply pursued her father's admonition to fight for her rights.[30] While she chose to pursue life on her terms, those choices prompted more critiques than accolades. This negative evaluation by others was likely due in no small part to her gender.

That she fascinated the public is without doubt. Green's activities, both business and personal, often provided fodder for the press. Her persona acquired a sort of iconic stature, giving rise to a 1905 song dubbed *If I Were As Rich As Hetty Green* and at least one racehorse that was named after her.[31] Even her visit to a beauty parlor, possibly undertaken to quell particularly hurtful published comments, was covered in the press, with the *New York Times* headline reporting "Hetty Green Taking Beauty Treatments."[32] Green's penny-pinching ways, such as her customary lunchtime custard, was sensationalized, but John D. Rockefeller's predilection for pie at nondescript lunch counters was not touted.[33] This sort of intense scrutiny, coupled with her private nature, only stoked her superficial perception by the populace. Green understood how she was regarded, commenting, "My life is written for me down in Wall Street by people who, I assume, do not care to know one iota of the real Hetty Green. I am in earnest; therefore they picture me as heartless. I go my own way. I take no partner, risk nobody else's fortune, therefore I am Madame Ishmael, set against every man."[34]

No one would ever confuse Green with Andrew Carnegie in terms of charity. Not all robber barons were so philanthropically inclined either. Certainly, Commodore Vanderbilt was not altruistic during most of his career. Neither did Green's parsimoniousness extend to the preclusion of all charitable matters. Upon her death, her son intimated that she had given numerous sums to charities during her lifetime, as well as regular incomes to approximately 30 families who had been long-time associates of her family.[35] She acknowledged lending money to churches at low interest rates and financing a school for boys.[36] Reports had also surfaced of a large donation presumably made by her in 1912 to flood victims in Ohio. She may have preferred to donate on an anonymous basis either because of her desire to discourage an endless stream of requests for donations or out of Quaker sentiments.[37] She herself commented that "One way is to give money and make a big show. That is not my way of doing."[38]

While Green may not have personified philanthropy, she did encourage saving. She once gave neighborhood children toy banks, each containing one dollar, to which she would contribute another if they later returned with additional savings.[39] Abhorring the excesses of the era, she believed that women spent rather than saved and disparaged this propensity.[40] She recognized the lack of financial literacy among most women and advised an early introduction to business training.[41] A woman could overcome any fear, Green believed, if she only "conducts herself properly and looks after herself."[42] No staunch proponent of a woman's right to vote, she declared in later years "I don't believe in suffrage, and I haven't any respect for women who dabble in such trash."[43] Still, she believed "what man has done, woman can do . . . it is the duty of every woman, I believe, to learn to take care of her own business affairs."[44] As for her daughter, she allowed, "My daughter hasn't been reared to be a business woman. She knows a good deal about business, and she'll be able to take care of what she may have, but I wouldn't want her to follow in my footsteps."[45] Instead, Green groomed her son as a business successor while providing that both children would equally share in her estate.[46]

Green was an ambitious individual and not one without flaws. Surely, her stature as the country's richest woman and most prominent female financier, coupled with her idiosyncrasies, thrust her more into the spotlight and its attendant glare than she would have liked. "I have been more abused and misrepresented than any woman alive," declared Green on her 70th birthday.[47] Despite surmised unhappiness, she also remarked that she knew of very few people other than herself who better combined business with pleasure and that "one of the rules of my life is never to worry uselessly about things."[48]

Like Tennessee Claflin and Victoria Woodhull, Green stood in stunning contrast to the Gilded Age's prevailing social norms. Each of these women challenged convention through their dealings undertaken with an underlying charge of reclaiming what had once been wrongfully taken. All spoke of a greater need for financial education and independence. They strove for and achieved wealth in different aspects of Wall Street's affairs. They did so with contrasting styles and with dissimilar political motivations. While the sisters courted attention, Green tried to avoid it. While they flirted and flaunted their physical beauty, Green covered up her femininity. The sisters saw their brief Wall Street careers as means to a political end, while Green, whose very success exemplified a woman's capacity to succeed in finance, sought no such greater goal.

More than 90 years ago, the *New York Times* got it right. When the paper published her obituary on the front page, it remarked:

> If a man had lived as did Mrs. Hetty Green, devoting the greater part of his time and mind to the increasing of an inherited fortune that even at the start was far larger than is needed for the satisfaction of all such human needs as money can satisfy, nobody would have seen him as very peculiar—as notably out of the common. . . . It was that Mrs. Green was a woman that made her career the subject of endless curiosity, comment, and astonishment.[49]

In fact, but for the circumstance of her gender, the Witch of Wall Street might really have become known as its wizard.

FIVE

Maggie Walker

. . . let us have a bank and factory, and let our cry be let us save the young Negro woman. . . .[1]

—*Maggie Walker*

A young girl trudged through the streets of Richmond, Virginia carrying a basket filled with clothes that she had helped her mother launder. Neither the spare change that Maggie received for her labor nor her familial circumstances added up to suggest that one day she would become the first black woman to establish a bank.

Born out of wedlock in Richmond on July 15, 1864,[2] Walker's mother, Elizabeth Draper, was a former slave working as an assistant cook for the wealthy Van Lew family. Her father, Eccles Culbert, was a white abolitionist writer. In the Confederate capitol, mixed-race marriages occurred rather frequently despite being considered illegal under state law. Ten months after Walker was born, her mother married William Mitchell, a butler in the home where she worked. Noted Walker in her diary years later, "He was the lightest skinned colored man she could find."[3]

Tragedy and poverty entered Walker's life early. At first, the Mitchell family, which now included younger brother Johnnie who was born in 1870, enjoyed a relatively comfortable life in the city. Her father had become a hotel waiter, and her mother worked as a laundress. Then, in February 1876, Mitchell disappeared, only to be found drowned five days later. Although the family believed that he had been robbed and killed, the coroner's report indicated suicide as the cause of death.

Thrust into dire economic circumstances, Walker assisted her mother with her laundry business. She recounted later, "I was not born with a silver spoon in my mouth, but with a laundry basket practically on my head."[4] One of few economic pursuits available to black women, laundry work was fairly common for those seeking income.[5] In fact, contemporary Sarah Breedlove, who would one day be known as cosmetics entrepreneur and millionaire Madam C. J. Walker, also worked as a laundress while a young girl in Louisiana.

The church and volunteerism rounded out Walker's school days. She became a member of the First African Baptist Church, the city's largest black congregation, in 1878. Three years later, inspired by her mother and her religious school teacher who were members, Walker joined the local council of the Independent Order of the Sons and Daughters of St. Luke. Organized in 1867 in Baltimore as a black benevolent society, St. Luke's cared for the sick and needy and covered funeral expenses for the indigent. Walker earned merit badges through the organization's youth arm, the Good Idea Council, and at age 16 was elected its secretary.[6]

Walker's public spiritedness did not preclude, and may have even undergirded her participation in the country's first black school strike. She and nine other high school classmates at the segregated Colored Normal School protested the school board's plan for separate commencement ceremonies for the city's white and black students. Although they did not achieve their aim for a unified celebration, Walker graduated with honors at age 16 in 1883 and then became an elementary school teacher. Teaching represented one of the few career paths open to single or widowed black women. With that occupation came a measure of prestige within the black community, and Walker found herself fraternizing with other successful professionals and leaders. In her spare time, she studied accounting in the evenings and worked part-time for an insurance company that provided life insurance to black women.[7]

Domestic events interrupted her budding career. Upon marrying Armstead Walker, a brick contractor, in 1886, she relinquished her position in order to comply with state law that precluded married women from teaching. New family responsibilities arose, with her mother living with the couple, and children soon arriving. Son Russell was born in 1890, followed in 1893 by another son, Armstead, who died seven months later. Her husband's niece, Margaret Anderson Payne, moved in with the family in 1895. Polly, as she was known, seems to have taken a place as a daughter and may have been adopted. Two years later, in 1897, son Melvin was born.[8]

Despite the bustling household, Walker delved further into the activities of St. Luke. Serving in various capacities, she chaired its committee to establish a juvenile branch that was successfully organized and boasted 1,000 members within its first year. Under her auspices as Grand Deputy Matron of the new branch, children received religious training and learned about individual empowerment, community involvement, and thrift.

Both locally and nationally, many blacks continued to struggle with poverty. Black women particularly found their roles circumscribed to the domestic front due to economic and political circumstances as well as to cultural attitudes pervasive within both black and white communities. For upper-middle-class white women, the women's club movement offered an avenue into a potentially larger societal role. At a time when many upper-middle-class white women participated in women's clubs focused on literary and charitable purposes, the General Federation of Women's Clubs declared its membership closed to blacks. Those black women who did manage to overcome the odds comprised the exception rather than the rule.[9]

Mutual benefit societies such as St. Luke's offered black women economic opportunities through paying jobs, such as membership recruiters and administrators.[10] Walker blazed her own upwardly mobile track by way of her activities with the organization. By 1899, at the time of its 32nd convention, St. Luke's struggled with declining membership. Walker stepped up to fill a leadership vacuum when, after a contentious vote, she was elected to the organization's highest position, Right Worthy Grand Secretary. Upon assuming leadership, she moved quickly to right the foundering group. She reduced her monthly salary by one-third, to eight dollars, and emphasized the organization's growth.[11] Just as significant was her commitment to elevating women, "[My] first work was to draw around me women,"[12] she later wrote in her diary. With the 1901 election of the executive board, women occupied six of the nine seats.[13]

Walker's frequent travel, business acumen, and hard work on behalf of the organization paid off. Membership rose modestly, the number of councils grew, and St. Luke's regained financial stability. Those achievements might have sufficed, but Walker had a larger vision. Using her formidable public speaking skills, she outlined her ideas in a memorable address to the annual convention in August 1901. Her strategic plan included the establishment of both a newspaper and a department store, but at its centerpiece stood a new bank:

What do we need to still further develop and prosper us, numerically and financially? First, we need a savings bank, chartered, officered and run by the men and women of this Order.

Let us put our moneys together; let us use our moneys; let us put our money out at usury among ourselves, and reap the benefit ourselves. Shall we longer continue to bury our talent, which the Lord has given us, wrapped in a napkin and hidden away, where it ought to be gaining us still other talents?

R.W.G. Chief, brethren and sisters, let us awake. Let us have a bank that will take the nickels and turn them into dollars. Then, as our patron saint went about doing good, how easily can this great organization now start and do good in our ranks. Who is so helpless as the Negro woman? Who is so circumscribed and hemmed in, in the race of life, in the struggle for bread, meat and clothing as the Negro woman? They are even being denied the work of teaching Negro children. Can't this great Order, in which there are so many good women, willing women, hard-working women, noble women, whose money is here, whose interests are here, whose hearts and souls are here, do something towards giving employment to those who have made it what it is?[14]

These ideas of Walker had not been borne out of pure fantasy, but emerged from observed realities. Calls for black business development by national leaders such as W.E.B. Du Bois and Booker T. Washington had spurred a growth in black-owned businesses. Those enterprises, however, encountered obstacles, stymied both by the frequent denial of credit by white-owned banks and a high degree of financial illiteracy within the black community. Although a handful of black banks operated in Richmond at the time, Walker perceived a need for another, one that might lift the fortunes of St. Luke's and the black community. Just two years after St. Luke's had teetered on bankruptcy, her bold and innovative plan was unanimously approved.[15]

In order to set up a bank, Walker required more than eloquent words. She needed to learn the business, as well as to establish its corporate governance and capital structure. By way of a courtesy extended by one of its former presidents, Walker spent time learning the fundamentals of banking at the white-owned Merchants' National Bank of Richmond. A board of directors consisting of the members of the 1901 St. Luke's Executive Committee was called upon to contribute capital, and Walker traveled to northern states to raise additional funds. On July 28, 1903, the state granted a charter for the St. Luke Penny Savings Bank.[16]

Almost immediately, Walker was referred to in the press as the first female bank president in the country. This accolade may not be accurate. That title has been alternately bestowed on Louisa Stephens, who assumed the position at the First National Bank of Marion, Iowa upon the death of her husband, the bank's president in 1883, and Anna Martin, a German immigrant, who established a family owned and operated bank in Texas in 1901.[17] If not the first woman, Walker was certainly the first black female bank president. The plight of black women continued to engage Walker, who had observed that few careers existed for them other than in domestic work, teaching, or within the church. Hoping to install women in the bank's leadership posts, she acquiesced to male pressure to refrain from gender exclusivity after a viable female cashier had not been identified. Eight of the initial nineteen board members were women, but a requirement that each director own $100 worth of stock caused half of the women to no longer qualify.[18]

Reaction to a black female bank president did not appear to have been as hostile as one might imagine. In fact, Walker appeared the beneficiary of a successful public relations campaign and a welcoming circle of commerce. Reported the press, "She commands the respect of both races here and has fine executive ability."[19] Walker stood alone among the black bank presidents in Richmond to be asked to join the Virginia Bankers' Association. The support of the local white banking professionals may have stemmed from a desire to tout the progress of black banks as a sign of advancement in Southern race relations.[20] Walker later recalled, "As soon as I was elected I received a very cordial invitation to join this white organization. I shall do so, and shall hope to so conduct myself as to reflect credit upon my race and people."[21]

On November 2, 1903, the St. Luke's Penny Savings Bank opened for business. According to the local paper, "The main office has been crowded all day with colored people representing all stations of Afro-American society."[22] Children received special incentive to save as they were given cardboard banks whose future contents could then be used to fund their very own accounts. That first day, approximately 280 customers, some of whom had traveled from as far away as New York, made small deposits that totaled $9,430.44. Walker herself may have been disappointed in the first day's business as it fell significantly short of the $75,000 she had forecast.[23]

A successful business builds over time and St. Luke's grew modestly in its early years. The bank's strategy focused on making services accessible

Maggie Walker in office. (National Park Service, Maggie L. Walker National Historic Site)

to small depositors through vehicles such as Christmas savings accounts and extending credit for mortgages and other customer loans.[24] Laundresses deposited their hard-earned wages and legend even grew of a shoeshine boy who had purchased homes for himself and his mother through the accumulation of interest in his savings account. By January 1906, the bank had carried out transactions totaling approximately $170,000.[25] Walker's stature as a successful leader increased. A comment in an Illinois newspaper remarked that ". . . she is quoted from frequently by her male contemporaries and shows that women can say things both pertinent and efficacious, other than house gossip and the fashions."[26] The following year, Washington cited her and the success of the bank in his book, *The Negro in Business*.[27]

Perhaps the greatest testament to the bank's sound management came as a result of new state legislation passed in July 1910 that required all banks to undergo state solvency inspections. The oldest and largest black local bank, True Reformers, closed that October after the commission deemed its credit overly extended in home loans. One month later, St. Luke successfully emerged from its own audit, only to face another regulatory burden enacted that same month. According to this new law, banks could no longer be a part of fraternal organizations. Forced to sever ties with its fraternal arm, the bank now changed its name to St. Luke Bank and Trust Company. Walker remained both president of the bank and Right Worthy Grand Secretary of St. Luke.[28]

Despite these hurdles, the bank thrived. Walker herself was no easy manager. She demanded loyalty and was particularly hard on her favorite protégés. To her customers, she embodied a welcoming hands-on approach, often greeting customers near the front door of the bank's new three-story building that had been built in 1911. From 1910 to 1920, deposits multiplied by 300 percent and reached over $376,000 in 1919. Facilitating credit within the black community remained a core commitment of the bank through loans extended to students, businesses, and homeowners.[29]

These years were busy ones for the order. Other parts of Walker's 1901 plan had also materialized. The *St. Luke Herald* began publishing in 1902 and three years later, the St. Luke Emporium embarked in retail commerce. The department store represented a particularly promising venture for larger scale female employment. Clerical pay scales exceeded that of most other jobs for women, yet few such opportunities had existed in Richmond for black women until then.[30]

Not everything in Walker's life went according to plan. The black community never embraced St. Luke Emporium. Their antipathy, coupled with retail competition, hostility from whites, and inexperienced management, forced the perennially unprofitable store to close in 1911. A far worse tragedy occurred in her personal life. Ten years after the Walkers had settled into a new home on "Society Row" and enjoyed an affluent lifestyle, 25-year-old son Russell accidentally shot and killed his father after mistaking him for an intruder. Walker remained loyal to her son through the investigations and the 1915 trial that ultimately found him not guilty. However, the legal victory did not absolve Walker from standing at her own political trial by detractors who requested her resignation as St. Luke's leader. Rivalries had developed over the years and critics called into question her domestic affairs as well as her consolidated power. At the 1915 St. Luke Convention, Walker nevertheless prevailed, earning a standing ovation and re-election.[31]

Walker could not only maneuver the politics of her organization, she also proved adept at sidestepping the woes of the Great Depression. Amid the harsh economic times, she approached the remaining black Richmond banks to explore options to augment their chances of survival. Ultimately, the St. Luke bank took over Second Street Savings Bank and established the Consolidated Bank and Trust that opened on January 2, 1930. One year later, the bank merged with Commercial Bank and Trust, resulting with Walker as chairman of an entity holding $864,000 in assets.[32] Later that year, the president of the National Negro Bankers Association remarked to the press, "I feel that you are also delighted to know of the splendid success which attended the consolidation of the three banks in Richmond. This delightful consummation was due in the largest manner to the genius and splendid good management and goodwill of that magnificent woman, Mrs. Maggie L. Walker."[33]

In her civic endeavors, Walker championed the same causes that animated her professional life: gender and racial equality, economic independence, and education. While remaining busy with her church, she actively participated in many other organizations. Among her undertakings, she founded the Colored Women's Council of Richmond, held leadership roles with the National Association of Colored Women and the National Association for the Advancement of Colored People, and served locally on the boards of two girls' schools, a hospital, and the Richmond Urban League and Interracial Commission. Less well-known deeds include a $10,000 loan that she once made to the city of Richmond so that the school year for black children would not be curtailed and her support for suffrage. In 1921, Walker became the first woman in Virginia to run for statewide office when she unsuccessfully ran for Superintendent of Instruction for public schools on the ticket of a black splinter group of the Republican party.[34]

Family matters figured prominently in her life, but not always serenely. The frequent absences of her husband, coupled with whispered innuendos of an affair of her own, belie notions of domestic bliss.[35] Relations with her sons may have become strained over her divided attention between work and family. Niece Polly Payne appears to have filled in for Walker, to the extent that son Melvin later recalled that he often regarded her as his own mother.[36] According to historian Elsa Barkley Brown, "her sons were disgruntled at the amount of attention and funds their mother expended on other people's children. Becoming prominent and successful (or even just engaging in community and/or wage work) had its personal costs. Maggie Walker seems to have paid them—usually quietly, privately, and for a few months quite publicly."[37]

By 1928, Walker's health had begun to fail and she was confined to a wheelchair. Her spirit and energy stayed vibrant. She remained chairman of the bank and leader of St. Luke's until her death on December 15, 1934. According to legend, her last words were "Have faith, have hope, have courage, and carry on."[38] Those words likely informed her personal life during the low points. In her professional life, that maxim underpinned her transformation of St. Luke's through the design and successful execution of an innovative plan. Her charismatic leadership energized a population victimized by prejudice. She challenged them to combat segregation by understanding that "The almighty dollar is the magic wand that knocks the bottom out of racial prejudice. . . ."[39]

Until recently, the bank that Walker had proudly led proclaimed its stature as the country's longest continually operated black bank. In 2005, Consolidated Bank and Trust retained its name while becoming part of Abigail Adams National Bancorp, the holding company for Adams National Bank, the first federally chartered bank owned and managed by women. Four years later, its new parent company, Adams National Bancorp, was merged into Premier Financial Bancorp and in 2010, Consolidated Bank and Trust relinquished its name and merged with four other subsidiary banks to become known as Premier Bank.[40]

Walker's legacy is far more nuanced than one that can be reduced to bricks and mortar or a dollar value. She inspired others to recognize the importance of education, the significance of financial literacy and economic empowerment, and the values of thrift and hard work. Her articulation of black financial empowerment highlighted that need for women. Using St. Luke's as a platform and model for female upward mobility, Walker urged women to work and become financially independent. In a 1909 address, she declared:

> Whatever I have done in this life has been because I love women. . . . And the great all absorbing interest, the thing which has driven sleep from my eyes and fatigue from my boy, is the love I bear women, our Negro women, hemmed in, circumscribed with every imaginable obstacles [sic] in our way, blocked and held down by the fears and prejudices of whites—ridiculed and sneered at by the intelligent blacks.[41]

Far removed from the gilded upbringing of Hetty Green or the bohemian lifestyles of Tennessee Claflin and Victoria Woodhull, Walker, who had confronted inequality from the time of her birth, articulated her version of the American dream. She exhibited her own business and banking competence while sounding the call for female economic independence. Although she enjoyed its material benefits, she sought prosperity less for her personal enrichment than for the equality and autonomy it might offer her race and gender. Savings and thrift undergirded Walker's banking discipline rather than equity investment or speculation. These banalities formed the essentials of capital accumulation needed by her community. While not directly tied to the securities industry and geographically distant from New York's financial district, she built an empire that did not reward her with as great a celebrity as Claflin and Woodhull or with as excessive a fortune as Green. Walker's legacy, however, inured to many more and endured far longer. We do not know what dreams the young girl lugging laundry may have entertained. We do know that what she delivered years later was a message of empowerment and the clout of large aspirations.

PART III

Patriots and Bankers

The colorful female characters of the Gilded Age's financial world did not give birth to a new generation of women financial leaders molded in their images. While they may have inspired some women to take their first investing steps, Victoria Woodhull's and Tennessee Claflin's aberrant behaviors and Hetty Green's eccentricities dominated their respective public perception. Maggie Walker, who left an enduring institutional legacy in Richmond, contributed most effectively to a model of upward female mobility engendered through financial empowerment, but her narrative was not largely acknowledged outside the black community.

Not until the wartime years did American women make further significant headway in finance. No firm societal foundation for such advancement even yet existed. A gradual recognition of women's rights began to take place prior to World War I. By 1900, married women in all states had gained increased control over their property and income. Suffrage efforts focused on individual state amendments and made inroads, especially in the western states. However, while women broadly supported the Progressivist agenda and generally favored labor reform, most did not seek employment outside the home.[1]

Change also came eventually to Wall Street, where bankers steered the rise of money trusts and industrial consolidation during a time of relative prosperity before the outbreak of hostilities. Financial institutions remained largely unregulated until 1913 and the creation of the Federal Reserve System. The introduction of a central banking system, though it represented a significant overhaul of the country's economic structural foundation, nevertheless paled beside the economic effects of World War I.[2]

While the world teetered on the brink of war in 1914, uncertainty gripped investors and sent stocks prices down. In late July, steep selling forced prices down as much as 30 percent and NYSE volume reached its apex since the 1907 Panic. As foreign exchanges closed, the NYSE also shut its doors on July 31 for only the second time in its history. Normal full-scale operations did not return until April 1915.

When the United States entered the war in 1917, the government needed to finance its costs. The nation embarked on a vast capital raising campaign, selling more than $21 billion of savings bonds over the next two years. Marketing these Liberty Bonds entailed the enlistment of Hollywood celebrities, as well as legions of private citizens who volunteered to pitch their sales. Women assumed the leadership of many of these bond drives and won acclaim for their prowess. Women also stepped into job vacancies created by both the draft of four million males and the creation of new positions brought about by wartime needs. For some women, a glaring anomaly remained their lack of enfranchisement during a war deemed by President Woodrow Wilson as a fight for democracy. As political pressure mounted, President Wilson eventually threw his support behind a national suffrage amendment in early 1918, which paved the way for passage of the Nineteenth Amendment two-and-a-half years later. In 1923, suffragist leader Alice Paul drafted the first version of legislation introduced in Congress that mandated equal rights for men and women and later became known as the Equal Rights Amendment (ERA).[3]

The American economy also had turned a corner. By the latter half of 1915, the initial dire forecasts of the war's economic effects had reversed. A prediction by the president of the National Association of Managers that the United States would ultimately emerge as the world's leading power with New York as the premier financial capital soon proved correct.[4] Foreign demand for American agricultural and manufactured products grew.

A great economic boom and bull market began. When hostilities ceased in November 1918, the United States had evolved from the world's largest debtor to its biggest creditor. Not even a bomb that was allegedly placed by anarchists outside the Morgan Bank in September 1920 and killed 40 people could disturb Wall Street's stature as the new epicenter of global finance. The market's near uninterrupted rise between 1922 and 1929 was powered by an array of factors: increased productivity, mergers, the growth of advertising and use of consumer credit, low interest rates, and the use of margin.[5]

As the American economy matured during the war, women's ranks within the labor market swelled by 400,000.[6] But no demobilization plans for them existed, and when the war ended, so, too, did their employment terminate within most traditionally male strongholds. With the exceptions of those employed in an expanding clerical workforce, women reluctantly returned home. On Wall Street there was a large need for clerical workers and women occupied pink collar jobs in banks and were even scattered among brokerages as switchboard operators, secretaries, and margin clerks.[7]

From the sidelines of the investing public, women certainly numbered among those who bid the stock market higher during the Roaring Twenties. Those heady times found its iconic essence in that of the flappers, who were young women who flaunted their seemingly rebellious behavior and flippant indulgences.[8] While they may have been partying, their more sober sisters did not shy away from stock speculation that figured as another excess of the times. The *Saturday Evening Post* reflected upon the new national pastime that attracted both genders:

Oh, hush, thee, my babe, granny's bought some more shares

Daddy's gone out to play with the bulls and the bears,

Mother's buying on tips, and she simply can't lose,

And baby shall have some expensive new shoes![9]

Mother was buying equities. No one specific catalyst prompted the widespread engagement of women in the market. Instead, a myriad of factors contributed to female participation in the overall speculative frenzy gripping the public: their enhanced financial literacy gleaned from World War I days as bond saleswomen and purchasers, the growing ranks of wage-earning women and savings bank depositors, and the rise in joint marital investment accounts. Women now had more money at hand, and more discretion to allocate it according to their wishes.[10]

From over 5,000 "specialty" brokerages catering to women that sprang up around the country, including within suites at the Waldorf-Astoria Hotel, "ladies of the ticker" purchased stocks.[11] Corporate shareholdings reflected the growing significance of female investors. The Pennsylvania Railroad even became dubbed "the Petticoat Line," as women comprised over half of its shareholders.[12] As the public embraced buying "Any Old Thing,"[13] one survey even suggested that "financial ignorance is largely responsible for the feeling many women have of waning social popularity."[14] Some male brokers complimented their new sources of commissions, albeit with a patronizing tone as they praised female common sense.[15] Despite its norm of entrenched institutional hostility toward outsiders, with the floor of the NYSE described as "better protected against women members than that of Congress,"[16] some women found a professional home on Wall Street. Twenty-two firms now had female partners, and Bank of America had hired the country's first Chinese woman bank manager for its San Francisco Chinatown office.[17]

With the public entranced by the market, personalities known for their stock picking prowess garnered acclaim. Among the luminaries was a woman who hailed not from the ordinary world of finance, but from the celestial realm. Since 1927, astrologer Evangeline Adams focused on predicting the market's future based on interpretations of planetary alignment. In her office above Carnegie Hall, she produced a monthly newsletter sent to over 100,000 subscribers, boasting of her "guaranteed system to beat Wall Street."[18] She attracted such clientele as J.P. Morgan, Mary Pickford, and Charles Schwab.[19]

The stars were indeed crossed as share prices began to drop in early September 1929. Still, debate over the market's general health remained divided. Its decline picked up steam in the second half of October, and on Thursday, October 24, only an agreement by leading bankers to prop up the market with a $20 million infusion helped calm tumultuous trading. Long lines of clients awaited the advice of Adams, who one day earlier had predicted the downturn. After telling them to expect an upturn over the next two days, she then instructed her broker to sell all of her personal holdings the next day.[20]

Prices bounced up on Friday, but selling returned on Saturday. When the market shed 12.82 percent on Monday and 11.73 percent on Tuesday of the following week amid panic selling and high volume, the sell-off knew no gender preferences. The speculative bubble had burst and the Roaring Twenties came to a screeching halt. Even though October 29 became known as Black Tuesday, the market did not reach its low until November 13, with the erasure of two-and-a-half years of gains. By the end of the year, a cautious upturn took shape that continued until the late spring of 1930. Although the market had by then recouped almost half of its losses of the past autumn, more economic hardship followed.[21]

Causes for the Great Depression can easily be attributed to certain factors. In the latter half of 1930, foreign trade stalled as a consequence of the protectionist Smoot-Hawley Tariff. Stock prices slipped for two-and-a-half years amid a tight money supply, bank failures, declining corporate revenues, and the largest tax hike in the country's history. Unemployment soared to over 25 percent, and productivity plummeted.[22]

For women, the Great Depression sent mixed signals. On the one hand, strong female leaders such as First Lady Eleanor Roosevelt and Labor Secretary Frances Perkins, the first woman appointed to the U.S. Cabinet, garnered the spotlight. It became more acceptable for women to work in order to supplement the family income. In addition to increased opportunities available through projects including the Civil Works Administration and the Works Progress Administration, women also benefitted from certain New Deal legislation that promoted fair labor standards, aid to dependent children, and prenatal care. On the other hand, wage-earning women were often seen as unfairly depriving males of income. Various state "right to work" laws discriminated against married women by barring them from certain jobs. Financial hardship also prevented more women from pursuing higher education. During the thirties, the number of married women who worked increased by 3.6–15.3 percent, while female college enrollment dropped by 3.5 percent and the ranks of professional women declined by 1.9 percent.[23]

For Wall Street, it was all too easy to gauge measures of financial distress. The DJIA totaled 41.22 on June 8, 1932, which was just fractionally higher than its 40.94 level on the first day of its existence in 1896. In October 1932, investors scrambled for safety and purchased Treasury bills even though they offered virtually no interest. Volume in equities withered from 1.1 billion shares in 1929 to 500 million in 1933 and NYSE seat prices tumbled along with the market's decline.[24]

With the market now reflecting dreary economic fundamentals instead of its previous froth, attention focused on regulation of the financial industry. President Franklin Roosevelt took office in March 1933 amid a banking panic, and quickly enacted a bank holiday to evaluate systemic soundness and restore confidence. One month later, he took the country off the gold standard. In May, President Roosevelt signed into law the Federal Securities Act, the country's first federal laws governing the securities industry. This legislation changed the face of Wall Street forever by requiring that all new securities issues be registered with the Federal Trade Commission and setting forth disclosure requirements.[25]

By early June, Congress passed the Banking Act of 1933. This legislation, often referred to by reference to its Congressional sponsors as Glass-Steagall, aimed to protect the commercial banking system by creating the Federal Deposit Insurance Corporation that insured deposits up to $5,000 and introducing a legal division between commercial and investment banks. Previously, commercial banks commonly engaged in securities activities, most often through underwriting in their growing bond departments. In the wake of widespread commercial bank failures following the 1929 Crash, this blurring of traditional business lines was blamed for increasing risk in the financial system. Banks now had to choose to either serve as depositary institutions that could not underwrite or sell securities or as investment banks that could not accept deposits.

Further reforms ensued. The Senate Finance Committee held hearings regarding Wall Street practices that led to calls for further regulation. The NYSE headed off some reforms by prohibiting certain practices such as investment pools and forms of insider trading. The Securities Exchange Act of 1934 went even further by establishing the Securities and Exchange Commission (SEC) and regulating secondary trading. SEC Chairman Joseph Kennedy, while promoting a moderate stance regarding regulation, quickly moved to stimulate the return of underwriting and lending. Volume gradually returned to the market, prices began to rise, and brokerages resumed hiring.[26]

As the United States became embroiled in World War II, the American economic engine powered forward. Between 1940 and 1944, the economy grew by 125 percent, but the stock market did not mirror its triumphant rise. The DJIA initially rose in the first days of the war, but soon trended downward until the end of April 1942. Stocks dropped from the end of 1939 to April 1942 as the French and British suffered losses, and did not recover until Allied victory became more likely. The DJIA exited 1945 at a level of 191.47, 27 percent higher than its level six years earlier. Though trading volume and prices had risen, there was not much enthusiasm or widespread public support.[27]

Americans had other uses for their cash. The doubling of disposable personal income that they enjoyed during the first half of the forties was spent on such sober-minded matters as reducing personal debt, spending more on life insurance, and augmenting their savings. Notably absent was any sizable interest of small investors in stocks, who had accounted for little more than 1 percent of the 125 million brokerage accounts in the early 1930s, and remained paralyzed by recollections of the 1929 Crash. Employment on Wall Street declined by nearly 26 percent between 1940 and 1947.[28]

Although the *New York Times* had declared on October 30, 1929, that "Women Traders Going Back to Bridge Games,"[29] females did not fold from the investing game completely. The 1929 Crash had sent speculators of both genders away from the market temporarily, but while the individual investor did not emerge emboldened from World War II, the American woman did. She had once again risen to the demands of war and her contributions were magnified to a greater extent than ever. Even on Wall Street, she had gained more of a toehold.

In the financial arena, the progress of women during the wartime years was initially achieved by individual efforts predicated on patriotic sentiment and exerted in collective action. Just as the women of the Revolution found occasions for action during a time of national and personal crisis, these women of the 1940s also broadened their skill base and demonstrated their capabilities to themselves and to a country needing their services. These experiences bred opportunities to forge new career paths, including in banking, where women staked out a new future. The United States commandeered global leadership as a result of the wars, and her women also marched further along, even breaching the chauvinistic boundary of the NYSE floor.

SIX

The Women's Liberty Loan Committee

When the United States went into war with Germany the business of bond selling was a field so new to women that all work within it has been genuine pioneering.[1]

—Secretary of the Treasury, 1918

"[W]e can not win this war by shutting up women's energies in a garbage can," asserted Helen Ring Robinson, chairwoman of the Colorado Women's Liberty Loan Committee.[2] Indeed, the trash was no place for the likes of the multitudes of women who would contribute their efforts to the cause of American victory in World War I. Rather than remaining idle along the sidelines of history, women found outlets for their patriotic fervor. In so doing, the Great War proved a transcendent movement in which women swept away much prior societal skepticism about female aptitudes and abilities. Lines blurred between separate gender-based spheres even in financial affairs.

Upon the outbreak of World War I, women still had not gained the right to vote, although suffrage had emerged as a strong political cause in the preceding years. Progress was also occurring on other fronts essential to female empowerment. State common law relating to matters of inheritance, earnings, and divorce had already bequeathed to women more economic rights. Although mostly as low wage-earning laborers in manufacturing and textile industries, women in increasing numbers worked outside the home. Once elementary and secondary education for females became more widely available by the 1880s, educational opportunities also broadened. Women's colleges opened their doors to a mainly white, middle-class clientele. In 1870, women comprised 20 percent of the 1 percent of Americans who attended college. By 1910, women accounted for 40 percent of the 5 percent of Americans receiving higher education.[3]

Many of these women joined together to form associations aimed at bettering society through further self-education, community philanthropy, and various social causes. Other non-college graduates also joined in the growing numbers of literary and social clubs that generally comprised middle-class women and sprang up between the Civil War and World War I. The origins of the women's club movement are commonly traced to Jane Cunningham Croly. She was a New York journalist who soon after being barred from attending an all-male dinner given in honor of Charles Dickens at the New York Press Club in 1868 established Sorosis, which became the first well-known prototype of such groups. Although Sorosis pursued educational and social activities for professional women rather than embracing a specific charitable or political purpose, most clubs that later sprang up shared a more civic-minded orientation. Many of these groups became affiliated with the General Federation of Women's Clubs, an umbrella organization that encompassed more than 60 other clubs, formed at the initiative of Sorosis in 1890 to unify the efforts of local clubs. Similar consortiums sprang up under the auspices of the National Council of Jewish Women in 1893 and the National Association of Colored Women's Clubs in 1896.[4]

As middle-class women enjoyed the luxury of indulging in volunteer activities, toughening economic circumstances forced less privileged women to earn wages. While most toiled in traditionally female jobs such as in domestic service or in the garment or food industries, the expanding pink collar sector offered opportunities. Approximately 600,000 women worked in offices by 1910, and seven years later, almost 99 percent of all switchboard operators were women.[5]

These changes were manifest on Wall Street where communications advances that facilitated efficient price dissemination had already contributed to the financial industry's growth. A 1905 *New York Times* article attested to the growing number of lunchrooms catering to working women in lower Manhattan's financial district. Recalling the days when Victoria Woodhull and Tennessee Claflin could not be seated at Delmonico's without an escort, the writer adroitly observed, "The only force which is strong enough to break down social convention is economic necessity."[6]

War also served as an extraordinary catalyst for change. The outbreak of hostilities jolted the nation from its relatively complacent Victorian era upper- and middle-class lifestyle of leisure and comfort into the grim circumstances of global strife.[7] A new harsh domestic economic reality demanded rationing and conservation that gave rise to both victory gardens as well as a new crop of American women eager to serve their country. Whether among the more than 25,000 women who served overseas as nurses, cooks, clerks, journalists, and entertainers, or remaining at home ensconced in relief work or filling labor shortages, women shouldered their share of wartime burdens.[8] Through their efforts as concerned citizens, they helped strengthen the cause of women's political and economic rights.

Women had broadly supported the war prior to official U.S. entry in April 1917. But although World War I ultimately accelerated the advancement of American women, some found it particularly vexing to reconcile President Wilson's call to "make the world safe for democracy"[9] with the legal status of women at home. Wilson's record on women's rights was hardly a bulwark of support. Initially opposed to a national suffrage amendment, he preferred to leave the issue to individual state decisions and largely ignored angry militant suffragists who repeatedly picketed the White House.[10]

Female leaders urged President Wilson to establish a national women's organization to support the war efforts. In April 1917, with the President's approval, the Council of National Defense created the Women's Committee that was charged with the mission "to coordinate the female preparedness movement."[11] Under the leadership of suffrage activist Dr. Anna Howard Shaw, the group did more than merely function in an advisory capacity. Drawing on the women's club movement as an organizational tool, the group established a network of state and local branches with the intent to mobilize every American woman.[12] Careful not to inject suffragist politics into the mission, Shaw admonished the women: "Do not mention suffrage in connection with this work. In my work on the committee I am only a patriotic citizen working for my country."[13]

At the outset, the Women's Committee focused on how best to assist the Red Cross and to promote food conservation and thrift. Before long, the country recognized the value of female volunteerism, even in financial matters. Turning to the capital markets to raise the necessary wartime funds, the United States authorized the issuance of the so-called Liberty Bonds. This debt instrument, offered in denominations ranging from

$50 to $100,000 and released through five campaigns occurring between April 1917 and October 1919, ultimately provided over $21 billion. Much of the manpower behind the bond drives that produced approximately two-thirds of the war's funding was provided by women.[14]

In order to sell these bonds, Treasury Secretary William Gibbs McAdoo embarked on a public relations campaign to effectively capitalize patriotism through Hollywood rallies and attention-grabbing posters. At first, the "Liberty Loan Volunteer Army"[15] did not rely heavily on the organized efforts of women. That soon changed. In early May 1917, McAdoo acknowledged the strong interests expressed by various women's clubs to distribute the debt and made public his plans to organize a women's committee: "I believe it can render service of the most effective sort in bringing the advantage of this loan to the attention of women throughout the land, who, I am assured, wish to manifest in a concrete and striking way the extent of their own resources and of their patriotism in this hour of the national need."[16] Within weeks, he appointed members to the newly formed Women's Liberty Loan Committee (WLLC) and installed his wife as chair.[17]

Eleanor Randolph McAdoo had big intentions. Prior to a September conference of women bond volunteers, she announced intentions for marshaling their energies with a nationwide scope, declaring that "We recognize that united effort of the women in the country is as essential to success as the united efforts of the men. It is our aim that there be a Liberty Bond in every home."[18] The WLLC became organized into geographically based subcommittees, of which some also established "colored committees."[19] Certain women held key positions in both the WLLC and the Women's Committee as the two groups tried to ally their operations. Eventually, all organized women's loan work fell under the official auspices of the WLLC.[20]

Few male leaders expected that the women would significantly contribute to actual bond sales, yet they achieved surprising success from the outset.[21] In her published history of the Women's Committee, executive office member Emily Newell Blair captured the disjuncture between ideology espoused by the government and reality first encountered by women:

> In May 1917 the status of women was a nebulous will-o'-the wisp. When speeches were made to mothers of boys, woman was the strongest power of the world, the noblest jewel in America's diadem; when food was wanted, she was the foundation stone on which our whole economic structure is

Women's Liberty Loan Committee. (Library of Congress, Prints and Photographs Division)

built; when labor was needed she was the great reserve of the industrial world; when pain and anguish wrung the brow or threatened to, she was a ministering angel. But when she asked for a definite status in the scheme of things, when she asked for the privilege of deciding how she should serve her country and what her contribution to victory should be, her status varied according to the group of men to whom she applied, from that of a mendicant on the doorstep begging for a chance to do all the drudgery of war work to that of a favored creditor, receiving financial aid, provided her desires were O.K.'d by her banker.[22]

The WLLC initially focused on publicizing and rallying support for the matter of war finance. To attract attention, they resorted to a degree of theatrics. Their activities included erecting a miniature replica of the Sub-Treasury building on Wall Street, installing neoclassical statues of winged women throughout Philadelphia, and engaging throughout the country in an assortment of creative outreach activities, even organizing community song and dance events.[23]

The WLLC also engaged in more substantive educational efforts. It explained to a relatively uninformed public various options available for financing the war and demonstrated the merits of government bond investments. The members themselves had significantly expanded their own financial literacy through their participation. In New York City, Wall Street executives led intensive weeklong training sessions in bond-selling techniques. In order to induce purchasers, many Americans first needed to be enlightened about investment generally. Anecdotes gleaned from WLLC canvassers shed light on the degree of financial illiteracy that they encountered. When asked which bond denomination she'd prefer, one elderly woman responded "Methodist."[24] Men didn't fare much better; a man responded to a request to purchase a Liberty Bond by exclaiming "Why I thought that Liberty Statue was paid for long ago."[25] To an unsophisticated population of men and women alike, government posters pointed out that bonds paid interest and underscored the safety of the security.[26]

Reminiscent of the selling tactics utilized during the Revolution by the Philadelphia Ladies, the WLLC emphasized thrift and rallied behind the slogan, "No New Dresses" at the outset of the Fourth Liberty Loan offering.[27] They, too, mixed an appeal to patriotism together with a dose of female charm. A training pamphlet cautioned volunteers that ". . . it is your duty as an American to stamp out all forms of arguments which will injure the total sales. Any attack on the Government or the Liberty Bond campaign is an attack on you, and should be reported AT ONCE to your captain."[28] That same brochure advised, "Smile! Smile if it hurts!! If you come in with a long face, the prospect will wonder who's dead!"[29]

Their methods worked. Whether due to patriotic fervor or a new appreciation of investment, the war bonds sold. Even in the face of personal hardship, women themselves bought the securities. Although 35 percent of the total subscribers in North Carolina to the Fourth Liberty Loan were women, not all of those investors possessed substantial assets.[30] There, an elderly woman invested her entire lifetime savings in a hundred-dollar bond, and bought it with a thousand dimes ensconced within an old jug buried beneath her cottage.[31] Her specific circumstances may have been unique, but similar scenarios of economic strain echoed throughout the country. In Wyoming, for example, Cecilia Hennel Hendricks recounted in 1918, "We ourselves have invested in five one-hundred dollar bonds. Of course we had to borrow the money, but it sure is the time to lend our credit to the nation now. We can pay off the money when our crop returns come in next fall."[32] Organizers in Alabama particularly noted the enthusiastic response from its black female community whose incomes ranked lowest among its citizens.[33]

Women! Help America's sons win the war—Buy U.S. Government Bonds, 2nd Liberty Loan of 1917/R. H. Porteous. (Library of Congress, Prints and Photographs Division)

The success of the Liberty Bond sales derived from both leadership within the WLLC and support procured from its audience that included substantial numbers of women. Although they had little, if any, prior investment experience, females accounted for nearly one-third of all the Liberty Bond purchasers of the first issue. In Los Angeles, women outnumbered male investors at a ratio of 7:3. At the outset of the Second Liberty Loan sale that commenced in October 1917 and included 60,000 women volunteers, Mrs. John T. Pratt, WLLC chair of the Second Federal Reserve District, outlined one of her goals as having "every woman who has bought a bond sells one to somebody else, and not necessarily to a woman, either . . . we want to be able to say that the women stood shoulder to shoulder with the men in every department of their Liberty Loan activity."[34] Over the course of the Third Liberty Loan campaign that commenced seven months later, women constituted 40 percent of the total bond subscriptions, and approximately a half-million women volunteers accounted for over a billion dollars worth of sales.[35]

Despite encountering pockets of continued bigotry and even occasional early tensions that arose with their male counterparts, a female chairperson represented the campaign in nearly every locality in the United States during the Third Liberty Loan sale.[36] As the war caused more men who had previously sold bonds to shift into military or industrial service, women increasingly shouldered the burden of selling the debt. Girl Scouts contributed their energies as well, with 500 scouts having sold a minimum of 10 bonds to 10 individuals and becoming eligible to receive a Liberty Bond Medal in June 1918.[37] By the following autumn, between 700,000 and 800,000 women actively participated in the activities of the WLLC.[38]

Grateful political leaders acknowledged the contributions of the country's women. Their service in support of the war, coupled with the women of Great Britain gaining the vote, had already caused President Wilson earlier in the year to support a constitutional amendment for suffrage.[39] Addressing Congress in September, Wilson urged:

> We have made partners of the women in this war; shall we admit them only to a partnership of suffering and sacrifice and toil and not to a partnership of privilege and right? This war could not have been fought, either by the other nations engaged or by America, if it had not been for the services of the women,—services rendered in every sphere,—not merely in the fields of effort in which we have been accustomed to see them work, but wherever men have worked and upon the very skirts and edges of the battle itself.[40]

Secretary McAdoo proclaimed October 5, 1918 to be "Women in War Work Day."[41] In his annual report, he elaborated on the work of the WLLC:

> No mere recital of results achieved can show the extent of the service which women have given to the Nation through their participation in war finance. That hundreds of thousands of women assumed the burden of a new kind of labor, not for themselves but for their country, is one of the most striking and characteristic facts in relation to the women of America that the war has developed. The Liberty loans have afforded a new proving ground where the women of the Nation have accepted the opportunity to demonstrate again their patriotism, their ability, their consciousness of the obligations of citizenship, and their steadfastness of soul in the great and terrible crisis which our country has met.[42]

Nearly 140 years earlier, the Philadelphia Ladies had similarly proved their willingness and prowess at stepping outside their comfort zones to sustain their country during a cataclysmic fight for national survival. While those volunteers helped underwrite the country's independence and so earned ephemeral praise, they did not secure lasting rewards for women. In contrast, as a result in part to the contributions of the WLLC, women won the vote. They were now vested political stakeholders. They also had invested in their own potential independent and professional futures. As Blair asserts in her account of women's wartime service, "No one event in history has done more to crumble that mortar [of division between male and female roles] than the Great War."[43]

Without formal plans for demobilization, however, women found themselves unwelcome in traditionally male positions once men began returning home. The American woman had gained the vote and helped win the war, but, particularly in the manufacturing sector, she lost the immediate battle to retain many of her occupational advancements.[44] Ironically, women achieved a more enduring legacy in finance, which had previously extended limited access to females. The WLLC merits acclaim for its hand in enabling that to occur. Showcasing their talents and aptitude at a range of disciplines not customarily open to them, including finance, the women of the WLLC became increasingly recognized by the public for "hav[ing] shown an organizing and business ability quite equal to that of men."[45] In so doing, they broadened their own financial literacy and that of the public, and whetted investment appetites.

Women even advanced within the private financial sector. Although some had worked in banks prior to the war, their jobs had been nearly wholly in clerical positions. These existing ranks found expanded opportunities as they provided the initial solution for financial institutions that felt the pinch of losing men to the war.[46] Women comprised 59 percent of all officers and employees of national banks on November 1, 1918. They accounted for 86 percent and 68 percent of the respective Chicago and Boston financial workforces.[47] New York City women, who comprised 48 percent of that city's employees in national banks, formed their own wartime assistance group, the Business Women's War Service, offering experienced administrative and clerical services to wartime relief groups.[48] But acknowledging the lack of trained female financial professionals, the president of one large Wall Street company fretted, "It is not as if we could reach out and grab some casual individual in the world at large to fill a given gap. We can't put women in the places of the men we lose, as Mr. Shonts is doing in the subway and as is being done in so many other lines of industry. It is not common labor that we need, but specialists, and specialists are few and hard to get."[49]

Banks began conducting training courses for women, who soon became immersed in nearly all bank departments.[50] Emphasizing the need to prepare women to replace absent men, Columbia University opened courses to women on the subjects of banking, higher economics, and corporate finance.[51] According to one female banker, "It was not until our men were called overseas that we made any real onslaught on the realm of finance, and became tellers, managers of departments, and junior and senior officers."[52] In 1917, Rochester engineer and business executive Kate Gleason stepped in to lead the First National Bank of East Rochester during the remaining wartime years when its president enlisted in the army. She became regarded as the country's first female bank president without familial ties to an existing institution.[53]

Women had gained a toehold in banking, an industry which itself was undergoing massive transformation as the country secured prominence as a global power and technological advances provided increased efficiencies for the international capital markets. Neither the United States nor Wall Street would ever be the same following the Great War. Likewise, the female role in finance would not be the same. American women had broadly been exposed to the investment rationale and displayed their business acumen to the public in a largely non-threatening way. While women had not truly secured their spot on Wall Street, the scales of change had begun to tip there in favor of female opportunities and advancement.

SEVEN

Women Bankers

So far, women bankers are freaks.[1]

—*Bank executive Anne Seward, 1922*

Virginia Furman set out only to tend to her personal banking one warm summer day in 1915. She had no idea that her errand would lead her to a prominent career in banking.[2] As she departed the Fifth Avenue branch of the Columbia Trust Company, a vice president interrupted her departure. He offered her a job. Incredulous, Furman asked, "Why? What could I do? I'm fifty-four and know nothing of the business."[3] The following morning, the officer called her and reiterated his proposition. And with such inauspicious beginnings, Furman's groundbreaking banking career began.[4]

In 1919, Furman's management of the bank's women's department led to her appointment as its assistant secretary. Her selection as New York's first female bank officer made headlines. Hailed by suffrage leaders, her appointment attracted female clientele and prompted competing banks to hire more women.[5]

The notion of businesses catering to females was not exclusive to the financial industry. Prior to the turn of the century, many department stores, post offices, and railroad compartments had offered similarly specialized services. Within financial institutions, women's banking departments had sprung up in New York, Chicago, Washington, D.C., and even smaller cities such as Rochester, New Haven, and Spokane.[6] These separate banking divisions often utilized separate physical office spaces apart from the main banking lobbies. In order to accommodate the practice of women carrying their deposits tucked into their hose, The National Bank of Commerce in Kansas City made headlines in 1903 when it opened a "stocking room," in which women could access their funds in private. This feature made headlines and was soon emulated by other banks. A conscientious effort was made to transform these areas so as to appeal to "ladies of leisure" by resembling comfortable extensions of one's home. Furnished to convey an aura of wealth, they shared a similar decor aesthetic. A female consultant hired to design a women's division for a New York bank described her plans that included thick rugs laid on teakwood floors, walls covered in tapestries, and mahogany furniture set forth in a suite comprised of a general banking room, sitting room, and dressing room.[7]

The ambience provided a comfortable backdrop by which to acquaint women with various facets of the banking experience. An 1894 account of a Brooklyn bank aimed at female depositors recounted that "Daintily designed checks and crisp new currency are always features of a woman's bank."[8] A Manhattan bank predicated the 1906 opening of its women's annex on several factors, including female confusion over figures "unless they were certain that their hats were on 'straight,'"[9] their apprehension over waiting in line while holding their possessions, and their lack of confidence in formulating decisions. Advising that tellers be male as they were more "convincing" to the patrons, a female employee charged with planning recommendations further cautioned, "We'll leave out the tea until we have considered further. But we must not forget a great need, and that is smelling salts. It is so necessary, when a woman finds that her account is overdrawn."[10]

At the time, bankers viewed women's departments more as nuisances satisfying relatively unimportant female budgetary matters than as serious endeavors.[11] An 1897 article that took note of the approximate half-dozen banks within the New York City environs operating women's departments provided mixed reviews on the female bank customer, commenting, "At the outset this particular feature took on the character of a primary school in banking, the tellers at the women's windows finding it necessary to give minute and rudimentary instructions to their patrons. That was some years ago, however. The average woman depositor is a very independent and self-contained bank patron now."[12] In that same article, a bank president applauded women for learning to write a check but chastised them for their proclivity to omit their signatures, "after finishing with the figures their minds seem to leave the check and pass on to some other subject."[13]

Bank Deposit
Copyright 1908, by Consolidated Art Co, Boston.

Woman with bank deposit, 1908. (Library of Congress, Prints and Photographs Division)

This "first wave"[14] of women's departments that catered to mainly well-to-do women with "Christmas present accounts"[15] evolved into a wider business pursuit in the following decades. Post-World War I female intrusion in the financial arena could be seen tangibly as women swelled the ranks of the ensuing investing craze of the 1920s. America was punch drunk on speculation, and women shared in the party. Participants included an emerging class of female investors that encompassed clerical workers, beneficiaries of corporate stock sharing programs, and the very wealthy. A 1926 article on the rise of female investors noted that women who used to fear handling a checkbook of $100 now invested hundreds of thousands of dollars. The article further commented, "Modern women have marched down to Wall Street and learned to battle with investments in stocks, bonds, and futures. To them the terms securities, common stock, preferred stock, marketability, income, increase and diversity are no longer the bugbears they seemed before the World War."[16]

True enough, but women still faced discrimination from many Wall Street professionals who resisted the purported emotionalism of female investors and also refused to hire female salespeople.[17] Loathe to altogether forego a source of commissions, more banks established separate women's departments and brokerages opened special customer trading rooms attracting the likes of "aggressive, guttural dowagers, gum-chewing blondes, [and] shrinking spinsters who look as if they belonged in a missionary-society meeting."[18] This segregation provided career opportunities for Furman and other women when managers sought to hire women to attract and cater to female clientele. In 1918, Evelyn Aldrich, head of the women's department at the American International Corporation, became the first woman to address the American Institute of Banking. In her speech, she professed that women and men shared similar business capacities, "Ability is not so much a matter of sex as of the individual."[19] With respect to the purported declining interest of female employees, she pointed out that "It is because of the attitude of the men in the bank, especially the young men. They make these girls think that the bank is man's field, that the girls are not welcome and only there because they are sorely needed; that there is no hope of their getting very far."[20]

Welcome or not, women proceeded to infiltrate available positions. In 1921, Cornell University graduate and bond saleswoman Elizabeth Ellsworth Cook, who began her career in 1908, founded the Women's Bond Club (WBC), a professional organization for women in financial services. Cook had counseled women of opportunities in finance in 1918 in the pages of the *Journal of the Association of Collegiate Alumnae*, concluding,

"There are still so few women in finance that each one stands as typical of her whole sex to a large group of men. It is of the utmost importance that each acquit herself credibly lest she be a stumbling block to those stronger, freer, better women who are to come."[21] By 1926, Empire Trust Company Assistant Secretary Anne Seward, noting the situation in Manhattan, commented that few banks in midtown and above did not employ women managers to oversee their women's departments.[22] Outside New York, certain advances had come even earlier and were more pronounced. Lena Riddle Steck had founded the Texas Women Bankers' Association in 1912 to forge closer ties between women interested in banking, whether as stockholders, directors, or executives.[23] In Tennessee, Brenda Vineyard Runyon had established the First Woman's Bank in 1919, the country's first "all feminine" bank, which specialized in lending to women and encouraging savings and investing.[24]

Largely held back from positions of broad authority, women working in large metropolitan financial entities found their niches as assistant secretaries, assistant cashiers, managers of the women's departments, and in general research units. Many of them had rudimentary financial knowledge gleaned from their wartime experiences but sported social connections in lieu of formal training. Furman's own background consisted of leadership roles during the Liberty Loan campaigns, high society affiliations, and a father who had been a bank president. She along with other recent banking newcomers Key Cammack, Nathalie Laimbeer, Mina Bruere, and Jean Arnot Reid formalized the emergence of women bankers and charted a course for their professional future. Their individual stories illustrate the circuitous routes that led them each to banking careers.[25]

Cammack, the next New York City female banker after Furman to gain widespread recognition, became assistant secretary of the New York Trust Company after a varied path. An early writing career foreshadowed her later focus on education, budgeting, and thrift. In a children's verse entitled "High Finance," she penned, "As he hurried up the stairs his fingers opened unawares; Two shining nickels skipped and spun, and through a deep dark crack slipped one. O Fortune, thou art fickle."[26] Subsequent wartime relief work led to a stint with the U.S. Department of Labor before entering banking.[27]

Fortune indeed proved fickle for Laimbeer. Left a "penniless" widow with three children by her noted broker husband in 1913, she attained similar acclaim eventually in her own career. At first a food conservation volunteer during the war, she entered banking in 1919 to organize the women's and new business departments of the United States Mortgage and Trust Company. She became manager of both units in January 1920 and assistant secretary six months later. In 1925, she served as the first female executive of National City Bank as assistant cashier and head of the women's department.[28]

Bruere had left a singing career for social work prior to serving for seven years as private secretary to the president of National City Bank. In 1921, she managed the new women's department of the Central Union Trust Company. Appointed assistant secretary the following year, she was described later as having lived according to her maxim: "Accept as a great adventure the challenge life offers."[29]

Reid, a former artist and overseas Red Cross director, encountered her career break upon her return home when a financial statement that she had prepared for a Red Cross hospital impressed a banker. This interaction led to an assignment to help organize the women's department at Bankers Trust Company. After a year of working in bank offices during the day and at the American Institute of Banking in the evening, she became manager of a midtown branch women's department.[30]

Clara Porter, a Smith College graduate, rounded out the group. An assistant secretary of the Guaranty Trust Company's bond department, she had studied municipal finance while serving as an editor for the New York Edison Company before embarking on her banking career in 1918.[31]

Meeting on February 25, 1921 at Furman's invitation "just to talk things over,"[32] the six women contemplated how they might best help each other professionally as well as the possible organization of a broader coalition of executive bank women. At the time, Bruere later reflected, "The men executives of the banks had no clear conception of the program they wished the women they were inviting into their organizations to enter upon. The women themselves had none either, because they had no precedent to follow, nothing to guide them in the new work they were taking up. They were starting out it in an entirely new direction and had to chart their own course by experience."[33] They met again, nearly two months later, and this time they attracted nine additional women intent on proving the growing presence of women in the industry and to increase their efficiency and exchange ideas.[34]

A month later, just one year after Congress established the Women's Bureau of the Department of Labor to address issues confronted by working women, the women bankers solidified their leadership structure and mission. An executive committee was formed, consisting of president Furman, vice president Laimbeer, secretary Bruere, treasurer Reid, program chair Cammack, and membership chair Caroline Olney, who was manager of the women's department of an uptown branch of the United States Mortgage and Trust Company.[35] The 16 members each paid $5 dues and approved a motion:

RESOLVED

That the purpose of this Association be

    To encourage mutual helpfulness and cooperation among its members with the end view in making themselves increasingly valuable to the institutions with which they are associated,

    To help not only its members but other women wishing to take up the same type of work; to take advantage of opportunities which may come to the attention of the Association from time to time.

    And at all times to uphold the dignity and integrity of women associated with (or employed by) banks.[36]

By late September, the group adopted the name "The Association of Bank Women" (ABW) and sought female bank executives with customer contact for membership. At this same meeting, Porter resigned but retained cordial relations with the group.[37] Although the official history of the early years of the ABW states that her "resignation was regretfully accepted in view of the change in the character of her work,"[38] one historian suggests that she may have grown uncomfortable with the separatism and potential career entrapment of women's departments.[39]

The ABW evolved in its early years to target membership, publicity, and education as its immediate priorities. The first non-local members joined in early 1922. That year also heralded the advent of monthly meetings and inauguration of a yearbook. Even more auspicious was the organization's presence and the warm reception received at the 1922 ABA convention. There was now impetus for the women to hold their own assembly. In September 1923, 43 women representing 13 states attended the ABW's first general convention. Held in Atlantic City to coincide with the concurrent meeting of the ABA, the women's function notably attracted an impromptu appearance by the ABA president who welcomed the women to the industry. Two months later, the group launched the monthly *ABW News*.[40]

External trade publications and the popular press alike provided ample coverage to women's departments and their female managers.[41] Even those articles most favorable to the developments, however, contained stereotypes concerning women's lack of permanence in the labor force, disposition toward gossip and flirtation, and natural disinclination to money and business.[42] While women's place in banking was acknowledged, their significance remained open to debate. Chief among the contentions was whether banking and motherhood were mutually exclusive. In 1922, British author Arthur Stuart-Menteth Hutchinson published a best-selling novel in which the banker heroine suffers the deaths of her three children, ostensibly due to her career choice.[43] Bank officer and writer Seward disputed this premise in a *New York Times* article while raising her own concerns: "But are women really bankers in the true sense of the word? Are they not sex instruments for their sex? Are they not in banks as buffers for the men officers, as social baits for the rich women clients, as ornaments for the women's departments?"[44]

Eye candy to a degree, they were also valuable and visionary. Evidence exists of increasing significance of female bankers and their business. Eighteen women delegates attended the 1922 ABA convention, which had no female officials 18 years earlier.[45] A 1924 survey by the Union Trust Company revealed that women's accounts were more profitable than men's by 9 percent.[46] Laimbeer, who had become ABW president in 1923, spoke optimistically in 1925 of a woman's place in finance, "I believe that the greatest development in any future phase of banking will be the development of the woman power in banks."[47]

Her outlook appeared borne out over the next several years, at least in terms of numbers. One New York bank that had only two female employees prior to World War I employed 1,000 by 1929. Outside New York City, especially within familial enterprises, women rose even faster to higher positions. While most of the customers were male, a women's savings and loan in the Midwest boasted all females among its officers and directors, and 90 percent of its stockholders. Nationwide, women comprised nearly 2,000 bank officers in 1929.[48]

But the 1929 Crash and the ensuing Great Depression stymied investing activities and brought with it the demise of many women's departments.[49] To the public, "Wall Street" became a dirty name. With no "easy" money to be made and trust in the financial system tarnished, many individuals withdrew remaining funds from the market and resorted to hoarding any savings.[50] Various educational outreach projects halted, and ABW membership dropped 23 percent between 1929 and 1933 to a total of 189, which was equal to its 1925 level.[51] The identification of over 4,000 potential members led ABW President Grace Stoermer to try to rebuild membership through promotion: "We must make the public conscious of the permanency and worth of the contribution which we as women bankers are making to the world of finance and business. . . . The emergencies of the times should be looked upon as a worthy challenge to the Association, which holds within its membership so many women of ability and intellectual attainment, of experience and vision."[52]

Not all female financial forays were extinguished. Despite diminished resources, women directed at least 73 percent of retail buying and comprised at least 40 percent of the stockholders of large corporations.[53] In 1935, politically conservative isolationist Cathrine Curtis organized the "Women Investors in America." Billed as "an outgrowth of a nationally spreading interest of women in financial and social problems,"[54] the group engaged in a mix of financial education and anti-New Deal lobbying that attracted 300,000 members by 1939.[55] On the other side of the political spectrum, feminist activist Harriot Stanton Blatch asserted the need for female economic empowerment, but thought few women managed their own money due to lack of training and confidence.[56] Mina Bruere believed that Blatch would be surprised to overhear the decisiveness of her female clientele. This trait she attributed to the wartime experience of women handling money matters in the absence of men: "they have never relinquished either their interest or their participation."[57]

Although the Great Depression wreaked financial havoc on both genders, the crisis actually provoked more women to enter the labor force. While men bore the brunt of layoffs from the male-dominated fields of manufacturing and heavy industry, many women sought wage-earning jobs outside the home to supplement the family income. Most opportunities existed for them in the traditional female-oriented sectors of domestic and clerical work, teaching, and nursing. ABW President Agnes Kenney, however, believed that Wall Street would also offer employment prospects, and stated at the 1934 convention, "I am not among those who view with alarm the job mortality among women in banks and think that their places will be taken by men. In all evolutions some mortality is inevitable. Instead I believe that as business improves there will be a greater demand for the services of women. Officers and customers have come to realize that the intelligent woman executive makes a special and valuable contribution to the banking profession."[58]

During the 1930s, the ABW redoubled its membership drive and publicity campaigns. It also urged continued cooperation with the American Institute of Banking in its public educational efforts. Ranking chief among its accomplishments stood the 1935 establishment of an internal library of speeches, clippings, and academic materials. Four years later, *The Woman Banker*, a successor to the *ABW News*, appeared. In the premier April 1939 issue, President Mildred Roberts editorialized that "More than ever before is there need in the banking world for qualified women to help in the gigantic tasks facing it. It is the quiet efficient mastery of these problems and the aid we give in the smooth working of our institutional machinery that constitutes our real worth to our banks and to our Association that most effectively promotes the interests of all women in the banking profession."[59] The editor of *Banking*, the journal of the American Bankers Association (ABA), hailed the new publication as "an event of historic importance."[60] His encouraging sentiments echoed that of other male bankers during this time who promoted the idea of ABW membership.[61]

The ABW not only weathered the storm of the 1930s, it ultimately thrived. The latter half of the decade showed steady growth in membership, reaching 272 members in 1939, which evidenced a growth of 1,700 percent from its inception.[62] In 1939, the *New York Times* also extolled the career of Mary Vail Andress, the only female officer at the country's largest bank, Chase National Bank, as symbolic of the advancement of women in banking. Lacking formal training when she entered the field with the Paris office of Bankers Trust Company in 1920, she specialized in assisting traveling Americans with foreign exchange matters. Upon her return home four years later, she joined Chase. Without restrictions limiting her to female customers or individual accounts, her duties also included public relations and the opening of a London branch. An active ABW member and staunch believer in mentoring, Andress suggested that female stockholders and executives needed to do more to help other women advance.[63]

Andress's advice hearkened back to the original purpose of the ABW founders. Describing the rationale underlying the original impetus to form the ABW, Bruere once explained that "By pooling our experience and our ideas, it was our thought that we women might evolve a workable set of ideals and standards, both for our own guidance and that of those who would in the natural course of progress follow us."[64] Certainly, the formation of the ABW marked a significant step toward professionalizing the advent of women in banking. By setting membership standards and establishing forums for communication and exchange of ideas, an infrastructure now existed to support and promote female financial executives.

On the eve of war in 1941, the ABW claimed 331 members.[65] While women bankers in their earlier forays may have been utilized predominantly as bait to lure potential customers, many of these women did their best to reel in substantive careers for themselves. To borrow from a well-known adage, the banks gave them a rod, albeit a small one, and they taught themselves to fish. The opportunities encountered by the women, coupled with their own professionalization and networking, would help lead in the ensuing decades not to the mere mention of the appearance of women in banks, but to the achievements of women bankers.

EIGHT

Rosie the Wall Streeter

New York's financial district has always taken the attitude that women can handle the money in the home, if their husbands are willing, but that they should remain at least a silver dollar's throw away from the Street.[1]

—*New York Times, May 13, 1945*

On April 28, 1943, 18-year-old Helen Hanzelin encountered catcalling, whistles, and jeers "as few Long Islanders outside the ranks of the Brooklyn Dodgers have ever faced."[2] She wasn't stepping up to the plate on the ball field, however. Instead, by merely showing up for work that day, she shattered the 150-year-old male-only preserve of the NYSE trading floor.[3]

Armed with a smile and dressed in a carefully composed tan gabardine corporate uniform, Hanzelin spent her first hour on the job posing for pictures and answering reporters' questions. Then, she began learning the nuts and bolts of her new duties as a telephone clerk in Booth X-J for Merrill Lynch & Co. (Merrill Lynch). A native New Yorker, Hanzelin had left her junior year of high school just that February in order to work in the Merrill Lynch wire room. The firm, like so many others, had already lost 275 employees as Wall Street ranks dwindled due to young men joining the armed services. Hanzelin was soon promoted to the order room where she identified share certificates relating to particular orders. One month later, she joined nine other male telephone clerks on the floor, half that of the pre-war number, and reported odd-lot trades.[4]

Newspapers nationwide carried Hanzelin's photo. Fan mail even included a screen test proposal.[5] Any additional reinforcements to Hanzelin's "lone Battle of the Sexes," cautioned the *New York Times*, "Should not be the kind that fluster easily."[6] Regardless of whether the deluge of publicity or a mere common cold caused Helen to be absent the last week of May, Merrill Lynch summoned Helen Kowalski to fill in. Eighteen-year-old "Helen the Second"[7] remained on the floor when Hanzelin, Helen the First, returned. Approximately six weeks later, the NYSE itself hired 36 young women to work as "quote girls" and "carrier pages" on the trading floor. Once again, attire merited careful consideration. Consultation with the secretaries of top exchange officials led to the selection of uniforms comprised of conservative blue wool blouses and skirts.[8]

Apparently, things went well for the female hires. Women filled in similarly on other exchanges, including the New York Curb Exchange and the San Francisco Stock Exchange. By early August, the *New York Times* reported that since the prevailing opinion that work on the NYSE floor was too emotionally trying for women was now discredited, the hypothetical possibility of future female floor members there had surfaced.[9] According to the article, although the exchange's status as a private club meant that it could arbitrarily rule against any membership application, it remained proud that it had never done so. This assertion must have seemed absurd to the many brokers who did not sport prestigious family lineages or academic pedigrees and instead conducted their business as members of the more ethnically and culturally diverse ranks of the New York Curb Exchange, the forerunner of the American Stock Exchange (Amex). Rest assured, soothed an NYSE official quoted in the article, "If an applicant is a person of good reputation, is financially responsible and knows the brokerage business, the decision is invariably favorable."[10] In fact, a woman of whom little is known was rumored to have unsuccessfully sought membership in 1927.[11] As it stood, approximately 90 women were "allied members" by virtue of being partners of stock exchange firms.[12]

While the appearance of a "girl" on the exchange floor struck a symbolic resonance, women had been making strides in finance since the days of World War I. Wall Street itself had evolved from a cult of high profile personalities to a more diverse group of players as business increased, in part due to cultivation of public investment stemming from the Liberty Bond sales.[13] The bonds themselves had stimulated job creation in both commercial and investment banks. For women in particular, the Liberty Bonds had served as their introduction to the securities world. According to ABW leader Mina Bruere, "Our first Liberty Loan was the most significant thing that ever happened to women in finance. It taught women what stocks and bonds were."[14]

Helen Hanzelin on New York Stock Exchange floor, 1943. (AP Photo/Pool)

Irma Dell Eggleston proved a particularly astute learner. She numbered among the cadre of women who forged Wall Street careers directly through opportunities afforded by World War I. On the day the United States declared war on Germany, she assumed a wartime vacancy at brokerage C.F. Childs & Co. The new position was admittedly "an experiment on both sides."[15] Lacking a college degree or any business training, she first worked as a manager's assistant before transitioning to trading, in which she excelled. She gained fame for holding a record in trading Liberty Bonds. She traded $30 billion worth in 10 years, which was almost double the total amount of $17.75 billion such bonds issued.[16]

Eggleston insisted that other women could have matched her record if given the opportunity. She did concede, however, that her feat "has not been easy."[17] Once, when confronted with a male customer who refused to deal with a woman, she simply directed a male to use his voice over the phone while she discretely directed the sale. Eggleston foresaw a bright future for women, commenting in 1927, "There is great opportunity for them in the financial field, but it takes a particular type of mind. Women have begun to prove aptitude for it, and I think the time is surely coming when they will be recognized as on a par with men. At present a woman has to work about three times as hard as a man to hold down the same job."[18]

By 1929, whether or not by working harder, hampered by trading restrictions, dismissed as decorations, or labeled as the biggest gamblers and poorest losers, women had become "an assured, if minor, denizen of Wall Street."[19] Not only did women invest in securities, but securities firms invested in them by hiring female employees. Two hundred forty-seven women belonged to the ABW and forty women awaited membership in the WBC.[20] Women had taken banking positions both in women's departments and as saleswomen who could "go out for whatever accounts they can get, masculine or feminine."[21] At least 22 exchange firms had female partners and one woman, Ethel G. Rich, even headed her own brokerage, Rich, Clark & Company.[22]

Journalist Eunice Fuller Barnard, a frequent chronicler of female financial activity, remarked that "the rise of women in financial occupations has largely paralleled the increase in the number of sisters with money of their own to invest."[23] Her June 1929 examination of professional women making progress in finance revealed their optimism despite their exclusion from certain brokerage offices, restrictions to working with female clientele, the comparatively lower wages that they were earning, and their lack of high-level representation. One female broker noted that women had already succeeded in sales positions, but had made few advances in "the higher positions within big investment concerns, involving the buying of securities, that women have not as yet had an opportunity to show whether or not they have ability. For these controlling officerships, attained usually through office contacts, are still always given to men."[24] Another saleswoman lamented that although she had never experienced discrimination, many female college graduates lacked the financial coursework and experience of their male peers, forcing them to begin their careers in more clerical positions. ABW leaders extolled research as an option for women. This advice concurred with that given by a male executive who characterized research as a venue in which women could excel behind the scenes. Barnard's article concluded by opining that "Woman has precipitately entered finance, but apparently she is settling herself for a long stay."[25] The economic downturn of the 1930s hampered this forecast, but some women survived. A few, such as Sylvia Porter and Isabel Benham, even thrived.

Haunted by the dire effects of the 1929 Crash on her parents, college student Porter decided to learn from it. She later recalled that "One of the things that turned me in the direction of personal finance was remembering how my ma and pa had lost money in Liberty Bonds by selling them at the wrong time, which is what a lot of people did after the First World War. Of course most of the Wall Street crowd knew what it was doing and sold the bonds when prices were high."[26] She switched her major to economics and began working for an investment firm in 1932. By 1934, she had begun a newspaper column on government bonds using her initials as her byline, though she did slip in references to her gender. Despite early hostility on occasion from men and women alike, her career flourished. She not only wrote about finance, she helped create it when her writing later paved the way for her input to the design of the next generation of United States' war bonds.

In 1936, the same year that New York City women represented 72 partners at NYSE brokerages, 250 members of the ABW, 4 bank presidents, and 2 vice presidents, Porter produced a 10-part series for the *New York Post*, profiling selected financial women: Bruere, Eggleston, Andress, Cook, investment firm owner Clara Taylor, writer Orline Foster, investment firm partner Louise Watson, investment firm partner Ethel Mercereau, trust officer Henriette Fuchs, and brokerage firm ombudsman Mary Riis.[27] She identified the bond market as a typical professional entry point. Eggleston concurred with this assessment. Paying particular attention to her subjects' femininity and personalities,[28] Porter found that "There are three outstanding characteristics of the modern Amazons of finance. The majority of them are unmarried, they all look younger than they are, and they're all remarkably serious-minded. Perhaps the three are connected."[29]

Benham, though not profiled by Porter, carved a niche for herself in the inter-war era and would eventually have a career that spanned more than

60 years. After graduating from Bryn Mawr College in 1931 as one of only five women with an economics degree, she enrolled in a course covering bond sales taught by the Guaranty Company. She hawked magazine subscriptions until landing a job in 1932 at the Reconstruction Finance Company, a lender to banks and railroads, despite not knowing the basics of mortgage finance. She next went in 1934 to R.W. Presspich & Co. She worked there first as a statistician and then as Wall Street's first railroad analyst when she inherited the duties of her boss who had been terminated.[30] Despite signing her correspondence "I. Hamilton Benham" in those early years, she claimed she never personally felt any gender discrimination. Her respected research reflected a keen attention to details that was a trait she thought intrinsic in women.[31] She became a partner at the firm in 1964 before going to Shearson Hammill & Co. and later to Printon, Kane Research. Benham believed that "A lot of firms hired women because I was a success."[32] Years later, she pointed out the irony that her first day of work at Presspich had coincided with April Fool's Day and confessed that she had lied at her interview when asked whether she could use a slide-rule. She quipped that she thrived nonetheless "Because I was the only person who could get the files out quickly."[33]

Benham was no joke; neither was the increasing sophistication of women investors and the overall extent of female advancement occurring in brokerages. Chastened by the 1929 Crash, women reportedly no longer sought quick profits but craved financial knowledge in order to fashion prudent plans tailored to their needs.[34] Despite the demise of specialized women's departments, the 1939 NYSE directory listed 67 women in firms accredited for floor trading. There had been only 12 women listed just 10 years before.[35] These women, however, did not capture the public imagination quite so much as soon would a fictional character who played a significant role in furthering the progress of women outside the home.

At the time of U.S. entry into World War II, approximately three million women worked in manufacturing capacities.[36] Then, beginning in 1942, "Rosie the Riveter" appealed to the patriotism of American women and inspired them to prove "We Can Do It!" By September 1944, an additional 6.5 million women joined the workforce with more than half entering manufacturing and clerical work.[37] While Rosie primarily reflected the need to have women step into assembly line industrial vacancies, she symbolized female strength, independence, and economic significance.

As they had during World War I, women again powered wartime bond sales. This time, however, the bonds themselves were engineered with female input. A 1938 article written by Porter described a practice of "free riding" in the bond market. The article caught the attention of Treasury Secretary Henry Morgenthau. He eventually collaborated with the financial writer to design the Series E Savings Bond, a 30-year non-fluctuating debt instrument used to finance the war.[38]

Morgenthau sold the first Series E Savings Bond to President Franklin D. Roosevelt on May 1, 1941, and in June 1942 established an official women's division that operated internally within the War Finance Division.[39] He mandated that the unit be fully integrated into the program with men's and women's committees working together.[40] An estimated 1,000,000 "bondadiers"[41] emulated their predecessors, the Philadelphia Ladies and WLLC, knocking on doors and offering "sacrifice bonds."[42] In August 1943, Woman's Division Chairman Harriett Elliott reported that "There is now an effective women's organization in every State and they take their responsibility as seriously as do the women in the uniformed services."[43]

In early 1942, Porter addressed the significance of the war for women. Optimistic for the creation of a new era, she nevertheless cautioned, "Out of the chaos brought on by conflict is developing a new era for women-an era in which women will have unprecedented financial independence, economic power and towering problems of social adjustment."[44] With her own star power rising, she revealed her gender later that year by using her full name in her byline for the first time in July.[45] She declared, "the first World War brought women into finance and the second World War is giving us our big chance. From this day on, you will write the story."[46]

Their story continued to unfold meanwhile in banking. While wartime obstacles limited travel and made national meetings difficult, the ABW focused on increasing membership and providing wartime support over the ensuing years.[47] At the group's 1942 annual conference, President Henriette Fuchs recognized the stresses now encountered by women assuming greater responsibility for household financial management in the absence of their spouses and promised the organization's help. She also urged additional training and assumption of greater responsibility by female bankers, and included a resolution calling "upon women in all walks of life to cooperate and lend support to women's endeavors in business and the professions."[48]

Professional and patriotic duties converged through ABW support of war bonds and stamps. Members were implored to explain the importance of savings in layperson's terms to engage prospective buyers within their communities. In November 1942, *The Woman Banker* underscored the significance of Rosie in finance: "As women in banking not only can you do your share by buying bonds yourself but also you can urge others to buy bonds with every dollar which is not needed for absolute necessities. In urging the purchase of war bonds, you are performing a service of tremendous importance to the prosecution of the war and acting just as effectively as the women turning out war materials in an industrial plant."[49]

At the same time the ABW was contributing to the country's sound future, it turned an introspective eye on its own prospects. Since 1941, the group had begun to conduct nationwide surveys regarding women and banking. The data detailed the number and sorts of positions females occupied, and characterized attitudes toward women and personnel standards. Public interest in the information was wide and varied, with requests for reports fielded from governmental agencies, vocational schools, and libraries from within the United States and abroad.[50] At the 1943 annual ABW meeting, President Fuchs acknowledged the importance of their research, "It cannot be denied that this survey has gained for the Association of American Bank Women far-reaching recognition. It further emphasized the fact that the possibilities for making greater contributions to the banking profession and to the cause of women in banking are unlimited."[51]

Not surprisingly, the data from September 1942 to September 1944 revealed a large influx of women into banking as they replaced absent males. The pre-war ratios of men to women were reversed in many instances. The survey placed a new emphasis on analysis of the statistics in hopes to attract more women into the profession and help them to advance. Incoming ABW President Helen Knox remarked in 1944 that "There is great fascination about banking for the ambitious woman who seeks a career in that field and many interesting tasks will be found to occupy her time."[52] Her comments rang true as the next survey, published in 1946, evidenced a decrease in gender prejudice and a rise in both promotions and merit-based salary increases. The number of female bank officers nationally had grown from 4,605 in 1944 to 5,635 in 1946.[53]

In 1942, when ABW membership had risen 74 percent over the prior two years, its president did not view peacetime demobilization as a threat to the careers of women bankers.[54] The future was differently understood on the floor of the NYSE. The very venue that would extol Rosie on Wall Street continued as a bastion of conservatism. The mindset of the NYSE at that time was evident when its board allowed floor access to Porter mostly because it was mindful that a refusal might lead to her editorial retribution.[55] The exchange passed a resolution stating,

"Sylvia is one of the boys. We hereby award her honorary pants."[56] The NYSE remained a boys' club, no girls allowed—except if no boys could be found.

In May 1945, while females served as 40 pages, 9 reporters, and 17 quotation clerks on the floor, a *New York Times* article opined on their dim future:

> As V-E marked the beginning of the end of the duration, these women began to realize that Wall Street means what it says, and that when the boys come back the girls will go back–home.
>
> . . . Of all who have worked in the Big Board since the war began, it is next to impossible to find one who has been able to make the break into more responsible fields leading eventually to trading . . .
>
> For Wall Street is not comparable to other industries in which women have established bridgeheads that they are planning to exploit in peacetime. . . .
>
> Most of the girls really don't care. They enjoyed the wolfish whistling that greeted the first feminine pages to step bravely out on the Exchange floor, but they have learned that Wall Street is not yet adjusted to the presence of women between 10:00 a.m. and 3:00 p.m.
>
> Even those who before the war and since Pearl Harbor, had fought their way up to researching and statistician jobs in brokerage and investment houses admit now that the day when women traders will be seen on the Exchange floor is probably as distant as the Buttonwood Tree, where the Exchange took shape in 1792.[57]

In fact, returning male employees reclaimed their positions, and women reappeared on the NYSE floor only briefly in 1948 during a strike of unionized workers. In so far as Rosie had graced center stage on Wall Street, she had been tolerated as a temporary wartime necessity in low-level positions, only to be booted when she was no longer needed.

Youthful Rosie may have been pushed from the financial world's epicenter, but many of her more mature sisters in banking were coming of age professionally while out of the limelight. Women were indeed establishing their own "bridgeheads" outside of deal-making and trading by making inroads in less glamorous and often lower paying areas of finance such as commercial banking and securities research. These areas were more removed from public attention and institutional confrontation. In its typically more high profile positions and within its inner sanctum, however, Wall Street remained unready to welcome women, nor were women yet primed to force the issue.

PART IV

Mavericks

From the 1950s through the 1970s, American women and Wall Street each encountered challenges as they staked their positions amid a changing cultural, political, and economic landscape. Both ultimately emerged revitalized from their growing pains. Where the two intersected, intrepid female leaders broke new ground at the crossroads of women and Wall Street.

Victorious in World War II, the United States swaggered in its aftermath with a new sense of power and optimism on the world stage and at home. Women, however, did not find themselves facing similar exciting opportunities. Instead of being able to explore further their expanded roles in the workplace, many were forced out of their positions upon the homecoming of the American veterans. While some embraced a return to domesticity, 80 percent of working women had not wished to relinquish their jobs. The government trumpeted Rosie's return home, however, and both suburbia and babies boomed.[1]

The idealized notion of suburban bliss in the early post-war years belied the existence of certain ironies. Even though women took charge of 75 percent of purchasing decisions, devoted wives and mothers played second fiddle to their husbands in the sorts of paternalistic families portrayed in such pop cultural icons as *Father Knows Best* and *Leave It to Beaver*. Housework increased despite advances in consumer-oriented technologies and daily life in planned communities caused female isolation.[2]

If women harbored much frustration, they did not publicly vent it during the buttoned-up 1950s. On the heels of U.S. entry into the Korean War in 1950 and intensification of the Cold War, the investigations of the House

Un-American Activities Committee and similar exploitations of the fear of Communism stifled expressions or activities that might be regarded as subversive. Civil dissent may have been restrained, but female discontent lurked beneath the surface. According to a *Fortune* magazine poll, one-quarter of women regretted that they had not been born male, and many wished to work outside the home.[3]

Women did find employment in the late 1940s and 1950s as ample job openings arose in the post-war economy. By 1959, women comprised 35 percent of laborers and began to be acknowledged as a permanent component of the workforce. Typically, they found work within the lower-paying education, social services, health care, and clerical sectors. Within professional and managerial spheres, little advancement occurred. In the financial services sector, networking efforts had continued. In 1956, female executives founded the Financial Women's Club of San Francisco. Six months later, after being denied admission by the Young Men's Investment Association, eight professional Wall Street women founded the Young Women's Investment Association, later known as the Financial Women's Association (FWA). The group aimed at sharing experiences and furthering the advancement of women on Wall Street. For the most part, however, female college graduates set aside their career aspirations in the face of vast cultural pressures in favor of the role of housewife. Few women attended graduate business schools and those women that did seek business careers tended to shy away from the finance industry.[4]

By the early 1960s, society had grown more aware and accepting of women's desires for challenges outside the home. President John F. Kennedy's election had galvanized the nation, and his concept of a New Frontier infused it with a spirit of optimism and reform. Initially conservative in his civil rights and feminist agenda, he nonetheless established in 1961 a Presidential Commission on the Status of Women. Chaired by Eleanor Roosevelt, the commission's work included documentation of employment discrimination and helped lead to passage of the Equal Pay Act of 1963. This legislation intended to abolish certain forms of gender-based pay disparity.

At the grassroots level, private activities also sent a siren call for change. In 1963, Betty Friedan penned the bestseller *The Feminine Mystique*. Describing a growing sense of dissatisfaction among American housewives, the book sparked awareness and interest in feminism. Three years later, Friedan co-founded the National Organization for Women (NOW), which was a group of 300 women and men who advocated for broad female participation in American society.

Concrete improvements in women's rights ensued through incremental victories. The cause to end racial inequity helped spark reform, much as abolitionism had once inspired earlier feminist leanings. In 1964, enactment of Title VII of the Civil Rights Act (Title VII) banned various forms of employment discrimination, including on the basis of gender, and established the Equal Opportunity Employment Commission to enforce it. The following year, the U.S. Supreme Court overturned an archaic Connecticut law that banned contraceptives. Meanwhile, passage of a constitutional equal rights amendment gained steam through NOW's advocacy and wider support. By the end of the 1960s, alongside the civil rights movement, Vietnam War opposition, and a developing counterculture, feminism emerged as a vocal and more powerful force.[5]

The 1970s continued the rapid ascendancy of women's activism and legislative and judicial success developed. In 1971, Gloria Steinem and others founded the groundbreaking feminist magazine *Ms*. The following year, Congress enacted Title IX to the Education Amendments Act that forbade discrimination in federally assisted educational programs and finally passed the ERA 49 years after it had first been introduced to Congress. The Supreme Court's 1973 landmark ruling in *Roe v. Wade* legalized abortion in certain circumstances by deeming it a fundamental constitutional right. In 1977, feminists organized the International Women's Year Conference, which promoted awareness of a host of political and economic issues affecting women.[6]

Even most women who rejected bra-burning sensibilities and did not label themselves as "feminists" supported causes such as equal job opportunities and access to daycare and abortion. Women no longer remained tied to their domestic chores either; over half of all married women worked outside the home by the end of the decade. Personal freedom also gained expression through more widespread use of the birth control pill, which had first become available in 1960.[7]

During these post-war decades, women's place in American society underwent significant questioning and transformation. No less a sea change in the ways in which Wall Street conducted business and interacted with Main Street also transpired contemporaneously in the financial establishment.

Although indirect individual participation in the stock market had grown during the 1930s and 1940s through the rise of pension funds, direct involvement by small investors remained limited in the early postwar years.[8] That would soon change. Several developments combined to create a new financial environment more hospitable and alluring to the individual.

The chief architect of a more Main Street-oriented brokerage was Charles Merrill. Beginning in the 1940s, he altered the traditional business model by removing brokers' commissions, implementing a sophisticated training program, and advertising widely. Recognizing a general lack of public knowledge of the securities markets, his ads included basic investing principles and portrayed his vision of an honest Wall Street staffed with competent professionals. Merrill's ideas translated into success. By 1960, his firm dwarfed its rivals, holding 540,000 brokerage accounts. As other firms replicated his methods, many old style smaller boutique firms disappeared in the shadows of a new landscape dominated by bulkier institutions.[9]

An expanding investor base gained confidence in the nascent field of securities analysis. The field was pioneered by Benjamin Graham who began teaching a renowned course on investment theory at Columbia Business School in 1928. His widely emulated method of identifying undervalued companies helped define analysis as a rigorous academic pursuit. The discipline was first designated as securities analysis in the 1930s. Investment firms began establishing more research departments and professional opportunities followed. By 1962, membership in the New York Society of Security Analysts had increased to 2,700, from its origin in the 1930s with only 20 participants.[10]

Possibly the most powerful factor in the changing perception of Wall Street was a rise in stock prices. A robust bull market always attracts public attention and a new one had begun in 1954 that was buoyed by the allure of President Dwight Eisenhower's talk of a balanced budget. The DJIA broke its pre-1929 Crash record level of 381.17 in December and prices continued to increase on the strength of underlying economic health, vigorous stock promotion, benign regulation, and a relatively limited supply of issues. The public ventured back into the market and stock tips once again provided popular cocktail chatter.[11]

By 1959, annual volume on the NYSE exceeded one billion shares. The doubling of retail investors over the preceding decade, of which women accounted for the biggest growth in participation, swelled this volume. Two years later, pension funds began annually investing approximately $1 billion in equities and $2 billion in bonds. Flush with inflow from the public, mutual funds also acquired greater stature. No longer did small investors just occasionally dip a toe in the financial waters; their firm imprint now made its mark through these products that allowed and aggregated modest investments. Mutual fund assets climbed from $500 million assets in 1940, to $2.5 billion in 1950, and to $17 billion in 1960.[12]

While stocks rose in the early 1960s, trouble surfaced in the commodities market. An attempted corner of cottonseed and soybean oil futures by an investor in 1962 threatened the solvencies of several firms. While Wall Street bankers were trying to find a solution to the fiasco, a different crisis erupted. On November 22, 1963, news of the assassination of President Kennedy sent the DJIA down 3 percent and the market closed early. The following day, both the exchange reopened and an agreement was reached for an orderly liquidation of one of the brokerages entwined in the commodities scandal. Heartened by the orderly transition of political power as well as the news of the exchange's assumption of responsibility for a member firm's failure for the first time, the market jumped over 32 points, accounting for its largest single day gain ever.[13]

The bull market resumed and the DJIA hit an intraday high of 1,000 in 1966. By the late 1960s, however, the tide turned. Business was almost too good. Prices stagnated while volume rose amid higher portfolio turnover and quicker price dissemination made possible in 1965 by the linkage of the ticker to an electronic display. Trading remained conducted on paper and by telephone while computers proved too cumbersome and expensive to afford relief. The rise in volume overwhelmed the system and caused errors in recording transactions. In early 1968, the NYSE even shortened trading hours by closing on Wednesdays in order to help alleviate the member firms' large backlog of paperwork. At one point, a staggering $4.1 billion in securities was lost in the system. Not until January 1969 did five-day trading weeks return. Even then curtailed hours were in place until May 1970. The advent of a central securities depositary in 1969 reduced the paperwork but did not provide a panacea. This turmoil translated not just into aggravation but also into lower brokerage profits.[14]

The bull market of the 1950s and early 1960s had stampeded out of sight. Inflation induced by the Vietnam War and the Great Society led to a hike in the discount rate to its highest level since 1929. Stocks declined. The DJIA dropped 15 percent in the first seven months of 1968, which was the steepest downturn in nearly 10 years. Volume fell, and brokerages suffered. To augment firms' capital, in 1970 the NYSE reversed its policy and allowed member institutions to sell stock to the public. Weaker firms failed and confidence eroded further when the SEC uncovered one defunct brokerage's prior practices of churning, fraud, and faulty record keeping. In order to assist troubled investment firms and shore up public trust, Congress soon created the Securities Investor Protection Corporation, a non-profit entity that would step into assist in the orderly winding up of a defunct brokerage and provide insurance coverage to investors. Still, the market slipped, firms closed, and Wall Street workers declined.[15]

President Richard Nixon's use of price controls provided a temporary respite to the ailing market; the DJIA broke the 1,000 closing level in January 1973. Once removed later that year, the economy stagnated and inflation soared. Amidst devaluation of the dollar and the Watergate and oil crises, both stocks and bonds plunged. Mutual funds lost much of their inflows, and bears ruled the Street. Industry professionals lost their jobs. A 28 percent drop in financial sector employment occurred over the approximately five-and-a-half-year span leading up to April 1974. The ultimate iconic image of Wall Street worth, the price of an NYSE seat, that sold for $500,000 in 1969 could now be purchased in 1974 for a mere $65,000, just two-and-a-half times the price of a city taxi license.[16]

The perils confronting Wall Street hastened constructive change from various players. In the face of declining volume and increased competition from regional exchanges, the NYSE instituted several internal reforms aimed at democratization of leadership and corporate governance. The boldest measure came when the SEC endorsed the NYSE president's idea to consider negotiated commissions. On May 1, 1975, the SEC abolished the longstanding concept of fixed commissions. Until then, investors had faced little competition from an industry holding greater leverage. The rules of the game now changed.[17]

The development of a more integrated national market system gained ground with passage of the Securities Act Amendments in 1975. This federal legislation gave authority to the SEC to foster greater linkages between the stock exchanges and other market participants. Nasdaq, which had already begun operating in February 1971 to disseminate data by computer on unlisted securities, received a strong boost and soon overtook the total daily volume of the Amex and the regional exchanges. With the advent of a consolidated tape and centralization of dependable information, competition increased and spreads narrowed.[18]

Not only had the way changed in which business was transacted, so too had who was conducting it. In 1974, the enactment of the Equal Credit Opportunity Act sought to redress discriminatory lending practices. This law factored into the development of women's banks. The insularity of old Wall Street was also receding. On the institutional level, larger firms pushed out old-time boutiques and their predominant WASPish male reserve. More Jewish bankers gained stature within firms not traditionally welcoming to them, and Chinese-American Gerald Tsai Jr. gained prominence as one of the new leaders within the world of money management. In 1967, Muriel Siebert became the first woman to purchase a seat on the Big Board; Joseph L. Searles III became the first black to do so three years later.[19]

During the turbulent 1960s and 1970s, various segments of the population called out for societal change. They sought greater equality and a more level playing field for marginalized groups. These voices screamed louder from outside the caverns of Wall Street than from within. The financial world, too, echoed a theme of building a future of more equal stakeholders, but changes there came about from different sources. The growing democratization of market participation and leadership had largely been enabled through the evolution of business structure and technology. Gradual entree and advancement of minorities within the financial system resulted primarily from certain individual efforts rather than through broad industry or corporate campaigns directed at diversifying the workforce. Women themselves stepped up their professional networking efforts when registered representatives at the NYSE formed the Women's Stockbrokers' Association in 1964.[20]

For the most part, the women in this era focused on their own careers and did not publicly lament concern over bias. Whether they remained silent due to lack of cause or whether they tended to harbor a more conservative approach to change is difficult to ascertain. A more cynical view might ascribe their relative complacency to a narrow pursuit of professional survival. After all, the Manhattan financial district was still a place where thousands of men turned out in 1968 to cheer the daily arrival of a particularly buxom bank worker.[21] Two years later, according to one *New York Times* reporter, Wall Street remained "a feminist organizer's Waterloo [because of] the tendency for its female minority elite to grin and bear the system."[22]

Siebert was not the lone female to register a "first" in the financial world during these years. Her name, however, is the best known and more than just symbolic. It is true that neither her seat purchase nor the achievement of milestones by other female financial contemporaries did immediately usher in the removal of bias, the riddance of hostility, or an onslaught of women financial professionals. But symbols are not devoid of substance. They hold the power to galvanize attention, inspire, and lead. The women in finance of this era did just that. These individuals represented a bridge from the prior era that had begun to see opportunities for women develop in commercial banking, bond sales, and securities research, and translate them into wider options in the realm of investment banking. This venue proved harder to infiltrate but not impenetrable. On occasion, tokenism may have mitigated some of the sting of residual gender bias, but in no way stood in for the aptitude of these women. Without female professional role models of their own, they persevered in their careers and navigated the shifting tides of what it meant to be an American woman against a societal backdrop of generalized calls for change and rising feminism—even while no such popular chorus sang out loudly for a greater presence of women on Wall Street.

NINE

Mary Roebling

Have your own power. Don't give it to a man.[1]

—Mary Roebling

Widowed for the second time and left with two children, 31-year-old Mary Roebling was apprehensive over assuming the presidency of Trenton Trust Company. In fact, she was not wholly unprepared for the duties. She had already assumed her late husband's directorship at his family-controlled New Jersey bank during the past year. Nevertheless, she doubted her abilities.[2] Both her father and father-in-law attested to her capability and the latter prodded her on by pointing out to her, "You have the rarest commodity in the world—common sense."[3]

This prudence and streetwise savvy served Roebling well as she undertook the duties of her new position. These qualities had been present long before she began this phase of her career, and would serve her equally well as she progressed. The very fact that Roebling decided to go ahead in banking testifies to her strong personality and determination. Given her financial comfort and a cultural climate unaccustomed to female business leaders, she might have chosen instead to shun personal involvement with her late husband's enterprise and focus solely on her children and social life. Although she later intimated that her inheritance was meager due to the bank's declining fortunes, her choice appeared informed at least as much by innate motivation as from any acute financial need. Her casting of the situation as one in which males persuaded her to pursue an expanded role, rather than one she herself coveted, also reflects a sensitivity to image and gender roles.[4]

Roebling herself had not been to the manor bred, despite her later attempts to portray that to Trenton society. Born on July 29, 1905, into a suburban New Jersey family, she was the eldest of four children of Isaac Dare Gindhart, Jr., a telephone company executive, and Mary W. Gindhart, a vocalist and pianist. Within a modest upbringing, she displayed tenacity, energy, a love of learning, and a hardy work ethic. These traits would also characterize her adulthood.[5]

Marriage, motherhood, and widowhood all came early for Roebling. At age 16, she left high school to marry World War I veteran Arthur Herbert and they had a daughter within one year. Within just two years, her husband died. Roebling then found work as a salesgirl at a department store. At a time when women were prohibited from taking daytime classes at the Wharton School of Business, she heeded her father's urging and attended night classes in merchandising and business administration. She became a secretary at a Philadelphia brokerage before being promoted to a customer consultant. Around that time, she also wed Hugh Graham. Their brief union ended several years later in divorce.[6]

She met her third husband, Siegfried Roebling, the grandson of Brooklyn Bridge builder Colonel Washington Roebling and founder of Trenton Trust, while working at the brokerage. He was a vice president and director of the bank, as well as a purported gambler and alcoholic. They married in 1933 and welcomed a son the following year. Tragedy struck again when Siegfried died unexpectedly in 1936.[7]

At the time of his death, Trenton Trust was faltering amid the Great Depression. Roebling, who had inherited her late husband's bank stock, subsequently appointed herself and her father to the board of directors in early 1936.[8] One year later, on January 21, 1937, she became president and was the first woman to serve in such position at a major commercial bank. Whether her appointment resulted from a self-styled coup that resulted in acrimonious board factions or whether she received the unanimous support to which she professed remains unclear.[9] Regardless of circumstance, when she greeted a press conference four days later, she epitomized poise and exuded confidence.[10] According to *Time* magazine, Roebling caught reporters off guard by first inquiring whether they were bank depositors.[11] The "prettiest bank president in the land" then reminded them that she numbered among 75 female bank presidents and 4,500 female bank officers.[12] She emphasized the significance of her gender by telling the assembled reporters that "So many women have deposits in banks, so many women are interested in retail and wholesale business . . . it is only natural that women are being elevated to positions of an executive nature."[13]

Roebling rose to the precarious occasion presented by the bank's frail health. Trenton Trust faced $4 million in debt and only $11 million in assets.[14] She later remarked that "Everybody was busted, and the bank was busted, too."[15] Taking over at the bank "was the greatest challenge I ever faced . . ."[16] She delegated the additional demands of a toddler and a teenager to others, enrolled in evening banking courses over six years at New York University, and also studied law for two years with a tutor.[17] Said her daughter years later, "She always worked, always studied. Even at night, she'd be at home reading books about finance."[18]

She harnessed publicity and marketing talents to augment the bank's position. A Trenton Trust customer might receive a toy bank upon opening an account, a shamrock on St. Patrick's Day, or an invitation to an art show. Known for her public relations flair, she initiated financial teas to educate wealthy women about trust funds, employed professional window dressers for the bank windows, and engaged in various community events and philanthropies. She viewed banks as "department stores of finance,"[19] sought to increase the female customer base by forming a women's division, and introduced the walk-up window, drive-in banking, a railroad depot branch, and bank credit cards. When not studying or at the office, she used her social skills to network among the city's businesspeople and leaders.[20]

Roebling also spoke on the development and significance of female economic empowerment. In 1938, at a convention of the Soroptimist International Association, an organization for business and professional women, she hailed the typewriter as "emancipating" women, and proclaimed that "Women are no longer an ornament of the home but a vital part of society, business and industry and their talents were needed as much as of those of men."[21] She explained that "Women's social emancipation started about eighty years ago through the typewriter. And now wise male business and industrial leaders are anxious to obtain the cooperation of astute women. They know there is something to this thing called 'the woman's touch.' And they know that if this delicate asset is directed into the proper channels, it aids the endeavor."[22] Optimism ran high among her audience. An attendee noted the present federal administration as making great strides in recognizing the abilities of women and cited Secretary of Labor Perkins and various other appointments. Another recited that "Of the capital stock of American corporations, women own $20,000,000,000. Forty-eight per cent of the persons bequeathing property large enough to be affected by the inheritance tax laws of five states are women. And women are the beneficiaries of a great proportion of the $100,000,000,000 insurance on the books of the American life companies."[23]

In 1941, Roebling became Trenton Trust's Chairman of the Board, the first woman chair of a major commercial bank. In the post-war years, female appointments to executive banking jobs became more common though still did not go unnoticed. In January 1945, the election of corporate attorney Mabel Walker Willebrandt to the board of the Hamilton National Bank in Washington, D.C. created a buzz. The bank's president supported its decision, stating that "The directors of the Hamilton National Bank for some years past have been conscious of the importance of women in the business and economic life of our country and now foresee an acceleration in participation by properly qualified women in policy-shaping bodies."[24] The following year, the Savings Bank Division of the American Bankers Association became the first of its divisions to appoint women to its committees. In 1949, Claire Giannini Hoffman became the first female director of financial giant Bank of America National Trust and Savings Association. She filled the vacancy left by her father who had been the bank's founder. That same year, the ABW established a national office in New York, a move that reflected the organization's increasing responsibilities. Growth of ABW membership had risen from 331 in 1941 to 540 in 1945 to 977 in 1949.[25]

In Trenton, Roebling had become one of the city's staunchest promoters. She sought expansion of its industrial base during the wartime boom as she managed the local finances of United States Steel Corporation and cultivated connections to powerful players in politics, journalism, and even Hollywood.[26] Her impact on behalf of the city was so profound that members of the American Institute of Banking and the ABA reportedly said that they no longer viewed Trenton in terms of its bank, "but in terms of Mary G. Roebling."[27] Roebling seemed to possess an "ability to dominate without being domineering."[28]

Still, she encountered critics, including a board rival who noted she "could be ruthless when necessary."[29] In 1954, an embezzlement scandal involving her friend New Jersey Governor Harold Hoffman threatened her professional and personal reputation. The governor, who kept funds at the bank, had appointed Roebling to the state unemployment commission. Eventually, Governor Hoffman confessed to absconding with $300,000 of state funds. Roebling maintained her ignorance of his illicit dealings.[30]

While executive positions may have begun to open to women, sexism had not ended. Although Roebling proved her banking prowess equal to that of men, she was viewed through an alternate prism. In fact, she herself sought to highlight her gender by promoting a "Banker in High Heels" media campaign in 1952.[31] Picking up on this theme, the *New York Times* profiled her with the opening sentence, "A vivacious financier in high heels today has a firm grasp on much of the phenomenal industrial growth of this old capital city."[32] The article next catalogued her physical appearance in more detail before going on to state, "Mrs. Roebling is far from the spare, unattractive, plainly dressed woman many men expect to find in a business office. It is difficult at first to realize that a woman with her natural charm built the total resources of her bank from $17,000,000 in 1936 to $70,000,000 today. She acts like the wife of a successful banker, not the banker himself."[33]

But Roebling was the banker, and a competent one. Longtime employees who had been interviewed for the article felt that she had understood the business from the moment she first served on the board. In the same piece, Roebling remarked that "I believe women have proven themselves to be equally capable with men and have shouldered their responsibilities in all phases of local, state and national affairs, as well as the most important fundamental principle of our lives—that of being a mother."[34]

Roebling had invoked the conventional norm of embracing and prioritizing motherhood, even though she herself juggled childrearing with her career. In most respects, her boundless energy enabled her to find ways to meld her professional and personal interests into a seamless mesh. Roebling later said that "I did nothing but work. I made work my hobby. I was lucky that way."[35] She possessed an indomitable work ethic. Her days stretched from the early morning until midnight and were jammed with both business and social functions. It was not unusual for her to wake at 2:00 a.m. to finish some correspondence for a few hours. She had a taste for extravagance and indulged in fashion, jewels, art, and opulent homes in Trenton and in Palm Beach. These luxuries were put to use in courting business and political contacts.[36]

That ability to appear to indulge stereotypical female pursuits while functioning professionally within a male-dominated world encapsulated the essence of Roebling. At once, she embodied both groundbreaker and traditionalist.[37] At a 1953 meeting of the women's forum of the American Institute of Banking, she addressed the topic of "Women in a Man's World." She opined that "women are an effective part of a team [with men], which can form an unbeatable combination."[38] Maintaining that the American woman neither seeks domination nor control of the economy, she asserted that she simply desires "the right and privilege of being a definite part of society, our economy, and our government [and that] also is what the discerning businessman wants."[39] Roebling's woman did not threaten the social order, she enhanced it.[40] In a 1958 column, food writer Craig Claiborne described Roebling as "equally at home discussing high finance, lobster thermidor, bank loans and vintage years."[41]

If Roebling up to this point had acted as the consummate hostess who served both clients and corporations without noisily jeopardizing the status quo, her next position sparked more than just idle dinner chatter. With Trenton Trust's assets now above $90 million, the Amex appointed 52-year-old Roebling as one of its three public governors and the first such woman. Noting that women comprised more than half of the nation's stockholders, exchange president Edward T. McCormick cited two factors underlying her selection: "first, because of her stature and executive ability in the business field and secondly because she is a woman."[42] The NYSE spokesperson retorted by stating that the Big Board "had no policy for or against naming a woman," and that the "only determining factor was whether a candidate would really represent the public."[43] Apparently, they could not find such a female prospect for another 14 years until economist Juanita Kreps became the first woman director of the NYSE in 1972.

At 11:00 a.m. on October 28, 1958, the Amex trading floor was "thrown open" to Roebling, and "Another male sanctuary had fallen to the opposite sex."[44] Although McCormick believed her appointment to the 31-member male group signified the first time a woman could go to a trading floor unescorted, that did not occur on her first day as she surveyed the floor accompanied by the exchange's top executives and a dozen photographers. At the time of her selection, Roebling held directorships in six companies, and belonged to multiple national and state organizations of different sorts. Yet, she regarded the Amex position as "possibly the most outstanding appointment I have had since becoming president of Trenton Bank," and hoped to make a contribution as she "learn[ed] more about the work of the American Stock Exchange."[45]

As a public member not directly affiliated with the investment houses of Wall Street, her function was "to report public reaction and thought to the Board of Governors."[46] Unless personally requested by the exchange president, attendance at meetings remained optional for the public members. Beginning in 1959, Roebling appeared at four meetings over a two-and-a-half-year span.[47] During her tenure, the exchange's top executives came under fire from a scathing report by the SEC regarding administrative practices that included criticism of the infrequent attendance of the public governors. The exchange's own internal investigating committee echoed many of the SEC's findings and in 1962 recommended reorganization of the board.[48] Labeled the "first lady of finance"[49] by McCormick, Roebling served as an Amex governor until 1962. It would be another three years until the exchange admitted any female members.

Although Roebling did not ultimately use her Amex position to advance any specific agenda, she had already been publicly espousing her views on the interrelationship of women and finance for more than two decades. Since 1938, she saluted the rising numbers of women stockholders and business owners. She thought that increased numbers of female consumers and entrepreneurs would benefit both women and business, and believed strongly in "equal pay for equal work with equal opportunity for advancement."[50] Employment also bestowed other rewards for women. In an interesting and rare moment of possible introspection, she advocated professional paths as "A career gives you a sense of accomplishment . . . it keeps you from being frustrated . . . or an alcoholic . . . or bored."[51]

The woman who had once acclaimed the typewriter as an emancipator of women became concerned that technology would bring obstacles to female progress. In late 1964, she foresaw gloomy days ahead when she predicted that most jobs currently held by women would be lost due to increasing advances in automation. Crediting the industrial revolution and World War II with providing the impetus for women to work outside the home, she said "The economic force that allowed women to escape from the home to work and to earn a livelihood will, within 20 years, turn like Frankenstein's monster and destroy the job opportunities which are now open to most women."[52] She noted that 70 percent of women held clerical jobs, which were the ones most likely to be lost and she called for action to avert a disaster.[53] Free enterprise was her mantra. She believed that employment provided the key to unlatch women from domestic boredom and supply them with material comforts.[54] Roebling bemoaned that "American women . . . do not use the influence their economic power gives them."[55]

In 1972, Trenton Trust merged with National State Bank and Roebling was elected chair of the new entity. Under her tenure, assets had increased to more than $200 million.[56] A new venture also beckoned and it was one that would further female economic empowerment. At the time, widespread gender discrimination in obtaining bank credit persisted despite federal regulatory efforts to boost female access to credit.[57] When several Colorado women approached Roebling in early

1976 about serving as chair of a new financial institution that would cater to the financial needs of women, she agreed.[58] According to her, "Women's banks can be better listeners for women and give them more time, advice and direction than an ordinary bank would give. It's a psychological thing, really."[59] In a 1977 press conference, she further elaborated on plans for The Women's Bank, explaining that "We want to translate the economic power of our women into a more productive and profitable resource for the whole community and thus it is basic to our purpose that we seek to provide top banking services to the entire community and not just the women."[60]

Many of The Women's Bank's 50 co-founders had been previously denied credit. In addition to serving as their mentor, Roebling's political savvy and expertise in rounding up capital played a critical role in obtaining the bank's federal charter. In 1978, The Women's Bank, N.A. opened and represented the first nationally chartered bank established by women. While The Women's Bank catered to female customers, Roebling remained mindful of the shaky fortunes of other financial entities that only served women and had lost money. Instead, theirs was "a business, not a cause,"[61] and she demanded that the bank serve everyone and do so with experienced professionals. The Women's Bank proved viable, receiving $1 million weekly during its first 12 weeks, and ultimately opening up access to credit. By 1981, it had accumulated over $21 million in deposits.[62]

Roebling's civic-minded endeavors extended into other spheres. Active in numerous non-profit organizations and often serving as the lone woman on various corporate boards, she thought women could bring more genteel qualities to leadership positions in business and government. A staunch Republican who had hoped for the nomination of a female vice president, she served as a civilian aide to the Secretary of the Army in several administrations and founded the Army War College Foundation. Her political leanings included support of the ERA, but did not extend to the sort of women's liberation agenda that included abortion and lesbian issues and had gained ground toward her later years. Instead, Roebling's philosophy could be described as that of "economic feminism,"[63] whereby female financial empowerment paves the way for greater overall autonomy. A firm supporter of Title VII, she implored women to take advantage of its promise and held them accountable for slow progress.[64]

Roebling remained at the bank until her retirement at age 79 in 1984. Her bank's assets at that time totaled $1.2 billion.[65] Often walking to a local branch and greeting employees, she remained interested in the bank's business as well as in women's affairs.[66] In 1988, she lamented, "I honestly believe women do not wish to assume the positions of executives because if women wished to advance they would push the problem."[67] She continued to remain as active as possible in her later years until finally succumbing to renal failure in October 1994. Her obituary in the *New York Times* restated an earlier *Forbes* magazine quote: "Mary G. Roebling didn't wait for women's lib, she was ahead of it, way ahead."[68]

Feminists come from all walkways, including those traversed by Republican bankers. While Roebling may have been clad conservatively in her couture and in her politics, she embodied professional success within a male sphere and promoted the idea of female economic empowerment. She purposely crafted an image for herself as a competent executive who still fulfilled the societal archetypes of a polished and genteel woman. She advised businesswomen to wear tailored attire and not to "play on your femininity,"[69] but accentuated many of those qualities in her own appearance and conduct.[70] A public relations employee commented that "She truly invented herself. She knew how to play the game and she projected an aura of power and confidence. Even if you were close to her, as I felt I was, you still felt that aura."[71]

Roebling herself revealed little of her sentiments and experiences in her groundbreaking career.[72] Her most telling statement may have come during a 1987 interview when she said, "Accomplishments are the most important thing in life, more important than even love. Love, especially romantic love, is fleeting. The person you love may leave for whatever reason."[73] In light of her own personal experiences of coping with loss, her message of economic empowerment seems more authentic than artifice. Amidst the conformist culture of the times during which she made inroads in banking, the packaging may have been considered, but the content seems genuine.

When her third marriage came to an abrupt end, Roebling created her own happy and financially secure ever after. Charging forward, she created even more opportunities for herself over her lifetime while exhorting other women to do the same for themselves. In many senses, she reflected attributes of the monument that her in-laws had built. Like the Brooklyn Bridge, she exhibited grace and strength and served as both symbol and workhorse. In fact, she had not just married into an engineering family. Roebling constructed her own bridges during a career that extended from commercial to investment banking spheres and straddled a rising current of feminism.

TEN

Julia Montgomery Walsh

I think it's one of the best businesses a gal can go into.[1]

—*Julia Montgomery Walsh*

Thirty-four-year-old Julia Montgomery (Walsh) knew her role as an Army wife had ended when she was handed the flag that had been used at her husband's funeral. What she did not know was how she would provide for her four children. She did not suspect that her future lay as a successful stockbroker; it was a notion she once thought "impossible."[2]

Born Margaret Julia Curry on March 29, 1923 in Akron, Ohio, she was two years younger than her brother. Her father toiled on the assembly line at Goodyear Tire and Rubber Company (Goodyear), and her mother had worked as a bookkeeper prior to marriage. These working class roots gave her the appreciation for a hard-earned dollar and the motivation that would later guide her to enter the securities field.[3] With a firm belief in free enterprise, she began investing at age 18: "I really believed in it, so it was easy."[4]

The extroverted Walsh excelled in high school. Displaying a knack for leadership, she became president of both her school and a citywide council of student leaders. Despite graduating as salutatorian, her father resisted the idea of her pursuing further formal education. He preferred her to take a clerical job. Her mother, however, encouraged her to apply for a scholarship to Smith College. Despite winning the award, Walsh turned it down due to her father's opposition. Instead, she accepted her parents' compromise for her to live at home and attend Kent State University.[5]

College provided a forum for Walsh to flex her leadership prowess. As one of 25 undergraduates from around the country selected to study world problems during the summer of her sophomore year, she met First Lady Eleanor Roosevelt. In her words, this was an occurrence that "was to change the course of my life."[6] The following year, she became student body president and decided to pursue a business degree: "The male-dominated field of business always interested me, because that's where the action is—if I was going to work to earn my own living, then I wanted to be well paid."[7] During a conference of student leaders held in her senior year, she again encountered Mrs. Roosevelt, who admonished the women attendees, "Just because you're female, don't tell me you can't do it!"[8] Inspired by the First Lady, Walsh gravitated toward public service.[9]

Opting to get a head start on her career, Walsh completed her academic requirements three months early. In March 1945, she sought employment in Washington, D.C., and secured an administrative position with the Foreign Service. In her autobiography, she writes, "I thought then and now that every girl should earn her own living before launching out into marriage."[10] But she adhered to traditional thoughts of division of labor within marriage. Writing to her parents who worried about her single marital status, she declared, "I have absolutely NO intention of being a career woman. This working for a living is strictly for *men* but I might as well be a success while I'm at it."[11]

In June 1945, Walsh graduated from Kent State. She was the school's first woman to receive an undergraduate degree in business administration. She passed the Foreign Services exam and received an assignment to Munich. While awaiting her departure, she reflected on her choices, "I was sure I would have no trouble in finding an import-export job in Akron after I returned; then I would marry, have children, and become a typical American housewife."[12]

Few women aspiring to be a housewife would have chosen to first embark on an international career. Walsh did so, and with typical gusto. As the administrative assistant in the personnel department of the consulate in May 1946, she witnessed the wartime destruction of Munich. Not content to merely mark her time, she organized a recreational facility for German women that also offered accounting training, bilingual classes, and day care after having observed that "One of the biggest problems was to get the German girls to think and act for themselves."[13] Walsh thought for herself and her future. She began building her nest egg by investing $20 per quarter.[14]

While in Germany, Walsh met U.S. Army officer John Montgomery and the couple became engaged in early 1948. She received an unwelcome surprise when she learned she would lose her job upon marriage. She recalled, "With my good record, it never occurred to me that I would have to choose between the Service and a husband."[15] When Montgomery was ordered home in October, Walsh agreed to follow in the spring: "Like so many women of that era, I disliked giving up my own meaningful work, but decided that marriage was more important."[16]

Domestic life now awaited. Settling in suburban Washington state, she became focused on her husband's career. She was not ready to leave the workforce entirely, however, and soon became a probation officer. The couple's first child, a son, arrived in October 1949. Her husband, who had reactivated his army commission, received a reassignment to California, and the family moved there where a second son was born in February 1951. Walsh, now an Army wife, was "too busy raising a family to regret my aborted career."[17]

Following an assigned relocation to Princeton, New Jersey, the family embarked for Istanbul in August 1951. While he served as a military attaché, Walsh worked as the executive secretary of the U.S. Educational Commission. As a member of the Turkish-American Women's Cultural Society, she took note that Turkish women enjoyed a spectrum of available job opportunities that paid wages equal to men. Four years later, her husband was reassigned to Washington, D.C.[18]

The transfer to the capitol heralded Walsh's entry into the world of capital. With their third son born in April 1955, Walsh took the first steps toward her future profession. Both to quell her boredom and as a potential means to stretch her husband's meager weekly military income of $40, she enrolled in a financial analysis correspondence course. Upon completing it in June 1956, she next enrolled in an investment course taught at George Washington University by George M. Ferris, Jr., who was an executive at his family-owned local brokerage, Ferris & Company (Ferris). After she completed an aptitude test, he offered her a position as an apprentice stockbroker. Walsh, "like other dutiful wives of the time,"[19] asked for her husband's advice. He encouraged her as he believed that the position might become their "best investment."[20]

Though expenses relating to commuting, clothing, and household help nearly overwhelmed Walsh's first profits, her husband was proven prescient. As the sole female broker in the office, her male co-workers "weren't used to having a woman colleague in the front office. They took the attitude that I wasn't serious, just a flash in the pan."[21] Nothing could have been further from the truth. Within six months, she passed the exam required to become a registered broker on the NYSE and larger commissions soon ensued. In the meantime, starting with only $25 per month, Walsh had been investing the family's savings. She began with a company, Goodyear Tire, with which she had firsthand familiarity from her childhood. Her portfolio increased and so did her family; a fourth son arrived in January 1957. She returned to work three weeks following his birth and maintained a busy schedule juggling work and familial obligations. Her mother-in-law soon moved in with the family to help out.[22]

Despite her weekly trips to the grocery to supply the family's requisite 24 quarts of milk, Walsh "always felt more at home in the stock market than in the supermarket."[23] Work proved more appealing than domestic chores. But it was not long before her new profession was to be sacrificed to again trail her husband. In the autumn of 1957, he was transferred to Ft. Riley, Kansas, while she initially stayed behind with her four young boys, ranging in ages from 11 months to 8 years, to conclude their house sale and her job. She later reflected, "It was hard to leave the job at the brokerage firm I had finally found a niche in, but like any dutiful Army wife, I 'paid, packed and followed.'"[24]

Unfortunately, no happy holiday reunion transpired. On December 23, 1957, while *en route* to join her husband, Walsh received a call from an army chaplain. John Montgomery had been killed in an accident. She broke the news to her children the day before Christmas.[25]

Many people might fall apart during such a crisis. Walsh put on a brave public face. By her own accounts, she was "in a state of walking shock,"[26] but was sustained by her religious faith and concern for her children. Opting to remain in Washington, D.C., she first unsuccessfully tried to re-establish her prior career with the Foreign Service and then resumed her prior position at Ferris.[27]

Walsh's own personal finances were strained. She rented a house, hired her mother-in-law to help her in the household in a profit sharing arrangement, and persevered until former clients returned and her income picked up. In March 1959, only 15 months after her husband's death, Walsh became a general partner of Ferris, and the only female partner of an NYSE member firm in the Washington, D.C. metropolitan area. She embarked on giving investing seminars, but "I worked too hard and tried to do too much."[28] After accidentally knocking over a coffee pot one day when exhausted, she suffered third-degree burns.[29]

Walsh's career moved forward, even while she vowed to take things a bit easier.[30] She attended the Institute of Investment Banking at the

Wharton School and as the first woman enrolled found, "It was not easy for me. When I first went to Philadelphia, seats emptied out on either side whenever I appeared. But from that experience, I learned many valuable lessons about the investment business and about the interpersonal relationship-building process known as 'networking.'"[31]

According to Walsh, the decisive moment of her career came when she attended the 13-week Advanced Management Program of the Harvard Business School in February 1962.[32] The grueling academic agenda was further toughened by her status as the first and only female participant, "at 39 I faced for the first time the full force of male chauvinism."[33] Physically isolated from her male peers due to separate accommodations, she felt excluded and feared failure. She considered leaving the program until a classmate invited her to join his study group. Ultimately, she "learned something valuable from the experience—I was as good as any of them, once I learned their system. I also discovered that the men had as many problems as I did."[34]

Walsh completed the program and, buoyed by the experience, put that self-assurance to work in her own finances. She invested the majority of her money in stocks that yielded a quadruple return within 18 months.[35] Although the program had been intended to put her on an advanced managerial track, it boosted her desire to continue in sales. She thrived in a marketing role and her celebrity grew as she gave seminars and appeared on television. Within just five years of becoming widowed, Walsh ranked as the highest income earning woman in Washington, D.C.[36] Her client roster included well-known figures, but she took special pride in serving widows with smaller accounts because "Making a few dollars profit meant so much more to them, and I knew what it was like to walk in their shoes. I used the experience of my own personal tragedy to help them fight their way back, too."[37]

In May 1963, she married real estate executive Thomas Walsh. This second marriage for both brought with it its own managerial issues. The combined family included his seven children, her four sons, and their own daughter who was born one year later. Children were divided among shifts for meals but all learned about the stock market.[38]

Despite the chaos that can occur even in the most well-managed households, Walsh, now in her forties, felt "all the pieces of my life seemed to fit."[39] In 1965, against a backdrop of female advancement across other industries, she and Phyllis S. Peterson, a broker at another local firm, applied for membership on the Amex. The exchange already included some female associate members but no woman had yet applied for full

Julia Montgomery Walsh. (Mark Montgomery)

membership in her own name. In November, the Amex broke its 116-year male-only tradition by admitting both Walsh and Peterson to its roster of over 600 members. Wrote Sylvia Porter, "Another barrier of prejudice in Wall Street finally is being shattered. The barrier is built out of protocol and prejudice—not out of constitutional rules or regulations. . . ."[40]

Walsh's extracurricular activities continued to expand, as did her paycheck. She sponsored many charities and served as co-treasurer of the Democratic National Committee in 1966. In 1968, when *Time* magazine published a feature on working women, the article noted her $200,000 salary and described Walsh as dividing her time between the office and "the rest in 'yours, mine and ours' domesticity" with her family.[41]

While feminist headwinds swirled in the 1970s, Walsh received offers to serve on corporate boards. Viewing herself as a substantive asset in the boardroom as an investment banker, she dismissed notions of tokenism and advocated for more women on boards. Nevertheless, in her early days of board service, she often found it difficult to make herself heard both due to her own inhibition and to the inattention accorded her by other male directors.[42]

Walsh received one particularly interesting board invitation. Arriving home one winter day in 1972, she unexpectedly found a florist's truck parked in front. The truck had delivered armloads of blooms sent by industry colleagues to celebrate her nomination for membership on the 33-member Amex board of governors.[43] Officially elected on April 10, she became the second such woman governor in the exchange's history. She followed Mary Roebling but was the first female who came from the securities industry itself. Walsh acknowledged that "I was thrilled over my nomination but I knew, in part, that my good luck came because the time was right for a woman—it couldn't have happened even ten years before."[44]

Walsh proved to be more than just a pretty face. At the time of her board service, the other national securities exchanges were challenging Amex for market listings. Smaller companies tended to select Nasdaq and larger ones opted for the NYSE. She helped formulate an options strategy that proved profitable for the struggling exchange.[45]

Amid a declining stock market in June 1974, Walsh was elected vice chair of Ferris. She continued to give seminars and particularly enjoyed mentoring her female clients in the basics of finance. She began regularly appearing as a panelist on *Wall Street Week With Louis Rukeyser* and after 18 years, became the first woman inducted into its Hall of

Fame.[46] Rukeyser later opined, ". . . in 1970, Wall Street was arguably the most chauvinistic profession in America. But a few bold pioneers had already been knocking down the sexist doors, and none more notably than Julia Montgomery Walsh. . . . At a time when too many women were frightened away from investing because arrogant men told them they lacked the ability and/or the funds, Julia offered both inspiration and encouragement."[47]

She also provided concrete opportunities for women. By raising funds and serving on the advisory board, she helped establish the business program at all women's Simmons College in 1975 and deemed her service, "One of the most satisfying experiences of my life."[48] Not long after, she was asked to serve as treasurer of the newly founded non-profit Women's Institute that aimed to broaden educational and career opportunities for women.[49]

Hearkening back to a notion of public service formulated in her youth, she believed that businesspeople had a particular obligation to public service.[50] Walsh actively participated in civic affairs, with her involvement with the Pennsylvania Avenue Development Corporation and promotion of women's causes figuring among her greatest sources of pride.[51] In 1977, her name surfaced on President Carter's short list for commerce secretary. Economist Juanita Kreps, the president of Duke University who had become the first female director of the NYSE in 1972, ultimately garnered the nomination. Offered a seat instead on the SEC, she reluctantly turned it down because of its required five-year commitment and attendant promise to refrain from resuming securities work for four additional years.[52] Walsh recalled, "The timing wasn't right. I was too young then to retire, and when I finished at age 59, I would be too old to develop another career. Yet I was ready to undertake a new challenge."[53]

Walsh was clearly not ready to retire. The end of the seventies heralded not only the rise of new investment vehicles, but in her view, a changing "relationship of *women* to the world."[54] Walsh wanted to be a part of both developments. She next took one of the greatest risks of her career: opening her own investment firm. Later, she reminisced that "After 20 years in the business, I wanted to prove that any woman with hard work and proper motivation could make a name for herself in a big way, as any man could."[55]

Julia Walsh & Sons opened its doors in June 1977. The firm's unique culture included a profit sharing plan for all employees and an emphasis on training and diversity. With Walsh at the helm, she envisioned a medium-sized regional brokerage focused on serving the Washington,

D.C. vicinity. The firm quickly achieved success. In 1977, it managed $100 million and had become the fourth largest in revenues among local dealers. In November 1979, only two years after its inception, the firm joined the NYSE. While her company flourished, the stress inherent in running a relatively large business, augmented by the country's economic downturn, may have contributed to a minor stroke that Walsh suffered that year.[56]

She nevertheless continued to maintain a full commitment to activities outside the office. Active in the Financial Women's Association, she had also become one of the founding members of the Women's Economic Roundtable, which was an organization formed in 1978 comprised of female corporate executives excluded from participation in its male counterpart. The group's aim was to foster entrepreneurship and financial independence among women. A staunch supporter of the ERA, Walsh admonished women to pursue financial independence as a route to political and economic independence.[57]

She engaged in various capacities in government service, including an appointment in 1983 to a presidential commission charged with examining the fair market value of coal leases. After U.S. Secretary of the Interior James G. Watt apologized for describing the demographical composition of the group as including "every kind of a mixture you can have—a black, a woman, two Jews and a cripple. And we have talent," Walsh relished introducing herself as "I am *that woman!*"[58]

That woman continued to steer her own firm. Believing that she needed a wider array of financial products to offer her 4,000 clients in order to remain competitive, she sold the business in 1983 for $6 million to Boston brokerage Tucker, Anthony & R.L. Day, Inc., a subsidiary of the John Hancock Mutual Life Insurance Company. Walsh served as managing director of the new entity that retained its original name.[59]

Following the merger, Walsh "felt free to focus on the investment business again and to become an 'elder' of the women's movement."[60] Yet she stepped up to other duties as well. In 1985, she became the first female president of the Greater Washington Board of Trade. Six years later, President George Bush appointed her as the only woman to serve on the Czech-Slovak American Enterprise Fund. Then, beginning in March 1993, she suffered a series of strokes. She penned her memoir in 1996 and died seven years later at the age of 80.[61]

Over the course of her life, Walsh witnessed a massive transformation in women's roles in society at large and in corporate America. As she saw the status of women in the 1990s, "We are no longer the exception but the rule in business."[62] She had, however, observed over earlier decades that a lack of networking opportunities represented a roadblock for women.[63] She credits the Harvard program for having "turned the tide for me in business—I became technically one of the boys."[64]

Walsh had "wanted to see whether, in my lifetime, I could put together something meaningful in the world of business; I was curious to see whether it could be done by a *woman*."[65] As much as she demonstrated that women could effectively compete and make significant contributions, she recognized that gender neutrality was not always present when navigating careers in the securities industry. Her own years at Ferris were not marked by significant displays of bias, and she believed that the performance-oriented commission structure of Wall Street offered equality. In 1972, she remarked, "The brokerage business has changed just as society has changed during recent years in its acceptance of individual talent."[66] Nevertheless, 24 years later she acknowledged her selection as an Amex governor as one based on gender, and despite all her accomplishments, "still consider[ed] herself a fringe-member of the club, the old boy network of brokers . . ."[67]

Walsh's reflections on her career identify a potential conflict inherent in advancing in any professional context: a need to fit in balanced with a sense of self. In her early days, "As a pioneer woman, I tried not to step on anyone's toes. On the few occasions I was invited into the smoke-filled, after-discussion groups with industry veterans, I *listened*."[68] Attentiveness mattered, not mimicry. She counseled that women must find their own styles, and not think "that being a corporate leader means dressing, acting, and thinking like a man."[69] She celebrated what she saw as a female propensity to view problems from a "humanistic" perspective that thereby provided balance to a more profit-oriented male vantage point. She believed that Wall Street's financial rewards provided a key to female independence and rued a relative lack of female attraction to the industry.[70]

While advancing in a male-dominated realm, Walsh retained her own unique persona and successfully joined her career and personal interests. Raising her children informed her critical career decisions. She typically brought one of her children with her on business trips, and chose to forego a New York City career, a potential U.S. Cabinet level position, and an SEC appointment at least in part due to their considerations.[71] She told an interviewer in 1984, ". . . I think the greatest mistake a young woman could make would be to deprive herself of having children in search of a career. It's not easy, but it is certainly possible to have both. And if you have married properly, it's fairly easy to have both."[72]

Beginning in her youth, Walsh alternated between observing and challenging the status quo. Her energy and determination merged with the paradigm of personal necessity to make her break from the mold of suburban housewife. Grounded by her beliefs in the importance of family and faith and powered by commitment, courage, and a desire to learn new things, she found success despite potential stumbling blocks. Her groundbreaking financial career reflected her belief that "Our most important freedom, as women, is economic freedom: for a young woman to achieve independence, she must be *financially* independent."[73] In her autobiography, she muses, "If I have accomplished anything worthwhile in my life, it is to have shown the next generation of women that with hard work and a little bit of luck they, too, can make it."[74] Chance surely plays its hand to a degree in one's life. For Walsh, it had always been pluck more than luck that held the key to her future.

ELEVEN

Muriel Siebert

When you hit a closed door and it doesn't budge, just rear back and kick it in—but hold it open so others can follow you.[1]

—Muriel Siebert

Far removed from broker Muriel Siebert's mind when she strolled one afternoon with her friend, fund manager Gerald Tsai Jr., was that their conversation that spring day in 1967 would prompt her to challenge Wall Street history or to become a role model to others. Siebert had no such grand mission; she just harbored a festering grudge. She resented that she did not get paid on par with her male peers who earned 50–100 percent more. She also felt confined by the limited capabilities of the small firm where she worked but did not view larger firms with their limited partnership opportunities for women as a viable alternative.

Up to this point, Siebert had decided not to take personally any perceived gender discrimination. She had shown determination from the beginning of her Wall Street career, when in 1954 as a 22-year-old she moved to Manhattan with only her Studebaker and $500. Siebert had left her Ohio roots behind following her father's death after a three-year bout with cancer. This ordeal contributed to Siebert's early withdrawal from college in Cleveland. There, she had been the only female to enroll in a banking course, but often skipped many of her classes to play bridge. She decided to strike out for New York where her older sister lived. Finance was not her targeted destination. Rejected by the United Nations, she next set her sights on Wall Street. She recalled the exciting floor action on the NYSE that she had once observed during a high school trip and had even saved a piece of ticker tape given to her then that read "Welcome to the NYSE, Muriel Siebert."[2]

Ironically, the exchange did not extend such a warm greeting to her when she later became a member; nor did the greater Wall Street community embrace her when she first sought employment. She applied to Merrill Lynch, but the firm rejected her because she lacked a college degree. Siebert then displayed the kind of spunk that would later typify her career. During her next interview, at Bache & Co., she lied about her uncompleted degree. This falsehood remained unrectified for 14 years. Accepting their offer, she chose to work in research, which was an area that paid less but appealed to her more than accounting.[3]

Numbers did not frighten Siebert. She relished her new job and thrived in it. Before long, she covered the aviation and motion picture industries. These were sectors that previously had not attracted much attention. She immersed herself in learning the intricacies of the two industries.[4]

Siebert was not the first woman transportation analyst; Isabel Benham had blazed that path as a railroad analyst two decades earlier. While other female analysts also worked on Wall Street, their numbers were few and they tended to cover industries viewed as appropriate for women, such as retail, food, or cosmetics. Siebert may have been selected for the motion picture and aviation industries by the erroneous judgment of management that they lacked bright futures. She, however, identified the potential lucrative income stream from televised movies and rode a flight to prominence in the aviation sector when the introduction of commercial jets revolutionized the industry.[5]

Siebert's analytical style consisted of focusing on a select group of companies and learning everything she could about their businesses. That depth of knowledge, coupled with probative questioning, impressed industry executives. Her gender also set her apart, but she felt that she was accepted by other analysts and the companies she followed who knew her work.[6]

Siebert's career nevertheless encountered turbulence. Although she had doubled her income in two years, her salary still lagged those of her male counterparts. She reasoned that she would have to change jobs to advance. Interviews at firms that had never employed a woman in any capacity other than secretarial proved unfruitful. One interviewer even advised her that in order to be hired, she would have to appear like the rest of the "girls" and wear a hat and white gloves in the elevator. Eventually, she landed a research job with Shields & Co. (Shields) in 1958—but only after the placement bureau of the New York Society of Security Analysts sent out her resume with her first name replaced by an androgynous initial.[7]

During her time at Shields, Siebert expanded the roster of companies she covered and obtained her industry license to sell stocks and solicit orders. Despite procuring several important clients, her salary remained significantly below that of the men. When rumor broke that another analyst had planned to start his own firm and to hire Siebert as a partner, the two were both fired. The pair joined the research department of Stearns & Co., where she became a partner. Disappointment quickly followed. The firm's focus on speculative stocks and an SEC investigation of its trading conduct convinced her of its limited growth potential.[8]

Siebert next joined Finkle & Co. and remained a partner there from 1962 to 1965 before going to Brimberg & Co. for the next three years. Her wealth meanwhile increased. In the absence of regulatory prohibitions, she had begun to invest in some of the companies she recommended. She parlayed $500 into $500,000 in under four years.[9]

The 1960s had already wrung change on Wall Street as a strong bull market took hold. Security analysts gained stature as institutional interest in equity holdings increased and advances in computers facilitated analysis. A more level playing field for all investors also emerged as the SEC began to develop new rules regarding full and fair disclosure of information.[10]

Although stocks gained, equal opportunities for those laboring within the securities industry did not. The passage of Title VII in 1964 prohibited job discrimination on the basis of sex, race, color, religion, or national origin. Yet, real advances remained illusory but for a select few. The next year, a *Harvard Business Review* study concerning senior executives reported that "In the case of both Negroes and women, the barriers are so great that there is scarcely anything to study."[11] The clubby veneer of Wall Street had begun to be chipped away by the rise of new competition in money management, but retained a conservative bulwark especially regarding women.[12]

Siebert, despite her success and financial comfort, chafed under conditions that impeded her career. She often could not attend luncheon meetings held at clubs that did not allow women. More important to her was the conundrum presented by an inability to bridge the practical realities of being a woman on Wall Street with her larger dreams. Her income still lagged behind men and she yearned to participate in dealmaking activity centered at the larger brokerages, which were the same firms that did not have female partners and were unlikely to offer her commissions.[13]

When she voiced these concerns to Tsai during their fateful walk, he admonished, "Don't be ridiculous. There's *nowhere* you can go. Buy a seat on the Stock Exchange and work for yourself."[14] Siebert recalled thinking that her friend had "gone off the deep end."[15] The seed had been planted, however, and that night Siebert reviewed the constitution of the NYSE. She found that membership only required a legitimate business purpose and a capability of paying the purchase price.[16]

Siebert was not the first woman to seek a seat on a national exchange. According to rumor, a woman may even have unsuccessfully sought NYSE membership in 1927.[17] Florence Stephens, who founded her own investment firm in 1928, never submitted an application. She opined nearly three decades later, "I think they'd drop dead if a woman applied."[18] More recently, in 1965, the Amex had admitted Julia Montgomery Walsh and Phyllis S. Peterson, who both conducted their business from their Washington, D.C. firms. The Chicago Mercantile Exchange made history in 1966 by becoming the first major commodities exchange to allow a woman to work on its floor when it permitted Sandra Stevens.[19] Overseas, the London Stock Exchange had recently rebuked "a prospective 'petticoat invasion.'"[20]

Six months elapsed before Siebert applied. When she finally did meet with an exchange official, she asked, "Can I buy a seat, or is this just a country club?"[21] According to her account, the official told her the NYSE would face legal risk if it rejected her application on the basis of gender.[22]

Siebert signed a conditional sales contract and paid 20 percent of the $445,000 purchase price on December 7, 1967. In the accompanying paperwork, she truthfully responded that she had attended college but no longer maintained that she had completed a degree. By attaining a seat, a member was entitled to execute transactions on the trading floor, which was a venue where females had only worked during wartime. Siebert, however, did not necessarily intend to transact business there unless circumstances warranted her presence. She did not see the floor as great income potential, and instead sought the seat as a means to retain a larger share of commissions.[23]

Other hurdles ensued. She later said, "You know, whenever you break a tradition that's 187 years old, not everybody's going to love you. People who had volunteered to sponsor me, when the time came, ran out the door."[24] Nine men turned her down before she secured the requisite two sponsors needed to champion her application. According to one sponsor, the exchange had asked about Siebert's personal life. This was a line of inquiry he had never encountered when recommending males. The NYSE next requested that she obtain a letter from a bank stating its willingness to finance the purchase price. This was another condition not previously requested from applicants, but one that Chase Manhattan Bank ultimately supplied.[25]

On December 28, 1967, 35-year-old Siebert received her acceptance. She walked out of her office to buy champagne for her office workers, thinking, "I still couldn't believe it was me. I was walking on cloud nine."[26] At a holiday party that day, an NYSE governor inquired, "How many more women are there behind you?"[27] The answer was not many. For nearly 10 years, she numbered the sole woman among the other 1,365 members. In May 1970, Jane R. Larkin, a partner in Hirsch & Co., became the second female member. She and Siebert never met during her brief two-month tenure before she lost her membership when her firm merged.[28]

Newspapers trumpeted Siebert's achievement, with headlines pandering to lowbrow sensibilities. The articles often detailed her physical appearance and personal life, such as "Muriel Siebert is unmarried, cannot cook, lives in the untidiest apartment on Manhattan's swank Upper East Side and admits to being at least ten pounds overweight."[29] Even her mother, whom she supported financially, showed some apprehension over her daughter's achievement. She worried, "What am I going to tell my friends?"[30]

Even as an official Big Board member, gender-related issues surfaced. Siebert launched her firm, Muriel Siebert & Co., Inc., on the first business day of 1968. Upon submitting to the NYSE a prospective ad announcing the opening of her firm that contained verbiage calling Siebert the "First Lady of the New York Stock Exchange," the copy had to be rewritten—because the exchange chairman felt that sobriquet belonged solely to his wife.[31] For months, she called officials in order to request an affidavit of membership, a document that the men who had been sworn in on the same day had received right away. She did not have to wait long, however, to become the recipient of a collection of toy miniature toilets sent to her by friends because no ladies' room apparently existed on the trading floor. After two years of marching upstairs to use the bathroom, a trader finally informed her of an existing ladies' room on the trading floor that had been built to accommodate female pages employed during wartime. Not until almost her third year did she venture into the Exchange Luncheon Club. Toilet trouble again ensued when in 1987 she successfully lobbied to have a ladies' room installed on the luncheon club floor after threatening to deliver a portable potty to the board of directors.[32]

At the time, women represented approximately 51 percent of American shareholders.[33] Siebert's interaction with women who contacted her, however, left her shocked to learn of an overwhelming ignorance of financial matters. She commissioned a survey of women's colleges and its results stunned her. The data revealed that 85 percent of graduates had never taken a single course in money management, a topic that college administrators deemed "not a proper subject for ladies."[34]

Although Siebert experienced inequities, she did not share in the tone and tactics of the budding feminist movement. Turned off by its stridency, she "felt there were different ways for women to go about demanding and achieving the opportunities to do what we were capable of doing."[35] Neither she nor Larkin chose to participate in a women's strike taking place on Wall Street in 1970; instead Siebert quipped, "I like men and I like brassieres."[36] But she did not turn her back on the issue of gender equality either, and in 1973 she helped form the Women's Forum, which was an organization dedicated to advancing issues affecting working women.

Siebert's way to effect change was to utilize the power that comes with money, and to do so with style and wit. When others told her that women did not frequent the exchange floor due to a female sensitivity to coarse speech, she "learned the language."[37] She wore designer outfits that emphasized the success she enjoyed. First year sales commissions totaling nearly $1 million helped finance her firm's foray into private placements.[38]

Meanwhile, the market itself was not faring so well. Regulators looked for remedies. The SEC began to liberalize the practice of fixed trading commissions that had existed since the beginnings of the exchange. Beginning in April 1971, the agency allowed negotiation of commissions on portions of orders exceeding $500,000, and lowered the threshold a year later to $300,000. The SEC's 1975 "May Day" ruling finally sealed the fate of fixed commissions by requiring fully negotiated rates for trading all listed securities.[39]

Siebert perceived the business opportunity afforded by the changing regulatory climate and repositioned her company as a discount brokerage. Observing that individual investors paid 10 times per share more than what institutions paid in commissions, Siebert "just felt that individuals weren't being treated fairly. If the larger firms had lowered the rates for the individuals then I never would have gone into that business, but they didn't."[40] This was not a popular choice among a Wall Street community already reeling from reduced profits. She persevered with her plan even when her firm's clearinghouse terminated their business dealings.[41] In September 1976, she extended discounting to retail investors by becoming one of the first deep discount brokers. Says Siebert of her decision, "My motives have always been pride, principle, and profit. I don't know how you stay afloat and sleep at night without all three."[42]

Not long after, in the spring of 1977, Governor Hugh Carey offered Siebert the position of New York Superintendent of Banking. He cited a commitment to hire women. According to rumor, President Carter had also contemplated naming Siebert to the SEC, but the New York appointment preempted any further consideration. Excited over the prospect of controlling a troubled system of 500 banks worth $400 billion in assets, Siebert accepted the job and placed her firm's operations in a blind trust during her five-year absence. During her tenure, not one bank failure occurred in the state as she helped foster a sounder economic environment by mandating reorganizations of troubled financial institutions and stimulating investment.[43]

Buoyed by her success and convinced that financial laws needed reform, Siebert tossed her hat into the ring for the 1982 New York Republican senatorial nomination. Her platform blended fiscal conservatism and a more moderate social agenda that included support for the ERA. She sought "to make the Republican power structure more sensitive to the real hopes and dreams of women."[44] She came in second in a field of three candidates.

Siebert's firm had suffered during her absence. Approached to sell the business, she refused, out of both affection for Wall Street and "a sense of obligation as a role model."[45] She set about making changes, including improving customer service, hiring promising talent, and embarking on a new public relations campaign. She again seized opportunities not readily apparent to her competition. Playing technological catch-up, she moved fast. Her firm became an early provider of dial-up telephone stock quotes 24 hours a day, and the first discount broker to house a branch within a bank lobby.[46]

Gender differentiation on Wall Street continued. Sometimes it benefitted her. When Congress ordered the government in 1987 to sell its stake in Conrail, Siebert obtained her firm's first major underwriting. Under the terms of the legislation, six minority-owned financial firms were to be named as special underwriters. Siebert picked up the phone and called the Transportation Secretary, saying, "I'm a woman. Deal me in."[47] He did, and Siebert successfully completed her portion of the offering.[48] Confrontations arise and enmities commonly develop, however, during a career in a fiercely competitive industry. For Siebert, "While always aware of making enemies, I never knew when the acrimony and ill will was gender-based."[49]

In 1996, her firm was flourishing and raking in approximately $14 million before taxes. Believing that industry consolidation was in the air, Siebert circumvented the conventional public offering route to obtaining stock. She engineered a merger with a publicly traded shell and created a holding company, Siebert Financial Corp. She defended her choice by citing a desire for marketable securities that would enable her to participate in potential mergers rather than a need for cash. Siebert has subsequently expanded her firm by establishing branches in California, Florida, and New Jersey, and obtaining a 49 percent stake in Siebert Bradford Shank & Co., L.L.C., the largest minority and women's municipal bond firm.[50]

Siebert's astuteness in harnessing technological advantage again came to the fore in 1998 when she introduced SiebertNet, among the industry's first electronic trading platforms. One year later, the company purchased two women's financial websites that formed the foundation for the Siebert Women's Financial Network, a venue meant to serve women's financial needs without the condescension she found in rival sites.[51] In an interview, she made known that men were also welcome, adding, "We're not sexist."[52]

At age 80, Siebert continues to lead Siebert Financial Corp., which trades on Nasdaq and encompasses a retail discount brokerage and investment banking business that produced total revenues in 2011 of $20.2 million.[53] In recognition of her achievements, she has rung the closing bell on several occasions at the invitation of the NYSE. Siebert has received a multitude of honors and served on many non-profit boards. She champions financial literacy and initiated a young adult financial education program in 1999 that has since been used in New York and New Jersey schools. Her political advocacy includes urging for day care and child support initiatives and speaking out on behalf of the small investor for financial reforms favoring greater transparency and disclosure.

"I'm a fighter," proclaims Siebert.[54] In the autobiography she penned in 2002, she concedes, "I don't know if I've ever broken into the old boys' network, but I've survived without it, and a lot of people who didn't accept me at first learned to respect me."[55] Over the years, the lack of significant advancement of women on Wall Street has concerned her. In her memoir, Siebert remarks, "For almost fifty years, I've been fighting, dodging and trying to derail the deeply ingrained misogyny of the financial community. . . . Women on Wall Street earn far more than those in other industries, and this 'golden muzzle' of high compensation makes being even a token woman on Wall Street attractive. The real issue is about being able to have meaningful, decision-making roles."[56] She has acknowledged the increase of women in asset management and public finance, but has bemoaned a relative lack of presence in corporate finance and in top leadership positions.[57]

Siebert did not embark on her career to become a role model, but she evolved into one. The defining moment in her career occurred with her entree into the NYSE. From then on, scarcely a reference to her would be made without noting that occasion which represented a milestone both in Wall Street history and in her own personal journey. Prior to that point, she had noticed discrepancies in the way women were regarded but worked within the existing system. Like other women trying to move ahead in male-dominated fields, including financial journalist Sylvia Porter and analyst Benham, she hid her gender behind initials when expedient and did not directly question differentiation. After becoming an NYSE member, personal inequities she had resented privately now turned into fodder for a more proactive commitment to combat gender discrimination for both herself and on a broader scale. Says Siebert, "I've seen things I've wanted to do and I've done them. In some cases being a woman was an obstacle, but it probably gave me more incentives than I would have had if I'd been a man."[58]

Siebert has never married. In her view, the times in which she made headway in her profession did not make it easy to combine a high-paced career with marriage. In 1981, she reflected, "I was growing pretty fast in my career and, when I look at the various people that I dated seriously over the years, they haven't kept up with me. . . . I don't regret that marriage wasn't possible in my time. You can't have everything."[59]

Risk and reward figure amply into Siebert's story.[60] In seeking an NYSE seat, she had calculated the inherent hazards and only did so after deliberate introspection. She had not desired public attention but financial opportunity and redress of personal grievances; she received both. Said Siebert, "Money represents power to men, but to me it represents freedom. Once I joined the exchange, I always felt I had to prove I bought the seat not for publicity but for the business."[61] Her seat purchase may have seemed a particularly bold and dicey investment when she paid a steep price for it in dollars and in privacy, but it represented a sound investment in her future. Through her professional success and extracurricular endeavors, Siebert has taken advantage of her standing as the First Lady of Finance to ensure that she would not be the last.

PART V

Icons

"You've come a long way, Baby," proclaimed a cigarette advertising slogan in the late 1960s and 1970s.[1] Indeed, she had. Vast societal changes had transformed family life, sexuality, politics, and the workplace. But further progress for the American woman soon stalled. Beginning in the early 1980s, a mixture of both anti-feminist backlash and a certain sense of complacency among the mainstream hampered the women's movement. Yet on Wall Street, women hit their stride. As they advanced, some women even achieved iconic status as their success coincided with the glamour that high finance itself appeared to embody. Others became more strident in defending their rightful place in a financial industry that was undergoing its own modernization.[2]

With the ERA failing to receive sufficient state ratification in 1982 and anti-abortion activism rising during a time of encroaching political conservatism, the broader feminist movement looked like it might have run aground. One had to look no further than in public and professional lives, however, to find continued advancement. The number of female elected officials rose by almost 2.5 percent between 1975 and 1981. Sandra Day O'Connor was confirmed as the first woman Supreme Court justice in 1981 and Geraldine Ferraro occupied the vice presidential slot on the 1984 Democratic presidential ticket. A majority of married women worked by 1980 and they were viewed as a permanent part of the workforce. Women comprised 40 percent of the entering classes of professional schools by the middle of the decade. Even in the military, women marched forward. The first woman matriculated at West Point in 1989 and females joined battlefield troops during the Gulf War.[3]

While these statistics sounded encouraging, inequities, particularly economic ones, lurked beneath the surface. Wages revealed an unjust reality. The percentage of women working had climbed to 60 percent by 1985, but women found advancement difficult and they earned only 55–57 cents for every dollar that men were paid. Even while time devoted to domestic chores declined, balancing work and family responsibilities continued to prove vexing. As divorce rates rose, so, too, did the feminization of poverty. Only 4 percent of women in 1984 earned more than $28,000. Women represented 80 percent of welfare recipients in 1990. This statistic was exacerbated by the rise of single motherhood that reached 24 percent in 1992.[4]

Sexual harassment in the workforce also came to the fore. In 1980, the Equal Employment Opportunity Commission (EEOC) promulgated guidelines that made sexual harassment a violation of Title VII. The Supreme Court generally affirmed this stance six years later in *Meritor Savings Bank v. Vinson*. The court held that such a violation may be established "by proving that discrimination based on sex has created a hostile or abusive work environment."[5] Ironically, it was the 1991 Supreme Court nomination hearings of Judge Clarence Thomas in which his former assistant Anita Hill testified of his alleged sexual harassment that galvanized public attention on the topic.[6]

Gender-related workforce issues encompassing charges of discrimination, bias, and harassment did not come to a head in the financial industry until the mid-to-late nineties. For the most part, women in the industry had previously championed their own careers rather than having led the prior decade's women liberation marches on Wall Street. Despite a survey of FWA membership in 1972 that revealed women earned lower incomes and received less training than their male counterparts, women had felt confident of their future prospects both in banks, which continued to provide more opportunities, and in brokerages.[7] Commented FWA Vice President and investment firm partner Anita Volz, "The next 10 years could see major change. Wall Street is going through a difficult period of structural change and uncertainty. Once these uncertainties are out of the way, the next step for women will be in management positions. They have already demonstrated they fill a functional need."[8]

The link between Wall Street's fortunes and advancement opportunities there for women was evident. Wall Street could not offer a promising future for anyone if it did not address stresses in its own technological infrastructure. The advent of the microprocessor in 1971 and the rise of the computer age promised hope. Wall Street quickly embraced the new technology. By 1978, the linkage of national and regional exchanges through the Intermarket Trading System produced a consolidated tape of all NYSE-listed securities irrespective of trading origination. Information forms the underlying core of any market, and the securities industry had been given a boost of paramount significance. Another soon followed. Installation of cables above the NYSE trading floor in 1981 enabled large electronic displays of data linked to the world's securities markets and major brokerage houses and transformed the appearance and concept of the market.[9]

While Wall Street upgraded its technology, the national economy remained stagnant. Stagflation, that fiscal environment marked by low economic growth coupled with both steep inflation and unemployment, raged during the latter half of President Carter's administration. The DJIA remained range-bound. In the commodities market, billionaire brothers Nelson Bunker Hunt and William Herbert Hunt unsuccessfully attempted to corner the world's silver supply.[10]

Carter's appointment of Federal Reserve Chairman Paul Volcker, a proponent of tight monetary policy, led to the highest interest rates in the country's history. Volcker's strict fiscal prescription initially seemed to cause even greater ills as it induced a severe recession. President Ronald Reagan replaced Carter in 1981, but the economic outlook looked no better in his early tenure as unemployment surged above 10 percent while corporate profits spiraled downward.[11]

The patient finally began to show signs of recovery. Foreign investors found high rates attractive and their Treasury bond purchases spurred the dollar higher. The DJIA began to slowly rise and the Fed cut the discount rate in mid-1982. Revived consumer spending, lowered capital gains tax rates, eased underwriting hurdles, booming merger activity, and the growth potential recognized in high tech and biotechnology stocks also helped awaken stocks from their doldrums. The DJIA climbed past 1,000 in the latter half of the year and continued on its near uninterrupted march to 2,000 in January 1987 and to 2,500 six months later.[12]

On August 25, 1987, the market reached a height of 2,722.42. Stock values slid over the next two months due to a myriad of factors that included foreign selling of Treasuries, economic policies, and Persian Gulf tensions. "Black Monday" arrived on October 19. Global sell-offs the preceding night led to New York opening under heavy selling pressure, which was exacerbated by computerized trading programs. By the close of trading, the DJIA had plunged 22.6 percent on heavy volume. Commented NYSE Chairman John Phelan, "[This is] the worst market I've ever seen, as close to a financial meltdown as I'd ever want to see."[13]

Despite popular allusions to 1929, this autumnal demise was different. Instead of contributing to another Great Depression, the market rebounded the following day and reclaimed its high within two years. Both investors and policymakers share credit for this resiliency due to increased sophistication leading up to and following the drop. Few investors had suffered complete collapse due to more diversified portfolios. A more mature Federal Reserve under the helm of Alan Greenspan immediately created liquidity by purchasing large amounts of government securities, and the Reagan Administration quietly encouraged corporate share buybacks. With the Fed acting decisively, panic was averted and prosperity returned to Wall Street. Although the 1987 Crash claimed the demise of two large brokerages, E.F. Hutton and L.F. Rothschild, as well as at least 60 smaller firms, Wall Street remained vibrant. By the end of 1999, the price of an NYSE seat reached $2.3 million. This price was more than double that of a seat in the mid-1980s.[14]

The allure of wealth and high finance soared along with rising equities. Personalities associated with Wall Street captured the imagination of the media and the public. A culture of excess and even greed was encapsulated in the Hollywood blockbuster *Wall Street* and author Tom Wolfe's novel *Bonfire of the Vanities* in 1989. Wall Street was minting celebrities as well as mega-millionaires and it seemed as if the age of the robber baron had returned. In a period of "momentous financial change"[15] marked by regulatory liberalization and product innovation, figures such as Rupert Murdoch, Carl Icahn, and Henry Kravis jockeyed to play kingmaker in their takeover games. A "Queen" had also arrived. Crowned not for any dealmaking activity but for her forecasting prowess, analyst Elaine Garzarelli had predicted the 1987 Crash based on a quantitative valuation model that she had created and honed.[16]

Some of the biggest stars also courted trouble. Insider trading scandals proliferated, which involved the likes of arbitrageur Ivan Boesky and bankers Martin Siegel and Dennis Levine. Michael Milken, the architect of the junk bond market championed by investment bank Drexel Burnham Lambert in the mid-1980s, was indicted in 1990. Fallout from that scandal drove the firm to file for bankruptcy and caused it to shut its doors the following year. At Salomon Brothers, irregularities in Treasury bond auctions claimed the ouster of its prominent chief executive officer, John Gutfreund.[17]

These incidents posed as distractions rather than obstacles to the market's continued upward march. Powered by broad market participation, financial innovation, an attractive dollar, and a recovering thrift industry, the strength of the Dow's 228.3 percent run-up in the 1980s continued into the next decade despite an early brief decline and volatility. Neither large derivatives losses suffered by Orange County, California, Procter & Gamble, and Gibson Greetings nor rogue trading incidents at Kidder, Peabody & Co., and Baring Brothers & Co., Ltd., had a significant long-term detrimental effect on the larger market beyond a downturn in 1994.[18]

The prolonged bull run found its champion in analyst Abby Joseph Cohen. Her outward manner could not have been more different than that of Garzarelli. However, she was armed with a similar work ethic, intellect, and quantitative-based approach and she became the market's muse. The financial market now appealed to a still larger audience. Technology again had paved the way for broader market participation as development of the Internet provided both a new crop of growth stocks and fostered greater access to information. The advent of online trading enabled individuals to bypass higher brokerage commissions and even lured some into the chaotic action of day trading. Others, some of whom may have been inspired by the breaking news in 1994 of First Lady Hillary Clinton's profitable trades taken some 15 years earlier by which her initial $1,000 investment returned $100,000 within approximately 10 months, dabbled in commodities speculation. Investment clubs flourished, with few achieving the fame of a group of older women in Illinois. The Beardstown Business and Professional Women's Investment Club (Beardstown Ladies) became media sensations and authored five books touting their success before the group's investment returns were audited and their widely publicized double-digit returns found misrepresentative. The nation had become accustomed to easy profits and this notion fed the securities market's frenzy. In 1996, Fed Chairman Greenspan cautioned of possible equity overvaluation and the market's "irrational exuberance."[19] Initially spooked by this comment, the market soon shrugged off this notion.[20]

A potential disconnect between appearance and reality echoed in the professional experience of women on Wall Street. The "complete globalization and integration of the world's financial markets in only a few years"[21] eased the professional ascent of women. As the financial industry expanded, it offered greater employment opportunities and served a broader investor base. The influence of successful commentators such as Garzarelli and Cohen was accentuated. In the 1990s, another woman, Amy

Domini, did not so much move the market as create one by demonstrating a profitable correlation between personal ethics and portfolio selection and breathing new life into an overlooked investment philosophy.

However, successes could not blunt the degree of discrimination that many other less well-known women endured in their career paths. Broker Pamela Martens led the charge to file the first gender-based class action suit against a Wall Street firm. Her 1996 suit against Smith Barney inspired a suit initiated by aggrieved women at Merrill Lynch the following year. Calling into question the way the industry did business, these cases publicized alleged entrenched discriminatory practices. They further led to an ending of compulsory industry arbitration of civil rights claims and to a greater examination of gender-based inequities in the financial industry.[22] It is probably no mere coincidence that increased networking activities by female financial professionals also took hold in the mid-to-late 1990s.

By the turn of the twenty-first century, women in finance had gone from quietly seeking to advance their personal careers to becoming more vocal and challenging the status quo. They had not led the feminist rallies on Wall Street during the 1970s, but their voices grew louder over the next decades despite a waning of the women's liberation movement. A predicate of political, legal, economic, technological, and cultural advances had altered female expectations generally. More women now by choice rather than out of necessity selected Wall Street by which to embark upon their own professional journeys; some now successfully forged strong identities within high profile careers.

TWELVE

Elaine Garzarelli

You just wouldn't believe how men doubt that a woman can do anything with numbers.[1]

—Elaine Garzarelli

The 1987 Crash did not just cause investors financial angst. For research analyst and money manager Elaine Garzarelli, it also triggered physical pain. Believing that she was suffering a heart attack early the following morning, she called her cousin who summoned an ambulance. Tension rather than coronary illness had provoked the symptoms, as accurately predicting the crash had proved far easier for Garzarelli than gauging its personal effects. One week following the market's drop, she admitted to a reporter, "I really don't know what's going to happen. This is the most uncertain time of my whole career."[2]

Doubt had never been something with which Garzarelli had much familiarity. Since her youth, she had always striven for excellence and recognition. Growing up in a conservative Italian-American family in suburban Philadelphia, Garzarelli enjoyed dancing, setting up chemistry experiments in her room, and watching *American Bandstand*. Despite this longing and her "wax doll"[3] looks, she was raised "like a boy"[4] within a competitive family. As the middle child and only daughter, she often felt in the shadow of her older brother. While he helped her learn math, science, and chess, she felt she "was always being compared to him—I wasn't as bright, I wasn't as good."[5] She longed to be number one.[6]

That early competitiveness would remain with her throughout her career, as would her penchant for coupling her individual style and behavior with a drive for perfection. Her mother pushed the children in all their activities and admonished her, "Don't come home if you don't win."[7] She never entertained thoughts of a career in finance despite her mother's urgings to "Get yourself into a man's business."[8] Academic success came easily, and she excelled in high school.[9]

Not until she went to Drexel University did her father, a bank executive and an experienced investor, urge her to pursue business. Instead, Garzarelli focused on a childhood interest, chemical engineering, with thoughts of a future career in medicine. She discovered her true passion, however, in an economics class. Finding that "It clicked. I just loved it,"[10] she changed her major and charted her future course on Wall Street.[11]

Garzarelli also reveled in her social life. Even so, she landed a part-time undergraduate job with Philadelphia investment firm Drexel Harriman Ripley as an assistant to chief economist Dr. Roy Moor. He assigned her the task of discerning the economic indicators most relevant to stock market direction. Garzarelli's professional calling in econometrics stems from this undertaking in which she embarked on formulating a novel forecasting model that merged macroeconomics with market dynamics.[12]

After graduating, Garzarelli joined Moor when he went to A.G. Becker Paribas (Paribas) in New York in 1971. While working full-time, she also pursued a master's degree program in business at Drexel by taking classes at night. Coupling hard work with hard play, she recalled, "I had a staff helping me, to start with. But that was so expensive they gradually cut it down to nothing. They were ready to give up on me. So I kept going, all by myself. I worked nights, I worked weekends, I worked all the time. I was never *not* working."[13] Nightclubs provided outlets for her stress-laden 10-hour days, and she ". . . [would] work or go to class until eleven o'clock at night, and then go crazy on the dance floor until one or two in the morning. I did that two or three times a week. It was a great release of tension, and great exercise."[14]

Her research produced meaningful results. Technological advances in computers had helped make statistical analysis more accessible in her search for quantifiable market indicators. By the late 1970s, she had identified approximately a dozen indicators that she considered key factors. Incorporating economic cycles together with monetary, valuation, and sentiment variables into mathematical equations, she identified market and sector direction that are essential components for determining stock performance.

Flourishing at Paribas, Garzarelli became the firm's first female managing director in 1982. She then moved to Shearson/American Express in 1984 when Paribas merged with Merrill Lynch. At Shearson, she continued her quantitative research to forecast market direction and to make stock recommendations. By now, she had become a well-known figure and made the rounds of popular financial television shows.[15]

Despite Garzarelli's professional success, her personal life suffered. Engaged in her early twenties, she apparently did not find a spouse supportive of her career. According to one report, a man even once threw her copy of the *Wall Street Journal* in her face.[16] Other romantic interests found her success threatening. According to her, "Whether it's money or some other thing, like being handy around the house, men don't feel comfortable if you're too independent."[17]

Sexism also occasionally surfaced professionally. Garzarelli, though, maintains that women were generally respected at Shearson.[18] Largely disregarded by male clients initially, she likewise paid scant attention to them and instead dove further into her work.[19] She explained later, "I've tried to use sexism as an incentive to work harder, to prove myself."[20] When given her first mutual fund to manage, the Sector Analysis Portfolio, in August 1987, one executive believed that the firm needed contractual protection in the event she left to get married. Garzarelli objected to such a provision and still gained stewardship of the fund that launched with an initial $470 million in assets.[21] To lure clients, many of them skeptical about a woman's financial aptitude, "I had to take each and every one of these guys out to dinner, and just keep explaining and explaining and *explaining* what I was doing."[22]

By the mid-1980s, Garzarelli was highly regarded on Wall Street. She had correctly called every market top and trough since 1980, and ranked as *Institutional Investor's* top quantitative analyst since 1983.[23] Her forecast of the 1987 Crash cemented her fame and solidified her celebrity.

Prior to the 1987 Crash, the bull market then running had seemed all but unstoppable to the majority of Wall Street. Only a few doubted the market's excesses, and those that did differed on their reasoning. For Garzarelli, a perfect storm of increasing bond yields, a hike in the discount rate, and a declining Japanese bond market led to such bearish sentiment that she divested the holdings in her $600 million Sector Analysis Portfolio by September 1. As her indicators ramped up their bearish stance, she began alerting 1,000 firm clients to her dire outlook on October 11. A few weeks later, she recounted, "Then we just waited, and 'boom' that was it. . . . Some were not believing. They kept saying that this time was different. But I wanted to get out and tell the truth. After a while, it sunk in."[24] Appearing on *Moneyline* on October 12, 1987, she warned of a collapse "like 1929,"[25] and did so again the next day to *USA Today*. Then, as she described her experience, she hid.[26]

On Monday, October 19, the market opened over 80 points lower. Garzarelli holed up at home. Later in the day, she tried to calm investors by telling them that Federal Reserve Chief Greenspan would surely take the necessary steps to soothe the market and that the swiftness of a correction in equities could be seen as beneficial. By the time the market closed, the DJIA had lost 508 points, a drop equivalent to a 22.6 percent loss in value. Virtually every stock and fund wound up deep in the red. Garzarelli's fund bucked the norm and closed up 5 percent, owing to its composition of 50 percent cash, 40 percent two-year Treasury bills, and 10 percent stock puts. Garzarelli celebrated at a bittersweet dinner with friends that night. She was happy with her fund's performance but saddened by her clients' woes.[27]

The suggested cure for Garzarelli's physical pain that manifested itself the next day was to avoid reading the newspapers. But newspapers were paying attention to her. The *Wall Street Journal* published an article that focused on her earlier forecast and, according to her, "It seemed after that article that my comments were being noticed each time I made one."[28] She felt awkward.[29]

Blamed by some pundits as causing the market tumble and the subsequent 157-point dip due to her continued dire outlook a week later, the "hottest Cassandra on the Street"[30] responded by telling angry investors that "No one individual affects the market."[31] According to Jack Rifkin, the firm's head of research, Garzarelli had neither wanted this celebrity nor tried to influence her indicators. Instead, she merely publicized what they revealed to her.[32] At 36, Garzarelli felt she had aged some 15 years.[33] She recalled, "My career was going very nicely until then, and it was too much attention. It was a lot of pressure. But the crash didn't shape the way I look at the market at all. It gave me even more confidence that the indicators are very good—that I should stick to them no matter what."[34]

Garzarelli adhered to her typical workaholic efforts and did not coast on her fame. She focused on continuing the success of her fund, whose worth had grown to over $770 million by the start of 1988.[35] For half of each month, she worked at home writing an extensive research report that was sent to thousands of institutional clients around the world. Rising early to check the London markets and retiring late to contact Tokyo, even during a few moments stolen on the beach, "I get my fun and my sun. But while the other people on the beach read a dirty novel, I'm reading my charts. I just always work. It's a hobby for me. It's my passion."[36]

Another of her passions stirred critics. Garzarelli's penchant for dressing in flashy attire made her "stands out like a Jackie Collins novel among the reference books."[37] Coupled with what was seen as flirtatious affections such as winking and nibbling on her pearls, she became scorned by some, including other Wall Street women, for her style.[38] Though she tried to reign in the winking and toying with her jewelry, she demurred in 1991 that "I don't look good in the clothes and ties that women wear on Wall Street. Why shouldn't I be stylish? And so what if I'm friendly and outgoing? I call it enthusiastic."[39] A male money manager noted, "Elaine is using every tactic she had to stay on top. A man would use every means available to get clients to like him. Why shouldn't a woman?"[40] The following year, she along with other prominent national figures appeared fully clothed in suits for a pantyhose advertising campaign. She put the proceeds that she received from it to use by endowing a scholarship for women majoring in economics at Drexel University.[41]

Garzarelli continued to excel, but her record did sport blemishes. In 1988, her fund lost 13 percent when she ignored her signals and stayed bearish for too long. Although she claimed that she would never again take an action contrary to her indicators, critics contended that her short-term decision making was often marred by her clamoring for press attention. Despite her 1998 blunder, she correctly called the 1990 bear market.[42]

The nineties provided fresh challenges. Some of these resulted from the changing financial landscape. Her firm in particular had undergone significant evolution since she had joined. As a result of a merger between Shearson/American Express and Lehman Brothers Kuhn Loeb in 1984, the combined entity became known as Shearson Lehman/American Express. Four years later, the firm acquired E.F. Hutton and took the name Shearson Lehman Hutton, Inc. until 1990 when it was renamed Shearson Lehman Brothers. In 1993, American Express Company sold the Shearson retail brokerage and asset management businesses to Smith Barney, and a year later spun off Lehman Brothers Holdings Inc. (Lehman Brothers).

No amount of dizzying corporate name changes, however, could obscure the fact that by the beginning of 1994, assets in the fund Garzarelli managed had shrunk to $130 million. In August, Smith Barney merged it into its Strategic Investors Fund. Two months later, as Lehman tried to rein in costs amid a sagging industry suffering from bond losses, Garzarelli was ousted her from her post as director of sector analysis just days after being named the top quantitative analyst by *Institutional Investor* for the 11th consecutive year. The media speculated over whether she had resigned at her own behest or was pressured to do so by the firm. She contends that she was fired when the firm learned that she wanted to leave.[43]

In early 1995, she formed Garzarelli Capital, Inc. that functions as a money management and research firm. Over the ensuing years, she has continued her sector analysis approach for institutional investors while intermittently managing several funds. Garzarelli still publishes her monthly report and manages her Sector Analysis Fund. On her website she touts her track record of market signals dating from 1982 that sports an impressive number of correct calls.

When Garzarelli joined Lehman, she was not the lone female employee. Women at that time comprised nearly half of the firm's research department. Interviewed by a reporter in 1998, Garzarelli ascribed the influx of women into research positions generally in part due to a female penchant for accuracy and detail. She conceded that "The media has helped women gain prominence. The TV people and the newspapers are much more willing to quote women now, thinking women have something to say. Fifteen to 20 years ago, you'd only see men giving their opinions."[44] Nevertheless, she did not believe that women on Wall Street compete equally with men: "You're not always in the loop with the political atmosphere. You don't play golf with the fellows. You don't work out with the fellows. You don't share off-color jokes. Men want to play with the men. I don't think they want women in the club."[45] To correct the problem, she maintains that "Women have to work harder to excel. You just have to be excellent in what you do."[46]

The scholarship fund Garzarelli had created at Drexel in 1995 evidences her support of women in business. Star performance and growing expertise, however, may bring pitfalls for women if men feel threatened by them once they compete with each other at higher levels. Reflective of her own experience, she reportedly once counseled that "What you do is go to a company when you're young and leave it in your 40s. Women are not good in corporations over 40."[47] She now believes the future for women on Wall Street "looks bright," and does not recall advising older and more senior women to step off the corporate ladder. Still, she contends they must work harder than anyone else to advance.[48]

Garzarelli received the ultimate accolade from her mother, the person perhaps most responsible for her determined work habits, who in 1988 remarked, "That little girl, I didn't expect she would go so far. But she earned it."[49] Garzarelli certainly earned it; her intellect and drive detected the perfect storm of economic conditions that presaged her bold and most famous call. With her fame came increased riches but also some drawbacks. She has been hailed as a hero for her prediction of the 1987 Crash but simultaneously cast as a scapegoat for the event.

For all the fame, whether thrust on her or courted over the years, Garzarelli learned to harness the power of publicity to the point of becoming a brand name herself. Undoubtedly, her renown increased her visibility and made her more of a target for criticism. For Garzarelli, unlike for most of her male peers, this meant that her appearance has provided additional fodder for attack. Throughout her career, she has not significantly altered her signature style. In fact, she has used it to both please herself as well as to create a distinctive persona within a relatively staid financial establishment.

Underlying her showy image lays an intellect that pioneered a quantitative analytical framework for the stock market. Pinpointing market direction is a combination of art and science. Garzarelli claims that her model could have predicted the 1929 Crash six months beforehand.[50] In those days, another woman had developed a unique forecasting model that warned of the imminent collapse. Evangeline Adams had based her forecast on celestial observations. Garzarelli's variables are of a more mundane nature, but they blasted her skyward in the late 1980s as the financial galaxy's newest star and continue to stand her in good stead during the present era. From that very public ride, she has orbited Wall Street while reflecting her own aura and enjoying an eventful career more enduring than any ephemeral shooting star.

THIRTEEN

Abby Joseph Cohen

I think that the addition of women and people of diverse backgrounds has had an enormously beneficial impact on not just the office culture, but on the quality of work that's getting done.[1]

—Abby Joseph Cohen

Not often does a wad of Silly Putty lead to any great economic epiphanies. But one gooey wad did just that in the hands of economist and market theoretician Abby Joseph Cohen. While fiddling with it one day in 1992, she saw something other than a mere toy. Noting its elasticity, she envisioned a model of a protracted bull equity market that led her to become "the muse of the bull market."[2]

Cohen's career has been anything but child's play. Her words, amplified and studied by investors, have often moved the market. While the rarefied atmosphere of high finance may seem a world apart from her more humble roots, she does not stray far from her down-to-earth upbringing or principles.

Cohen grew up in a middle-class neighborhood of Queens, New York. The daughter of accountant Raymond Joseph, himself the son of Polish immigrants, and Polish-born Shirley Silverstein Joseph, she has described herself as "a first-generation American."[3] Certainly, the work ethic imbued in her and embodied by her parents could be seen as reflective of the immigrant experience and ethos of education and diligence. Working full time, Cohen's father received two degrees from New York University.

Her mother, a Brooklyn College graduate, worked in the controller's office at General Foods Corporation until she had her first child. Four years later, in 1952, Cohen was born.[4]

Growing up, Cohen thought she might become a teacher. At her public high school, she distinguished herself both academically and socially. Cohen was active in various extracurricular groups; she was a leader of the honor society and won two Future Scientists of America awards. Amidst the charged atmosphere of the sixties, Cohen felt "no need to rebel at all. My parents were very aware of the times and willing to bend."[5] Prompted by her strength in the natural sciences, they thought she might pursue medicine. They counseled her to ignore stereotypical gender-based paths and instead to "Reach out for what you want to do."[6] In 1969, she graduated among the top of her high school class.[7]

College bore the imprint of significant choices made by an independent-minded and determined Cohen. She attended Cornell University, which then was one of the few Ivy League institutions open to women. Having initially decided to major in physics, an unpopular path for women, she discovered new interests in even more heavily male-dominated fields when she stumbled upon economics and computer science. She switched her major to economics at the end of her second year and was fascinated by its intersection with mathematics. Capable of building databases and conducting econometric analyses, she earned money by helping graduate students with their research. Gender bias also surfaced. She found it amusing that no ladies' rooms existed in some of the buildings other than those housing liberal arts classes. Another incident proved more vexing but displayed her resolve. Upon trying to enroll in a graduate-level computer science class her senior year, the professor informed Cohen that she was not welcome. Cohen refused to be deterred, regardless of whether it was due or not to her being a woman, and completed the course.[8]

Following graduation in 1973, she married her college boyfriend, David M. Cohen. They settled in Washington, D.C. where he attended law school and she pursued a master's degree in economics at George Washington University while working as a research assistant at the Federal Reserve Board. Finding that her interest in the financial markets was of a more practical bent than academic nature, she decided against obtaining a doctorate.[9]

Cohen's stint at the Federal Reserve during the mid-seventies included reviewing the agency's inflation forecasting model. She attributes her later willingness to question existing economic theories to this experience. According to her, "Parts of the economic model the Fed used had stopped working because they hadn't been adapted to reflect changes that had taken place in the economy. This was a fabulous lesson to me to be flexible in my analysis and to look beneath the usual rules of thumb to the underlying dynamics."[10] She enjoyed the Federal Reserve's professional and intellectual climate and never saw her gender as a determining factor of success. She regards her status as one of the few women there as "a generational thing. There were certainly a larger number of women in my age category than in the older categories, so we were the vanguard in terms of being the first large group of women academically trained in economics and beginning to move through the ranks."[11]

Despite her confidence in the agency's meritocratic structure, Cohen accepted an offer from Baltimore-based mutual fund company T. Rowe Price in 1976. Her boss at the Fed had become the firm's chief economist and he wanted her to join him. During her eight years at T. Rowe, Cohen concentrated on analyzing business conditions from an investment perspective and building econometric models. Advances in computer technology aided her research, but certain aspects of business culture remained stagnant. Few women worked in the econometrics field, and, Cohen experienced her first brush with workplace discrimination: "I realized firsthand that the field on which we were playing wasn't level. Sometimes the discrimination was so ingrained that others weren't even aware of it being a problem. On several occasions, when I arrived at meetings around town, people at the locations would look at me and say, 'Sorry, you can't go in there. We invited only the analysts, not their secretaries.' "[12]

In spite of potential prejudice, Cohen rose to become the firm's youngest vice president in 1978. Practical grievances still lurked. Denied health insurance for her family due to the company's guidelines that only primary wage earners were entitled to that benefit and their implicit assumption that women would not hold such status, her attorney husband found precedent that proved such a rule was illegal. When she showed the case to her supervisor, she gained coverage for herself and firm policy soon changed.[13]

Known as "the quant," Cohen was courted by firms eager to build modern computing methodologies.[14] Heeding "the siren call of Wall Street,"[15] Cohen left T. Rowe to head to Drexel in 1982. Hired as a portfolio strategist by the firm's research director, she devised quantitative and economic-based investment strategies. In addition to her specific duties, she was attracted to the position by her general perception of opportunities available for women at the firm.[16] She also looked forward to residing in the same New York neighborhood in which she had grown up and that allowed her to be near family.

Fully engaged in her new job at Drexel, she "loved the strategy role right away. Everybody in this business has a view on the markets. Now I got to spend my entire day working on mine."[17] In mid-1987, Cohen was promoted to chief strategist. Not long after, the October stock market crash caught her by surprise. Although she and her colleagues had believed in August that equities were overvalued, they had not foreseen any significant correction.[18] In the days following the crash, she advised clients to purchase stocks and bonds.[19] She regards this call as one of her proudest moments, "It was one of those cases of 'ignoring the noise,' looking at what was a traumatic market event and recognizing 'this is not going to have a notable economic impact,' that the economy was in reasonably good condition, and that stocks were inexpensive based on any thoughtful outlook for 1988 earnings."[20]

True to her disciplined habits, she scrutinized the cause of her error. By her reasoning, an emphasis on locating sudden changes in economic conditions overlooked examination of financial markets for potential structural defects, "an aspect of risk that I've paid more attention to ever since."[21] While the market eventually recovered, Drexel soon shut its doors in the wake of government fraud charges. Cohen teamed with other research department members and went to work for a subsidiary of Barclays Bank.

Cohen's career at Barclays was short-lived, yet marked her introduction to the fickle nature of press attention. Following a negative forecast for stocks in early 1990 that led to the *Wall Street Journal* calling her the most bearish analyst, ". . . I realized that being on the negative side—even though I was right—was not a popular place to be. Stock traders, company executives, and news reporters first called me a Cassandra and then blamed me for contributing to the downturn."[22] Within several months, the British firm's foray into American stocks stalled. Fortunately for Cohen, opportunity beckoned. In the fall, she joined The Goldman Sachs Group, Inc. (Goldman Sachs) after being recruited by Steven Einhorn who was the firm's global research chief.[23]

An offer to join Goldman Sachs had long been seen as the apex of one's Wall Street's career. As the industry's last remaining exclusive partnership, the firm paid handsomely in dollars and prestige. To Cohen,

Goldman Sachs represented " 'the gold standard' of the financial world"[24] and boasted a strong research department. As the firm's market strategist, Cohen's influence could be quite substantial. Although Einhorn was the senior of the two, they shared the title of co-heads of the firm's investment committee and both adjusted the model portfolios.

To attribute Cohen's rise to the fortuitous circumstance of a mere glob of putty found on her desk at home, would belie the rigor of her analysis. Already bullish since February 1991, just several months fresh from the DJIA bottom of 2,365, the toy did help her to visualize her thoughts when she twiddled with it while working at home one Sunday in 1992. Noting its ability to stretch and hold its shape, she considered the likelihood of a prolonged economic expansion and bull market that would be predicated on corporate growth in a benign inflationary environment that could be maintained over a protracted period. Dubbing her model "the Silly Putty economy,"[25] she later recalled that "It's said that the five scariest words about the market are 'This time it is different,' but sometimes it really is different."[26] While other market forecasters reversed stances during the market's short pullbacks, Cohen remained positive. She approached Einhorn in the fall of 1994 to advocate for a more aggressively bullish posture and he agreed.[27]

As her own confidence grew, so did her skills as a communicator.[28] Reminiscent of the style popularized several decades earlier by financial journalist Sylvia Porter and by contemporaneous columnists such as Jane Bryant Quinn, Cohen possessed the ability and savvy to explain sophisticated economic concepts into language that the average interested individual could understand. Both professional and retail investors listened. She herself has admitted, "I always thought it was amazing that I would say something at our 7:30 morning meeting, and the markets would move in response at 9:30 a.m. opening."[29] In November 1996, prices slipped on a rumor that she had turned bearish. The market reversed course only after Cohen arranged an internal conference call to Goldman Sachs' global trading and salesforce to confirm that her views remained unchanged.[30] She "was bemused by it. First, that such a story could be circulating. Second, that it could be distributed so quickly, and third, that we could correct it so rapidly."[31]

Named to *Institutional Investor's* all-star analyst rankings beginning in 1993 and elevated to its top spot in 1997, Cohen's record is not untarnished. In the mid-1990s, she did not consistently time accurate calls to invest in commodities or large cap stocks. Still, her thoughtful insights impressed clients.[32] Her methodology consists of projecting corporate earnings by considering macroeconomic trends while analyzing every quarterly earnings report by each company in the S&P 500. This strategy gives her a level of comfort despite the enormous required amount of effort and immersion in detail. She consistently searches for miscalibrations and potential systemic flaws as her "own worst critic."[33]

As the bull market enticed more individual investors into the market, Wall Street personalities acquired near-celebrity status. Garzarelli may have gained fame for predicting the 1987 Crash, but Cohen's celebrity eclipsed most in the financial industry. She did not just analyze the market, she seemed to personify it. Financial commentator Louis Rukeyser observed in 1988 that "A year ago, when Abby was inducted into our Hall of Fame, I said she was the most influential woman on Wall Street. But now I would say that she is the most influential market forecaster, period."[34]

Given such a high level of celebrity, approbation, and respect, it surprised many when Goldman Sachs passed her over for partnership in both 1994 and 1996. At the time, a Goldman Sachs partnership could equate to a reported annual average income of several million dollars. While that perceived snub resulted in even more notoriety, Cohen remained tight-lipped. Instead, she maintained that the quality of her work would ultimately prove the dispositive issue.[35]

Cohen herself does not ascribe gender considerations to those partnership decisions.[36] Thirty-four-year-old banker Jeanette W. Loeb had become the firm's first female partner in 1986, which was well before the 10-year estimate for that milestone that had been forecast by the firm's co-chair 2 years earlier. But Goldman Sachs was a firm previously besmirched for allegedly maintaining a less than hospitable environment for female employees. In 1985, a Goldman Sachs recruiter had queried female applicants from Stanford University as to whether they would be willing to undergo abortions to preserve their career. Although the firm denied that the questioning represented policy, nine anonymous female associates and officers sent a letter to the deans of various business schools complaining of alleged inequities. In the aftermath of this incident, Goldman sought to display a more hospitable attitude toward its female employees, but its image toward women continued to suffer.[37]

Within the firm, carving a path toward eventual partnership by anyone, male or female, could prove daunting. For the smaller number of women working toward that goal, the task was that much steeper and lonelier.

Cohen recalls:

> I had no mentor at Goldman Sachs. There was nobody looking out or block-
> ing and tackling for me. Now, we work hard to provide mentors—especially
> to women and minorities—but there was not much awareness or concern at
> this time that this was missing. Men weren't very receptive, and there were
> very few women in the industry ahead of me, so there was no one to whom
> I could reach out along the way.[38]

Two years after being named a managing director, Cohen gained ad-
mittance to Goldman Sachs' 1998 partnership class of 57 inductees. Two
other women also became partners that brought their total number to 17 of
the firm's 246 partners.[39] Cohen took her selection in stride and observed
later, "Objectively, I should have been a leading candidate for promotion.
So, becoming a partner in 1998 wasn't really a surprise. It was also bittersweet, quite frankly. My father was going through a health crisis at that
time, and that took much of the pleasure out of the promotion. Also, the
public speculation ahead of time about my promotion was disturbing."[40]

Hers was the final partnership class on the eve of the firm's 1999 public
offering. As a new partner, Cohen had a lesser financial stake in the firm
than many more senior partners, and she did not express the kind of angst
as did others regarding potential dilution of the firm's culture once it no
longer operated as a private partnership.[41] The business of the firm continued, as did Cohen's career. Her responsibilities broadened to include
participation in certain policy committees and she continued to capture
the imagination of the public.[42] "Never underestimate the power of Abby
Joseph Cohen," wrote a *New York Times* reporter in a tongue-in-cheek
article that continued, "While Ms. Cohen has been ubiquitous on Wall
Street, the rest of the world is badly in need of her guidance."[43]

As the bull market receded, Cohen's prognostications proved less accurate. She became a ready target for criticism by the media when she did not
pinpoint the broad equity decline in early 2000.[44] In 2002, she was named
chair of the firm's investment policy committee. In an interview that year,
Cohen responded to the media's quick and at times misleading labeling of
her positions by saying:

> I'm amused always by the way I get portrayed. It was in 1999 and early 2000
> that I was criticized for not being bullish enough and, in fact, in March of 2000
> when I suggested to our clients that they sell some stocks and be especially care-
> ful about technology stocks, I was blamed for substantial decline in the Nasdaq.
>
> And so what we have always focused on, what I always have focused on,
> is trying to analyze the fundamentals as I see them.[45]

While few analysts predicted the dire consequences of the housing bubble, Cohen's failure to forecast the 2008 market demise also caused critics to scrutinize her track record. In December 2007, Cohen, by then the firm's senior investment strategist, thought that the S&P 500 would reach 1,675 the next year.[46] Several weeks later, however, she did ratchet down her forecast in light of changes in the forecasts for the economy by the firm's economists.

Cohen remains among the most respected analysts on Wall Street. The subject of a Harvard Business School case study, she has been honored by many organizations including the Financial Women's Association, the NYSE, and is a member of the *Wall Street Week* Hall of Fame. She continues to lead Goldman Sachs' Global Markets Institute, which is a select team that provides advisory services to worldwide clients and focuses on long-term issues, particularly those that arise at the intersection of governmental policy, the economy, and fiscal markets.

Cohen's professional achievements may be measured by others keeping score, but her perspective is more nuanced, "I take great pride in my work, but work is not my only metric of success."[47] For her, "Being a happy family person is one of the most important things for me. I believe that being part of a warm family gives me greater insight and helped me keep different perspectives in mind."[48] When she described making partner as "not the defining moment of my life, but it was very pleasant,"[49] that kind of understatement appears authentic. Throughout her career, she has been described as supportive of her staff and motivated more by the drive to produce quality work than reward. For years, Cohen commuted to the office by bus from her middle-class Queens neighborhood and eschewed the glitzier city life afforded her. Family life figures prominently into her values. While guarded of her private life, she credits her ability to manage her extended workdays to the support of her spouse, children, and extended family.[50]

Extracurricular pursuits include activities that center on faith, education, and public policy. She was the first woman to lead the board of trustees of the Jewish Theological Seminary, and serves on the White House-appointed Innovation Advisory Board for economic competitiveness and as presidential councilor at Cornell, as well as on various boards including those of Weill Cornell Medical College and The Brookings Institution. She has been honored by many groups, including the Chartered Financial Analyst Institute which she formerly chaired and from which she received the Distinguished Service Award. Among other honors she has received was being chosen by the NYSE for its millennium trading bell series that recognized twentieth century leaders. Chairman Richard Grasso selected Cohen whom he regarded as "a beacon of what can be accomplished in finance as a woman."[51] She responded with flair, by breaking the gavel on the century's penultimate trading day.[52]

Cohen relates that she can recall discriminatory incidents, even as far back as at age 12 when she was turned away from trying out for a ball boy position at the national tennis championships. However, these events did not significantly alter her life.[53] She credits her mother's intellect and decisiveness for her resolve, "Like her, I am willing to go against conventional wisdom. If I've done my homework and I believe that I'm right, I really don't care if people agree with me or not."[54] Otherwise, Cohen lacked a female mentor in her profession. "I ask myself, 'Did I have any role models early in my career?' and the answer is, 'No,' ... But now we are finally at the point where there are some women in senior positions and there is a large enough population of women to move into the next level. We may have the critical mass and the right circumstances to make the profession much more women friendly."[55]

Cohen does not shy from citing research that shows a female propensity toward intellectual methodicalness and discipline. At a 2010 U.S. Treasury symposium addressing women in finance, she recalled these findings in support of her observation that women are well equipped for financial analysis.[56] In early 2011, however, she drew popular criticism for appearing relatively indifferent to the limited numbers of women in finance. In an interview with the *New York Times Magazine*, she responded to a question as to why few women populate the senior ranks of Wall Street by saying, "Let's think about it in the following way: We can only deal with the pool of young women who make themselves available and express interest in investment banking."[57] When questioned as to why women only comprise 12 percent of the partners at Goldman Sachs, she responded, "I don't think that we are proud of it, and I think we do have aspirations of improving the numbers."[58] Cohen says she does not mind being criticized for her views but wishes the critics had been able to judge her based on what she really said. According to her, the journalist used a heavily abridged excerpt taken from a broader conversation about strides being made in the advancement of women and the quotes are thus out of context and do not accurately reflect her views. She believes the firm has made great strides towards the advancement of women, including an increased number of women at the managing director level, and she has personally sponsored and mentored junior women to help them move forward in their careers.[59]

In fact, Cohen is a staunch advocate for ensuring that the firm's hiring practices accurately reflect the numbers of qualified applicants. She relishes serving as a role model and believes that both women and men benefit from seeing women succeed. She has worked both within the firm and across industries to foster development of the next generation of female leaders. She cautions against the possibility of overprotecting women and members of other historically underrepresented groups where doing so might limit their eventual advancement. Instead, she favors keeping a watchful eye while offering challenges that may more readily display talent and yield further opportunities.[60]

Given that Cohen finds both fun and meaningful purpose in her work, perhaps it is not so surprising that through her analysis and creativity she had aptly ascribed the name of a simple toy to an econometric paradigm that underlay the bull market of the 1990s. Years later, the putty also makes an apt metaphor for her career. Adaptable to the extent necessary to withstand changing market and industry dynamics and occasional unreceptive attitudes, she holds her own. In an environment that stretches most to their limits, Cohen bounces back, ready to meet the next challenges.

FOURTEEN

Amy Domini

So don't worry that you are a pioneer, breaking into a new and untested field.[1]

—*Amy Domini*

Whether investing is for the birds is a question often answered in consideration of market dynamics. For Amy Domini, however, it took on a different meaning in 1980. When a client voiced concerns over holding shares of a paper company whose actions caused harm to birds, the matter prompted Domini to devise a new investment strategy that accounted for ethical considerations in portfolio selection.

Domini's idealistic notions began at a young age. Indeed, they perhaps even permeate her DNA if genetics have a hand in determining personality traits. Hers hold a curious mix—a paternal grandfather who had been an Italian socialist party leader and a maternal great-grandfather who was a patrician attorney.[2] Those heritages melded when she was born in 1950 to Italian immigrant Enzo Domini, a food distributor, and blue-blooded elementary school teacher Margaret Cabot Colt.[3] She reflects, "As a child, I saw how hard it was on my father, who came to this country in the 50's when Italians were a scorned minority group, to be an unwanted immigrant. My American grandfather, on the other hand, was a Wall Street insider. . . . Perhaps the combination, my father, the outcast, and my grandfather, the insider who railed at fat cats, formed me more completely than I guessed."[4]

Growing up in Newtown, Connecticut, she later described herself as "a shy and unremarkable girl in a rural dairy community."[5] That purportedly reticent girl became a leader of an unorthodox investment approach whose basics took root in an inauspicious way—in the garden with her grandfather:

> One day we were talking as we weeded the garden. He scowled at me and said, "Amy D. It is time you learned a thing or two." He dropped the gardening tools and marched me back to his home, where he pulled out a stack of annual reports and proxy statements. He told me that companies have owners. He said that companies had to report to their owners and that these were the reports. He said, "Here's how you read an annual report, you start at that back. That's where the auditor's report is."[6]

So they started reviewing business documents. For years, the pair discussed financial statements. While doing so, Domini's grandfather would criticize the excessive compensation earned by corporate directors and executives.[7] The balance of Domini's time outside of school included attending Sunday School and participating in scouting. As a teen, she participated in the social service club at the Massachusetts boarding school she attended. These activities proved formative experiences in Domini's mind. She recalls that "I was brought up repeating, 'I promise to do my duty to God and my country, to help other people at all times.' It was, in many ways, just a silly line. Still, it framed me. Explicit encouragements of strong ethical behavior matter."[8]

She first attended Wheelock College before taking a year off and returning to Boston University from which she graduated in 1973 with a degree in international economics.[9] Without a definitive career focus, she completed a typing class and found work initially as an administrative clerk at the Boston brokerage of Tucker, Anthony & Co. before becoming a secretary to the firm's chief executive officer.[10] While stocks declined during the early 1970s, Domini observed that, "People were losing money, and I saw all these guys who looked like they were very important men helping them to lose their money, and I thought, 'I could do that, too.'"[11] Spurred by boredom, "in a moment of complete naïveté I asked to be trained as a broker and the boss said yes."[12]

Domini became the branch's only female salesperson in 1975. While building her client base, Domini took her first step in 1978 toward implementing a values-based approach when she decided not to tout the firm's recommendation to purchase shares of a defense contractor as that was at odds with her anti-war sentiments.[13] Over the next several years, she noticed that some clients chose not to invest in certain industries, such as coal, tobacco, or defense. Once her avid bird watcher client, aggrieved over a paper company's activities that might lead to defoliation and harm to birds came to see her, she no longer was content to merely observe investor concerns. Says Domini of that moment:

> And that hit me somehow. I sort of thought, "Hmm, there's something in this." After that, I got very curious and started looking around. It was during a period when South Africa was really getting more and more noticed in the early 1980s. And the South African debate was really a flashpoint in investing with values. It kind of changed the landscape for everybody. So at that point, I knew I was on to something.[14]

Domini had stumbled upon the concept of socially responsible investing (SRI). In fact, the idea of using business activity to promote a common good dates to ancient times. In the United States, this concept had found proponents as far back as the mid-eighteenth century when faith-based groups spearheaded values-driven commercial efforts. Quakers avoided slave or war-related profits, and Methodist leaders advised investors to spurn "sin stocks,"[15] such as those of alcohol, gambling, and tobacco companies.

Not until the twentieth century did further significant developments related to this concept occur. In 1928, Protestants established a mutual fund that avoided alcohol and tobacco companies. Decades later, corporate boycotts spurred by the 1960s civil rights movement and anti-war protests heightened investor awareness of business activities. More ethically based mutual funds were established in the 1970s. In 1971, Methodists organized a fund that shunned war-related companies, and in 1972 the Dreyfus Corporation introduced a fund that evaluated companies based on environmental, occupational health and safety, consumer protection, and equal employment considerations. Several anti-nuclear funds existed for a short time in the early seventies. In 1982, Calvert Investments, Inc. launched the first fund to oppose apartheid by screening for companies with business ties to the repressive system.[16]

The divestment campaigns to rid South Africa of apartheid proved the turning point where SRI came into its own. The movement had been taking shape in the United States primarily through the advocacy of religious organizations. When consumer advocate Ralph Nader spearheaded a successful drive that placed shareholder resolutions concerning board diversity and emission standards on the proxy ballot of General Motors Corporation in 1970, others took notice. Two years later, a coalition of faith-based groups formed the Interfaith Center on Corporate Responsibility (ICCR) to challenge banks and companies doing business with the apartheid regime. In 1977, a voluntary code of conduct known as the Sullivan Principles served as guide by which corporations might choose to conduct business and apply pressure to the South African government. Activists urged large institutional investors to divest and organized shareholder resolutions condemning racial segregation. As the campaign strengthened, socially responsible investing became more mainstream and no longer "dismissed as a refuge for churchgoers or aging hippies who didn't understand business."[17]

Despite these developments, no central resource existed that catalogued corporate behavior. Domini began to research the topic more fully and develop her thoughts. Believing that screening alone would not provide an effective means for change, she looked to shareholder activism as another tool. That method already enjoyed a colorful history. After shareholder Lewis Gilbert could not successfully raise his questions during the 1932 annual meeting of Consolidated Gas Co., he and his brother, John Gilbert, began accumulating shares of target corporations while often using theatrics such as dressing in costume at shareholder meetings to gain publicity. Ten years later, the SEC adopted a rule giving shareholders the right to submit resolutions regarding corporate governance for inclusion in corporate proxy statements.[18]

Public relations consultant Wilma Soss joined the fray in the mid-forties, taking particular aim at perceived corporate sexism and trying to stimulate financial literacy.[19] She founded the Federation of Women Shareholders in American Business in reaction to her rude treatment at a 1947 board meeting of U.S. Steel when she tried to inquire as to the possibility of appointing a female director.[20] Claimed Soss, "if they had treated me better there would have likely been no Federation of Women Shareholders."[21] Soss based her arguments on ethical and business grounds and has been seen as "the first moderate social issues activist, a serious investor willing to confront management regarding a non-financial issue."[22] Evelyn Y. Davis entered the scene in the early 1960s and the self-dubbed "queen of the corporate jungle"[23] continues today to unleash her particular brand of grandstanding at shareholder meetings and in the annual newsletter she publishes.

Domini did not need theatrical props to put her developing ideas into practice. After an editor read the description of an adult education class she was teaching, Domini agreed to write a book outlining her investment strategy. Published in 1984, *Ethical Investing* sets forth her premise that ethical dimensions underlie investments and that personal standards should consciously be applied to portfolio selection. She outlines in its pages her three-prong approach that encompasses stock screening, shareholder activism, and community investment.[24]

The book launched Domini as the preeminent voice of socially responsible investing. Her timing could not have been better. Publication coincided with momentum building in the South African divestment movement. In 1986, federal legislation banned new American trade and investment in South Africa.

The divestment movement galvanized Domini's commitment to ethical investing, "That left me a passionate advocate. I knew I had to remove barriers at the top and inspire grassroots at the bottom.... . Investors made the difference."[25] In the meantime, her own career path took her from portfolio manager at Franklin Research and Development Corporation to trustee at the wealth management firm Loring, Wolcott & Coolidge. In 1988, she co-authored *The Challenges of Wealth: Mastering the Personal and Financial Conflicts*, a money management book.

While preparing for the Chartered Financial Analyst examination, she was taught that restricting a portfolio on any non-financial grounds would limit its returns. Given that a money manager's job is to selectively choose stocks to build a profitable portfolio, she believed this concept preposterous and that a benchmark was needed to determine whether choices informed by ethical considerations might hinder investment performance. In 1989, she, together with husband Peter Kinder and Steven Lydenberg, formed the research firm KLD Research & Analytics, Inc. (KLD). Says Domini, "I wanted to remove the barrier that existed, and the main barrier was that you couldn't make money this way."[26] After evaluating corporate behavior including labor, customer, community, and environmental practices, they composed an equity index that included approximately half of those companies listed in the S&P 500 plus an additional 150 smaller corporations.[27]

Operating from Domini's home, KLD launched the Domini 400 Social Index on May 1, 1990. While the principals had visions of licensing the index and marketing their research, KLD was met with a lack of interest from mutual fund companies. Undeterred, Domini founded the Domini Social Equity Fund that tracked the index and represented "the first socially and environmentally screened index fund in the world."[28] With a $600,000 founding investment from a friend, operations began in June

1991. As the fund's only salesperson in its early years, Domini pounded the pavement seeking capital, "No audience was too small."[29]

Cash dribbled in slowly until the fund began to outperform the S&P 500. By 1993, the fund had amassed $10 million in assets, which grew to $100 million in 1996. With technology firms far outnumbering industrial companies in the index, the tech boom of the nineties propelled the Domini Social Equity Fund to average 30 percent annual returns for the latter half of the decade.[30]

Domini had other objectives in addition to cash inflow. In 1992, she co-authored *The Social Investment Almanac*, which was a compilation of articles on socially responsible investing from industry leaders, and the following year she co-authored *Investing for Good: Making Money While Being Socially Responsible*. That same year, the fund departed from the usual practices of the mutual fund industry and published its proxy voting guidelines that delineated its approach to shareholder activism. In 1994, the Domini Social Equity Fund filed its first shareholder proposal when it requested that Wal-Mart Stores, Inc. disclose employment diversity statistics. Fifteen years later, the fund had filed or teamed with investor coalitions to co-file over 200 resolutions concerning a variety of issues with 83 companies.[31]

The Domini Social Equity Fund began the new millennium as one of the country's fastest growing funds. Assets totaled over $1.5 billion in early 2000, but the ensuing technology stock bubble and subsequent recession inflicted losses and resulted with the fund holding approximately $677 million by the end of 2011. Market turbulence affects all investments; for the fund, selection of companies in accordance with its criteria also poses questions.[32]

Given the subjective nature of certain investment criteria, even likeminded ethically conscious investors may find reasons to disapprove of the composition of the index. Domini welcomes opportunities to engage in potentially fruitful dialogue. She explains, ". . . we are entering the belly of the beast of the financial/corporate juggernaut and we are shaping it."[33]

Selection methodology may be debated, but the notion of a valid and successful socially responsible investment model has been validated. In 2000, the Domini Social Equity Fund was the 15th fastest growing U.S. mutual fund and a poll revealed that one out of eight households owned an SRI fund.[34] Ironically, the mutual fund industry that had initially rejected the concept now marketed various socially screened products. Optimistic over the future of social investing, Domini stated, "I think we could be at a tipping point in history here and we could slide toward the better."[35]

The issue of corporate transparency, essentially the concept of full disclosure of governance practices and business activities, matters to Domini. In 2001, the corporate entity she had formed in 1997 requested that the SEC mandate that mutual funds disclose their proxy voting. This was an unpopular notion among leaders of non-SRI funds. Two years later, the SEC agreed with Domini's position.[36]

Over the next several years, Domini championed shareholder activism and wrote a guidebook for investors. Then, in 2006, she reached a difficult decision in light of fund underperformance. Following shareholder approval, an institutional investment advisory firm now actively managed the Domini Social Equity Fund and the Domini Institutional Social Equity Fund. That change meant the funds would no longer passively mimic the index, but would instead shift their holdings in relation to industry concentration or specific stock selection.[37]

Statistics indicate that women are more inclined to SRI and comprise more than 60 percent of socially responsible investors.[38] SRI funds often take into consideration a corporation's diversity policies and behavior. Domini's first book includes a listing of leading industrial, financial, and retail companies with women board members, but she has observed that gender diversity did not become a central concern for most SRI investors until 1994. The Domini Social Equity Fund subsequently introduced screens for gender diversity in corporate management as well as for records of purchasing from or investing in women- and minority-owned businesses, and for employee benefit programs addressing work/family issues. On the flip side, women have from early on numbered among leading SRI proponents. Leaders have included Joan Bavaria and Joan Shapiro, who in 1981 co-founded the Social Investment Forum (SIF), the industry's trade group; Elizabeth Glenshaw, who led a community banking program for Vermont National Bank in 1989; and former Neuberger Berman Group executives Joyce Haboucha and Janet Prindle, who spearheaded an internal team that developed SRI expertise and created the Neuberger Berman Socially Responsive Fund in 1994.[39]

During participation in a 2002 panel, Domini encountered a question about whether she would invest in a company that benefitted society but had only male board members. She responded, "I would invest in them, and file a shareholder resolution."[40] In an industry dominated by males, Domini does not recount personal brushes with gender discrimination. Instead, she encountered a more general cultural antipathy toward women in finance. The culture was one in which she initially may have had to work harder to gain credibility with both professionals and customers due to her gender and her youth. She credits a suit alleging discrimination by Merrill Lynch in the early seventies for opening the door to her employment.[41] She herself had entered the working world during what she describes as a window in time in which women generally did not see themselves in business careers or were not expected to go to graduate school. Her own grandfather had visualized the ideal path for a woman with lofty business aspirations as one where she might become secretary to a corporate board. Her great-aunt saw things differently. She foresaw potential in her niece for making a difference in the world and imparted this view during their weekly dinner dates that they held for over a decade during Domini's early adulthood.[42]

Domini acknowledges that asset management, with more of an emphasis on building long-term personal relationships and less on acquiring a short-term "economic torpedo," is an area of finance in which more women build long-term careers.[43] In many ways, Domini's path echoes that of her peers, as evidenced by a report conducted in 2005 by a consulting firm on women in the asset management field. The firm interviewed 10 top female executives, including Domini, who had entered asset management in the late 1970s and early 1980s. Often functioning within workplaces that could exhibit subtle resistance to female advancement but without mentors or developed networks, the women in the report were identified as having strong work ethics, perseverance, and adaptability as common characteristics among the women. Said one executive, "Even women I know who have stayed with the same firm often end up taking the new thing, the broken thing, the off-the-beaten path thing. And so, by default, what ends up happening is women who succeed have adapted and overcome incredible odds. They take the hard assignments and excel at them."[44]

In the same report, Domini comments, "To the extent that I had any work-family balance, it was a work-hard/play-hard approach. On vacation, I go to a deserted island. . . . I take a very intense, long time off that stays with me for the first couple of months after I return."[45] Her first book was dedicated to her parents and acknowledged their "babysitting on short notice."[46] Seven years later, she dedicated *Socially Responsible Investing* to her two sons, who "never signed on to give their mother up to another book but took it in stride nonetheless."[47] She and her husband divorced in 1997 after 17 years of marriage, and she remarried 10 years later.[48] In 2009, she related, "The big picture might sound glamorous, but the nuts and bolts of my job can get pretty tedious. Sometimes I forget why I do what I do. Then my children remind me."[49] When her 13-year-old son showed interest in international issues, "Suddenly I felt my activist and parent worlds collide. We don't talk much about the greater goals of socially responsible investing or the mutual fund industry. Nonetheless, this kid felt that what he did on a Saturday morning half a world away might matter to someone. My son was addressing world globalization in his own way, just as I, through my work, try to leave the planet a little better for him."[50]

Domini has established a considerable legacy. Although she was not the originator of SRI, a financial executive notes, "Amy has been more successful at promoting the [SRI] concept and keeping it in front of people. It was the index that helped more than anything to prove that socially responsible funds could deliver investment performance."[51] According to the Social Investment Forum, over $3 trillion in total assets employed a socially responsible investing strategy in 2010.[52] A burgeoning market for public relations professionals specializing in producing corporate citizenship reports has developed as corporations both reveal and spin their records. In 2009, when accepting an award for professional ethics from Villanova University, Domini acknowledged, "Today my field is accepted. All the greatest research houses sell corporate social responsible information. 4,000 corporations have voluntarily published CSR reports globally, some admittedly more worthwhile than others, but all representing legitimacy."[53]

Despite competition, her flagship fund continues to be ranked among the top performers of its peers. In 2011, Domini Social Investments encompasses the flagship fund, an international fund, a bond fund, and a money market account all meant to achieve a competitive triple bottom line of financial, social, and environmental returns. Domini has received numerous accolades that include being honored by ICCR and named by *Time* in 2005 to its list of the world's 100 most influential people and by *Investment Advisor* in 2010 as one of 30 most influential advisors. She has served on numerous boards, including the Church Pension Fund of the Episcopal Church in America, the National Association of Community Development Loan Funds, and ICCR.

Domini continues to frequently pen articles and speak out on issues while remaining as Chief Executive Officer and Chief Investment Officer of Domini Social Investments and a trustee of the wealth management firm Loring, Wolcott & Coolidge. Having changed the vocabulary and conversation on investing, she feels she has not yet come across another voice who carries her message.[54] She has allowed that "There is something wonderful in trying to find a way to be immortal."[55] Perhaps that quest has informed her litany of accomplishments. In her words, ". . . the key thing is to think about the fact that the way you invest builds the world that your children are going to live in, that your grandchildren are gonna grow up in, and to think about, is it really all about making the most money right now, or is it really about building wealth for all of us and having a better tomorrow for all of us?"[56]

Instead of mindlessly slapping on labels in vogue for marketing the supposedly more civic-minded activities of a corporation, she appears genuinely inspired by what she first called "ethical investing" almost 30 years ago. That passion led her to pursue its advancement. Rather than contending as some female money managers did with building careers in the less glamorous areas of the business foisted on them, she worked in such a field by her own choice. In doing so, she made a name for herself and for the discipline she championed.

Domini often recounts the "starfish story," a popular parable adapted from an essay by writer Loren Eiseley in 1978. Featured as a prominent page on the Domini website, it reads:

> Thousands of starfish washed ashore. A little girl began throwing them in the water so they wouldn't die.
> "Don't bother, dear," her mother said, "it won't make a difference."
> The girl stopped for a moment and looked at the starfish in her hand.
> "It will make a difference to this one."[57]

The parallel between the tale and the tenet of socially responsible investing is obvious. So, too, is the idea of determination and Domini's perseverance in the face of industry skeptics.

Less apparent is how the tale also echoes Domini's relationship with her grandfather, the person responsible for cultivating her interest in finance. She reveals that:

> My grandfather never read my book—it upset him too much, the idea of mixing sloppy values with money making. He loved to hear of my work. . . . But he could never understand that for me, when a tobacco executive lied about tobacco, and through those lies, killed people, he'd broken a commandment. For me, finance and capitalism are not exempt from right and wrong. Investors are not innocent in the actions of the teams they enable. How was I able to overcome his reluctance to acknowledge my work? I had permission, granted at a very young age, to seek out ethical behavior.[58]

This "permission" intertwined with the gardening and economic lessons she learned at an early age by her grandfather's side in the flower patch. Through her pioneering work, Domini has securely grafted a values-based branch onto the financial tree. She has altered the investing landscape forever by crafting tools that stakeholders can use to empower themselves and plant their own seeds for change.

Conclusion

Nineteenth-century banker Henry Clews was indeed wrong. In the intervening century since he disparaged the notion of women finding fortune or character on Wall Street, women have certainly found both. But their paths have not been easy, nor is the future for Wall Street women without remaining challenges.

Women have made their marks whether as financiers or philanthropists, bankers or brokers, swindlers or speculators, investors or asset managers, traders or treasurers, and regulators or researchers. The historic roots of their progress can often be traced to taking part in management of the household income. As women became more accustomed to handling domestic finances, they reached further, often animated by personal necessity. When the country needed help, they stepped up to raise funds or to fill job vacancies. Yet, often they were pushed out once normalcy returned.

For some of these women, however, normalcy now meant continuing their financial forays, whether by augmenting their personal investing activities or by seeking to advance professionally. In so doing, their economic independence increased. However, popular acceptance of the ideal of a financially sophisticated and autonomous woman remained elusive in the years prior to the civil rights and feminist awakenings in the 1960s and 1970s. Even now, it is not uncommon to encounter a cultural bias to regard women as less astute in topics of finance than men.

On Main Street, the percentage of women in the labor force continues to rise. In 2010, women comprised approximately 47 percent of the total labor force.[1] They are also increasingly assuming the role of primary breadwinner in married households. *Time* featured this topic in a cover story in March 2012, in which Liza Mundy, author of *The Richer Sex*, explores the potential social and political ramifications of this phenomenon. Wives earned more than their husbands by nearly 40 percent in 2009, a 50 percent rise over the previous two decades.[2] Yet other news is less sanguine. On both ends of the wealth pyramid, women fare poorly. The poverty rate for women registered 16.3 percent in 2011, virtually unchanged from the prior year although the rate for males declined 0.4–13.6 percent, and at the apex, women account for only 104 of the 1,226 individuals on the 2012 *Forbes* billionaire list.[3]

Popular media frequently fans the flames of gender warfare with sensationalized headlines, yet real issues remain unresolved as evidenced by a lingering wage gap. For similar work, a woman brings home only 81 percent of what a man earns.[4] Women themselves bear partial responsibility when it comes to their level of financial knowledge. A survey of over 10,000 women conducted in February 2012 revealed that although 90 percent of respondents saw themselves as their family's primary purchaser and bill payer, 60 percent characterized their investing and financial planning skills as below average but less than half sought resources for assistance.[5]

On Wall Street, much has been accomplished. Women participate in roles throughout the financial services industry and have ascended to greater positions of responsibility. A woman, Catherine Kinney, even took the helm of the NYSE presidency between 2002 and 2008. But there is more progress to be made.

In the years since the first class action suits against major Wall Street firms in the 1990s, continued institutional improvement has at times appeared elusive. Although the industry's regulatory and self-governing bodies backed away from compulsory arbitration of civil rights claims, some firms stepped up their internal practices of requiring arbitration. Spates of gender discrimination suits against brokerages also have occurred. Notably, in 2004 the EEOC joined with aggrieved parties to file a suit against Morgan Stanley in a high profile case involving top-level female employees. For the first time, it appeared that the agency was poised to challenge a major Wall Street firm in court over gender discrimination.[6] Even a step forward can be modified to a sidestep. The firm settled the case for $54 million just prior to trial by agreeing to pay $12 million to the lead plaintiff, and to support diversity programs and anti-discrimination training for institutional equity trading.[7] Although Muriel Siebert characterized the dollar amount as so trivial to the firm that "It may spill off their coffee cups in the morning,"[8] she also commented, "There had to be something there or they wouldn't come up with $54 million."[9] More disappointing than the monetary sum was the non-pecuniary price given, which was that of confidentiality.[10] The firm could keep details hidden of the behavior giving rise to the settlement. Until such secrecy is lifted and grievances are publicly aired, journalist Susan Antilla wonders how significant change will take root.[11]

Although sexual harassment and discrimination claims arise, most agree that the overtly hostile workplace has largely disappeared. A more subtle gender bias persists, however, that is harder to prove but attested to through a significant pay gap, sparse representation at senior ranks, and a disproportionate share of industry layoffs affecting women that resulted from the 2008 financial downturn.[12]

A financial career may be less alluring to many as the industry still reels from difficult economic conditions, increased regulatory scrutiny, and heightened public criticism. For women, a disparity in income is even more troubling. According to 2010 census data analyzed by Bloomberg, women who work across the spectrum of financial services jobs face the largest gender pay gap of any industry. These women earn 55–62 cents for every dollar made by their male colleagues.[13] Female financial managers, a group encompassing bank tellers and executives, earned just 63.9 cents for every dollar that men made in 2000.[14]

Firms have stepped up their attempts to increase workforce diversity and monitor their progress. Many firms now employ chief diversity officers in charge of inclusion strategies for retention and recruitment. Despite these efforts, a study by the United States Government Accountability Office on trends in the financial services industry between 1993 and 2008 found that overall workforce diversity in management positions "did not change substantially."[15] In 2011, women comprised 55.4 percent of financial services employees but only 16.6 percent of executive officers.[16] The Dodd-Frank Wall Street Reform and Consumer Protection Act of 2010 included provisions requiring the creation of Offices of Minority and Women Inclusion among certain federal agencies in order to help correct racial and gender imbalances in the financial sector by monitoring the agencies' diversity efforts and those of their contractors. While annual reporting obligations will shed light on the extent of internal progress made on the hiring practices within these governmental bodies, it may be less clear to discern the legislation's impact on their business partners.

Even while pundits waxed poetic about how the 2008 credit crisis might have been averted had women ran Wall Street, many leading female financial professionals lost their jobs in its wake. Prior to the downturn, three women had overwhelmingly been favored as possible candidates to become the first female head of a major Wall Street firm: Citibank executive Sallie Krawchek, Morgan Stanley Co-President Zoe Cruz, and Lehman Brothers Chief Financial Officer Erin Callan. Within a 10-month span ending in the fall of 2008, each of them lost their jobs. To add insult to injury, their departures also provoked published personal attacks that included criticism over their appearances. This sort of disparagement would not likely have occurred to such a degree had the executives in question been male.[17] Also of note, few women occupy board seats of Wall Street firms and only one sat on the board of Lehman Brothers at the time of its demise.

The corner suites and corridors of financial power remain lonely places for women and bastions of male culture. Within the federal government, although the post of Treasurer of the United States has been occupied by women continuously since 1949 and six of these women have been Hispanic, no woman has been appointed Secretary of the Treasury. Even in 2010, when many of the leading regulators of the financial services industry were women, Congressional Oversight Panel Chair Elizabeth Warren remarked at a Women in Finance Symposium, "The good news is there's no line for the ladies' room."[18]

There is no singular route nowadays to a financial career. Economic globalization and technological advancements provide more avenues for participation, and women have made strides in fields such as securities law, financial journalism, economics, and accounting that intersect with Wall Street. Within conventional fields of finance, regulatory walls between commercial and investment banking have blurred over the years, but cracks in the glass ceiling still arise more frequently for those women occupying typical commercial banking posts. In 2012, Beth Mooney took over as Chief Executive Officer and Chairman of KeyCorp, a Cleveland-based bank ranking among the 20 largest U.S. banks. She does not have a female peer at a major publicly owned brokerage. One of the largest privately held financial services companies, Fidelity Investments, named Abigail Johnson its president in 2012, and she appears likely to be appointed chief executive officer when her father steps down. Women are also more readily found at top executive posts in smaller firms.

In November 2012, when JPMorgan Chase & Co. named Marianne Lake as its chief financial officer, she joined Ruth Porat, who has been chief financial officer at Morgan Stanley since 2010, as two of the highest-ranking women on Wall Street. But when will a woman take the helm of a major Wall Street firm? Provided that available candidates boast a breadth of experience that showcases their potential and that the prevailing culture is receptive to an ambitious and powerful woman, this development may not be so distant given an existing array of talented female financial executives. When this happens, media attention will flock to cover the news and her tenure may come to be defined less in terms of her managerial efficacy than for her apparent embodiment of female progress. True advancement, however, will have been attained when accomplishments rather than identity represent the measure of success.

More importantly, will it usher in an era of gender equality in the financial industry? No doubt, a woman at the top will be a powerful image that may inspire others. What is meant by equality, though, can be hard to define. Does it simply require elimination of overt discrimination or does it call for affirmative action? Does it entail recognition that estrogen and testosterone are not pre-determinants of financial ability or does it postulate that greater gender diversity at executive levels breeds better decision making?

The past informs the future and several issues encountered in the preceding pages echo today. When addressing how to nurture an industry infrastructure that fosters advancement, especially in these times of heightened challenges to Wall Street's ingrained ways of doing business, it makes sense to reflect on these topics: networking, work/life balance, and financial education.

As far back as the early twentieth century, women in finance have recognized that benefits of networking extend from outreach and education to business opportunities and mentorship. Recent data reveals a need for female executives to go beyond mentors and seek sponsors, who are influential individuals who will advocate for the advancement of careers within an organization. Such relationships are critical to promote a flourishing pipeline of future leaders.[19]

The search for work/life balance has become a greater area of concern in general for society. Women naturally confront the issue of how to integrate family and career when faced with childbearing and typically bear the larger responsibility for childrearing. In finance, although businesses have become more "family friendly" with a growing number of firms offering benefits such as more generous parental leave policies and corporate day care, difficulties over achieving work/life balance remain a concern.[20] Throughout the securities industry, 4 percent losses occurred between 2001 and 2003 in both the numbers of women working on Wall Street and those holding executive management posts. Women left for

various reasons, with many noting the lack of flexible employment possibilities.[21] Limited part-time job positions exist in a service-oriented field
that often demands 70-hour workweeks and frequent travel. Women have
been more successful at carving niches for themselves in areas such as
research and asset management that lend themselves to more manageable
hours, and in which the availability of measurable forecasts, quantifiable
customer rosters, or revenue streams document their contributions. The
extent to which creative solutions can be imagined and technology harnessed to offer greater job flexibility across more subspecialties will play
a part in determining whether finance can more readily attract and retain
promising employees.

Finally, if women are to advance on Wall Street, then girls on Main
Street need to hear messages of the importance of financial literacy. Yet,
the signal received is often garbled. Popular culture amplifies the acqui-
sition of material goods without often bothering to transmit responsible
financial decision-making skills. Indeed, the overall financial illiteracy in
this country is woeful. There are lessons to be learned by both male and
female, young and old, that are critical to self-empowerment regardless of
career choice.

Wall Street is no longer marked by physical bounds, but barriers for
women have not entirely crumbled. Lists that rank "the most powerful"
women in finance abound yet testify to the reality that the achievements
of these leaders may still be eyed through the lens of gender. While one
may speculate over the timing of the ultimate crowning of a female head
of a major firm, what is certain is that the history of women on Wall Street
has been shaped by a confluence of factors arising from the evolution of
American society and business. Not to be minimized amongst this dynamic is an individual's ability to affect change through the person's own
aptitude and ambition to excel, as exemplified by the women profiled in
these pages. The future of women on Wall Street will be similarly in-
fluenced by individual effort coupled with further societal and industry
changes as the next generation chips away at the remaining glass ceiling.

Appendix A

Leading Ladies

Adams, Abigail—early investor in government debt, 1777.

Adams, Evangeline—astrologer and stock newsletter publisher who reportedly predicted the 1929 Crash.

Aldrich, Evelyn—first woman banking executive to address the American Institute of Banking, 1918.

Bache, Sarah Franklin—leader of Ladies Association of Philadelphia that raised money for Continental Army, 1780.

Bair, Sheila—chair, U.S. Federal Deposit Insurance Corporation, 2006–11; considered one of leading regulators during 2008 financial crisis.

Banuelos, Romana—founding partner of Pan American National Bank established to serve Latinos in Los Angeles, 1964; first Hispanic woman to serve as U.S. Treasurer, 1971–74.

Barker, Penelope—North Carolina colonist who organized boycotts of British goods and hosted Edenton Tea Party, 1774.

Bavaria, Joan—co-founder of SIF, 1981, and Ceres, 1989; founder and CEO of Trillium Asset Management, 1982–2008.

Bay, Josephine Perfect—first woman named chair and president of a major NYSE member firm when filled deceased spouse's position at A.M. Kidder & Co., 1956.

Beardstown Ladies—investment club of older women in Illinois who became media sensations until the group's investment returns were later found misrepresentative, founded 1983.

Benham, Isabel—first woman railroad analyst, 1934; president of WBC, 1948–50; first female partner at R.W. Pressprich & Co., 1964.

Bradley, Lydia Moss—first woman director of a national bank board, First National Bank of Peoria, 1875.

Brent, Margaret—colonial Maryland businesswoman appointed executor of the governor's estate, 1647.

Bruere, Mina—co-founder and first secretary of ABW, 1921.

Butterworth, Mary Peck—alleged operator of New England counterfeiting ring, 1716.

Cammack, Key—co-founder and first program chair of ABW, 1921.

Claflin, Tennessee—together with sister Victoria Woodhull became the first women to found a Wall Street brokerage, 1870.

Codding, Janet—co-founder and first president, Financial Women's Club of San Francisco, 1956.

Cohen, Abby Joseph—economist and market theoretician renown for championing 1990s bull market.

Cook, Betty—founder of the WBC, 1921.

Cremin, Marybeth—lead plaintiff in 1997 gender-based class action suit against Merrill Lynch that settled in 1998.

Curtis, Cathrine—founder of Women Investors in America, Inc., 1935.

Darnell, Linda—first woman rumored to sell securities on New York Curb Exchange, 1941.

Domini, Amy—investment adviser and SRI advocate who launched the first socially and environmentally screened index fund, 1991.

Douglas, Jennie—first woman employed by the U.S. Treasury, 1862.

Dunne, Jean—first woman stock specialist, National Stock Exchange, 1973.

Edwards, Christine—first woman general counsel of major Wall Street firm, Dean Witter Reynolds, 1990.

Eggleston, Irma Dell—bond saleswoman who held record in trading Liberty bonds during the 1920s.

Elliott, Harriet—chaired the Woman's Division of the War Finance Committee, 1942–46.

Furman, Virginia—co-founder and first president of ABW, 1921.

Garzarelli, Elaine—financial analyst and money manager renown for forecasting the 1987 Crash.

Gillis, Christine—founder, Women Stockbroker's Association, 1964.

Gleason, Kate—first woman president without familial ties at a national bank, First National Bank of East Rochester, 1917–19.

Glenn, Marian—*Forbes* writer whose column "Women in Business" was published in the magazine's debut issue, 1917.

Glenshaw, Elizabeth—SRI advocate who created a community banking program for Vermont National Bank, 1989.

Gray, Georgia Neese Clark—first woman appointed U.S. Treasurer, 1949–53.

Green, Hetty—first significant female financier during the Gilded Age.

Greenberg, Lynn—first woman floor trading member at Amex, 1977.

Haboucha, Joyce—SRI advocate who led creation of Neuberger Berman Socially Responsive Fund, 1994.

Hackett, Karen—one of first female NYSE trading floor pages, 1971; first woman NYSE floor governor, 1999.

Hansen, Virginia—one of first two women admitted to Chicago Board of Trade (CBOT), 1969.

Hanson, Janet—first woman promoted to sales management at Goldman Sachs, 1986; founder of networking organization 85 Broads, 1997.

Hanzelin, Helen—telephone clerk who became first woman to work on NYSE floor, 1943.

Hoffman, Claire Giannini—first woman director of Bank of America, 1949.

Howe, Sarah—founded Ladies Deposit Bank that offered fraudulent investment schemes targeted at Boston area women, 1880s.

Jarcho, Alice—first woman member of NYSE who regularly worked as a floor broker, 1976.

Jarrett, Valerie—first woman chair of Chicago Stock Exchange, 2004.

Jay, Sarah Livingston—early investor in bank shares, 1794–95.

Johnson, Abigail—president, Fidelity Investments, 2012.

Kahn, Lotte—broker and author of *Women and Wall Street*, one of first investment guides directed at women, 1963.

Karmel, Roberta—attorney and first woman SEC commissioner, 1977–80.

Kennedy, Margaret—mutual fund broker and first woman to become partner of an NYSE member firm, 1952; first woman to have name added to firm, Lubetkin, Regan & Kennedy, 1957.

Ketcham, Ginger—first woman specialist on Amex, 1977; first woman floor official of Amex, 1983.

Kinney, Catherine—first woman president of NYSE, 2002.

Kowalski, Helen—telephone clerk who became second woman to work on NYSE floor, 1943.

Kreps, Juanita—economist and first woman director of NYSE, 1972–77; first woman U.S. Secretary of Commerce, 1977–79.

Laimbeer, Nathalie—co-founder and first vice president of ABW, 1921.

Larkin, Jane—partner of Hirsch & Co. and second female member of NYSE, 1970.

Loeb, Jeanette—first woman partner of Goldman Sachs, 1986.

Loomis, Carol—writer and editor at *Fortune* magazine who reportedly rebuffed President Johnson's interest in appointing her first woman SEC commissioner.

Martens, Pamela—broker in Smith Barney branch office who initiated first gender-based class action suit against a Wall Street firm, 1996.

Martin, Anna—founder and president of The Commercial Bank of Mason, 1901.

McAdoo, Eleanor Randolph—chair of the WLLC, 1917–19.

McFadden, Rosemary—first woman president of U.S. futures exchange, New York Mercantile Exchange, 1984.

Middleton, June—first black woman broker for NYSE firm, Hornblower & Weeks-Hemphill, Noyes, 1965.

Mogavero, Doreen—founder of first fully woman owned and operated brokerage based on NYSE floor, 1989; first woman member of NYSE Board of Executives, 2004.

Morton, Azie Taylor—first black woman U.S. Treasurer, 1977–81.

Newkirk, Amy—first woman specialist, NYSE, 1980.

O'Bannon, Helen—successfully challenged gender bias on Merrill Lynch broker entrance exam in class action lawsuit, 1973.

O'Bannon, Marsha—first woman officer of NYSE, assistant vice president, Planning Services, 1976.

O'Brien, Edna—investment advisor who catered to women, including Amelia Earhart and Anne Morgan, the sister of J.P. Morgan; convicted of grand larceny, 1935.

O'Bryan, Mollie—first woman to hold seat on a mining exchange, Cripple Creek Mining Stock Exchange, circa 1900.

Ogorek, Peggy—first woman director of CBOT, 1991.

Olney, Caroline—co-founder and first membership chair of ABW, 1921.

Ovitz, Carol Jane—one of first two women admitted to CBOT, 1969.

Pankey, Gail—first black woman member of NYSE, 1981.

Peters, Aulana—attorney and first black SEC commissioner, 1984–88; first black woman director of NYSE, 1989.

Peterson, Phyllis—first woman to gain seat on major stock exchange, Philadelphia Stock Exchange, 1965; one of first two women to gain seat on Amex, 1965.

Phillips, Susan—first woman commissioner of Commodity Futures Trading Commission (CFTC), 1981–83; first woman chair of a federal financial regulatory agency, CFTC, 1983–87; Board of Governors of Federal Reserve System, 1991–98; director, Chicago Board Options Exchange, 2009–present.

Porter, Clara—co-founder of ABW, 1921.

Porter, Sylvia—financial journalist who helped design Series E Savings Bond and popularized personal finance writing.

Prindle, Janet—SRI advocate who led creation of Neuberger Berman Socially Responsive Fund, 1994.

Procope, Ernesta—first black female owner of a major financial business located on Wall Street, 1979.

Pyle, Gladys—Secretary of Securities Commission of South Dakota and first woman permitted onto floor of New York Curb Exchange, 1931.

Redel, Donna—first woman appointed board of governors of U.S. futures exchange, Comex, 1989; first woman chair of U.S. futures exchange, Comex, 1992.

Reed, Esther deBerdt—founded Ladies Association of Philadelphia that raised funds for Continental Army, 1780.

Reid, Jean Arnot—co-founder and first treasurer of ABW, 1921.

Rodriguez, Evelyn—first Hispanic woman member of NYSE, 1984.

Roebling, Mary—first woman commercial bank president, Trenton Trust Company, 1937; first woman chair of major commercial bank, 1941; first woman governor of national stock exchange, Amex, 1958.

Runyon, Brenda Vineyard—founder and president of the first U.S. bank entirely run by women, First Woman's Bank, 1919.

Savage, Terry—founding member and first woman trader, Chicago Board Options Exchange, 1973.

Schapiro, Mary—first acting female chair of SEC, 1993–94; CFTC chair, 1994–96; president of regulation, National Association of Securities Dealers (NASD), 1996–2002; vice chair, NASD, 2002–06; chair and CEO, NASD, 2006–08; first woman chair, SEC, 2009–12; considered one of leading regulators during 2008 financial crisis.

Schieffelin, Allison—lead plaintiff in gender discrimination suit against Morgan Stanley, 2001.

Schoenleber, Gretchen—first woman member of a commodities exchange, New York Cocoa Exchange, 1935.

Schulder, Peggy—first woman elected president of NYSE member firm, Auerbach, Pollak, & Richardson, Inc., 1969.

Selander, Joyce—first woman to trade financial futures on CBOT, 1977.

Shapiro, Joan—co-founder, SIF, 1981.

Siebert, Muriel—first woman to become member of NYSE, 1967; founded own firm, 1968; first woman New York Superintendent of Banking, 1977–82.

Soss, Wilma—founder, Federation of Women Shareholders in American Business, 1947.

St. John, Lilia—first black woman who passed NYSE exam; worked for Oppenheimer & Co., 1953.

Steck, Lena Riddle—founder of Texas Women Bankers' Association, 1912.

Stephens, Florence—attorney who founded own investment firm, F.W. Stephens Co., 1928, and Graphic Financial Charts Co., 1945.

Stephens, Louisa—president of the First National Bank of Marion, Iowa, a predecessor of Wells Fargo, 1883.

Stevens, Sandra—first woman to work on floor of major commodities exchange, Chicago Mercantile Exchange, 1966.

Talley, Madelon—first woman fund manager, Dreyfus Leverage Fund, 1970.

Walker, Maggie—first black woman bank founder and president, St. Luke Penny Savings Bank, 1903.

Walsh, Julia Montgomery—one of first two women to gain seat on Amex, 1965; second woman governor of Amex, 1972; founded own firm, 1977; first woman inductee *Wall Street Week's* Hall of Fame, 1992.

Warren, Elizabeth—chair, Congressional Oversight Panel, 2008–10; considered one of leading regulators during 2008 financial crisis; special advisor to Consumer Financial Protection Bureau, 2010–11; U.S. Senator, 2013.

Woodhull, Victoria—suffrage advocate who together with sister Tennessee Claflin became the first women to found a Wall Street brokerage, 1870; unsuccessfully ran for U.S. president, 1872.

Young, Cathy—first woman floor broker, Boston Stock Exchange, 1972.

Zuger, Nancy—co-founder and first president, Young Women's Investment Association, 1956.

Appendix B

Selected Chronology

1600s–mid/ late 1800s	emergence of she-merchants and deputy husbands.
1716–23	Mary Peck Butterworth operates New England counterfeiting ring.
1759–60	women comprise 61 percent of subscribers to Pennsylvania's Indian Commission Loan of 1759–60.
1766	colonial women begin to boycott British goods.
1774	Penelope Barker hosts Edenton tea party.
1777	Abigail Adams first purchases bonds.
1780	Esther deBerdt Reed forms Ladies Association of Philadelphia.
1792–99	women comprise 11 percent of the stockholders of the Insurance Company of North America.
1794–95	Sarah Livingston Jay invests in bank shares.
1810	women comprise 12.5 percent of subscribers to public offering of Commercial and Farmers of Baltimore.
1862	Jennie Douglas hired as first woman to be employed by U.S. Treasury.
1865	Hetty Green begins purchasing greenbacks.
1869	Victoria Woodhull makes fortune during Gold Panic.
1870	Woodhull, Claflin & Co. begins operations as first female-owned brokerage.

1875	Lydia Moss Bradley becomes first woman member of a national bank board.
1879–88	Sarah Howe founds Ladies Deposit Bank that fraudulently preys on women investors in Boston.
1883	Louisa Stephens becomes president of the First National Bank of Marion, Iowa, a predecessor of Wells Fargo.
1890–1919	banks establish women's banking departments.
1900	Mollie O'Bryan becomes first woman to hold seat on a mining stock exchange.
1901	Anna Martin founds The Commercial Bank of Mason and remains president for 24 years.
1903	Maggie Walker founds St. Luke Penny Savings Bank and becomes first black female bank president.
1905	women's lunchrooms open in Wall Street area.
1906	Goldfield Stock Exchange founded by several women to trade mining shares.
1907	Hetty Green attends J.P. Morgan's emergency bankers' meeting that halts Panic of 1807.
1912	Lena Riddle Steck founds Texas Women Bankers' Association.
1917	WLLC established; Kate Gleason becomes president of First National Bank of East Rochester, the first woman to head an existing bank without familial ties; Marian Glenn writes about women and business in *Forbes* magazine's debut issue.
1918	Evelyn Aldrich becomes first woman to address the American Institute of Banking.
1919	Brenda Vineyard Runyon founds First Woman's Bank, first bank run entirely by women; Virginia Furman appointed New York's first female bank officer.
1921	ABW and WBC founded.
1922–29	women participate in rise of stock market and begin to hold pink collar jobs on Wall Street.
1924	Margaret McCann claims to be first woman broker and opens firm that dissolves four years later following her grand larceny conviction.
1927	woman rumored to have unsuccessfully sought NYSE membership; Irma Dell Eggleston sets record for trading Liberty Bonds;

National Bankers Association founded to advocate for minority and women-owned banks on legislative and regulatory issues.

1929 Astrologist Evangeline Adams predicts 1929 Crash.

1931 Gladys Pyle becomes first woman permitted onto floor of New York Curb Exchange.

1934 Isabel Benham becomes first woman railroad analyst.

1935 Cathrine Curtis founds Women Investors in America; Gretchen Schoenleber becomes first woman member of a commodities exchange, The New York Cocoa Exchange.

1936 Sylvia Porter pens series on professional Wall Street women for the *New York Post*.

1937 Mary Roebling becomes first woman president of a major commercial bank.

1939 NYSE directory lists 67 women in firms accredited for floor trading, in contrast to 12 listed in 1929.

1940 Sylvia Porter helps design Series E Savings Bond.

1941 Mary Roebling becomes first woman chair of a major commercial bank.

1942 Sylvia Porter reveals her gender in column and also granted NYSE floor access.

1942–44 influx of women into banking to fill wartime vacancies.

1942–46 official women's division operates within War Finance Division of U.S. Treasury to sell bonds.

1943 Helen Hanzelin becomes first woman to work on floor of the NYSE.

1945 sixty-six women work on the NYSE floor before being replaced by returning veterans.

1947 Wilma Soss founds Federation of Women Shareholders in American Business.

1948 women briefly work on NYSE floor during strike of unionized workers.

1949 Claire Giannini Hoffman becomes first woman director of the Bank of America; Georgia Neece Clark appointed first woman U.S. Treasurer.

1952 Margaret Kennedy becomes first woman partner of an NYSE member firm.

1953   Lilia St. John becomes first black woman to pass NYSE exam.

1956   Josephine Perfect Bay becomes first woman to head NYSE firm; Financial Women's Club of San Francisco and Young Women's Investment Association founded.

1957   Margaret Kennedy becomes first woman to be a name partner of an NYSE firm.

1958   Mary Roebling becomes first female governor of Amex.

1962   NYSE premiers short comedy film "The Lady and The Stock Exchange."

1963   Lotte Kahn writes *Women and Wall Street*, one of first guides to investing directed at women.

1964   Christine Gillis founds Women Stockbroker's Association; Romana Banuelos founds Pan American National Bank.

1965   Phyllis Peterson becomes first woman member of Philadelphia Stock Exchange; Julia Montgomery Walsh and Phyllis Peterson become first women members of the Amex; June Middleton becomes first black woman registered representative of an NYSE-member firm.

1966   Amex permits women data clerks on floor for first time since World War II; Sandra Stevens becomes first woman to work on floor of the Chicago Mercantile Exchange.

1967   Muriel Siebert becomes first woman to purchase seat on NYSE.

1969   Peggy Schulder becomes first woman to be elected president and chief executive officer of an NYSE member firm; Virginia Hansen and Carol Jane Ovitz become first women admitted to the CBOT.

1970   Jane Larkin becomes second woman to own seat on NYSE; women return to NYSE floor as pages and clerical workers; Madelon Tally becomes first female fund manager.

1971   Romana Banuelos becomes first Hispanic woman to serve as U.S. Treasurer.

1972   Julia Montgomery Walsh becomes first woman from within securities industry to be appointed an Amex governor; Juanita Kreps becomes first woman director of the NYSE; Cathy Young becomes first woman to work on floor of Boston Stock Exchange.

1973   Helen O'Bannon successfully challenges gender bias on Merrill Lynch broker entrance exam; Terry Savage becomes founding member and first woman trader on the Chicago Board Options Exchange; Jean Dunne becomes first woman stock specialist, National Stock Exchange.

1975   Sylvia Porter writes best seller *Sylvia Porter's Money Book*.

1976   Alice Jarcho becomes first woman NYSE floor broker; Marsha O'Bannon becomes first woman NYSE officer.

1977   Muriel Siebert becomes first woman New York State Superintendent of Banking; Roberta Karmel becomes first woman SEC commissioner; Azie Taylor Morton becomes first black woman U.S. Treasurer; Lynn Greenberg becomes first woman Amex floor trading member; Ginger Ketcham becomes first woman Amex specialist; Joyce Selander becomes first woman to trade financial futures on CBOT floor.

1978   The Women's Bank, N.A., the first nationally chartered bank established by women, opens in Denver.

1979   Ernesta Procope becomes first black woman to own financial business on Wall Street.

1980   Barbara Thomas becomes second woman SEC commissioner; Amy Newkirk becomes first NYSE woman specialist.

1981   Gail Pankey becomes first black woman member of NYSE; Susan Phillips becomes first woman commissioner of CFTC; Joan Bavaria and Joan Shapiro co-found SIF.

1983   Ginger Ketcham becomes first woman Amex floor official; Susan Phillips becomes first woman chair of CFTC.

1984   Amy Domini writes *Ethical Investing*; Aulana Peters becomes first black SEC commissioner; Rosemary McFadden becomes first woman to serve as president of U.S. futures exchange; Evelyn Rodriguez becomes first Hispanic woman member of NYSE.

1986   Jeanette Loeb becomes first woman partner at Goldman Sachs.

1987   Elaine Garzarelli predicts 1987 Crash.

1989   Aulana Peters becomes first black woman NYSE director; Donna Redel becomes first woman governor of Comex; Doreen Mogavero opens first fully woman owned and operated brokerage based on NYSE floor.

1990   Christine Edwards becomes first woman general counsel of major Wall Street firm.

1991   Peggy Ogorek becomes first woman CBOT board member; Bankers Trust women launch Global Partnership Network for Women.

1992   Julia Montgomery Walsh becomes first woman inducted into "The *Wall Street Week With Louis Rukeyser* Hall of Fame"; Abby Joseph Cohen becomes celebrated muse of the bull market; Donna Redel becomes first woman to chair a futures exchange.

1993   Mary Schapiro serves as first acting woman chair of SEC.

1994   Beardstown Ladies publish best-selling investment guide; news breaks of First Lady Hillary Clinton's profitable commodities trades between 1978 and 1979.

1995   Deutsche Bank launches annual Women on Wall Street conference.

1996   first gender-based Title VII class action suit filed against Wall Street firm, *Martens v. Smith Barney.*

1997   second major gender-based Title VII class action suit filed against Wall Street firm, *Cremin v. Merrill Lynch & Co.*; Janet Hanson founds 85 Broads, networking association originally of Goldman Sachs women.

1998   New York Attorney General holds public hearings on gender discrimination in securities industry.

1999   United States Commission on Civil Rights applauds industry efforts to address Wall Street diversity but cites "a dismal lack of progress"; NASD eliminates mandatory arbitration of employment discrimination claims; firms strengthen diversity and anti-harassment policies; Karen Hackett becomes first NYSE woman floor governor.

2001–03   4 percent losses in numbers of women working on Wall Street and holding executive management posts.

2002   Catherine Kinney becomes first woman NYSE president; American Express Financial Advisors enters into consent decree notable for documenting discriminatory allegations and requiring detailed corporate action.

2004 $54 million settlement in gender discrimination suit brought by EEOC and lead plaintiff Allison Scheffelin against Morgan

Stanley; Doreen Mogavero becomes first woman member of NYSE Board of Executives; Valerie Jarrett becomes first woman chair of Chicago Stock Exchange.

2005 two women, Cynthia Glassman and Annette Nazareth, serve concurrently as SEC commissioners for first time.

2008 Sheila Bair, Mary Schapiro, and Elizabeth Warren known as chief federal regulators dealing with financial crisis; executives Sallie Krawchek, Zoe Cruz, and Erin Callan lose jobs.

2009 Museum of American Finance opens "Women of Wall Street" exhibit.

2012 Beth Mooney becomes chair of KeyCorp; Abigail Johnson becomes president of Fidelity Investments.

Notes

INTRODUCTION

1. John Steele Gordon, *The Great Game: The Emergence of Wall Street as a World Power 1653–2000* (New York: Scribner, 1999).

2. Charles R. Geisst, *Wall Street: A History* (New York: Oxford University Press, 1997), 4–5.

PART I: REVOLUTIONARIES

1. Charles Mackay, *Memoirs of Extraordinary Popular Delusions and the Madness of Crowds* (1852; Project Gutenberg 2008), 89, http://www.gutenberg.org/files/24518/24518-h/24518-h.htm.

2. Ibid., 55.

3. Vivien Jones, ed., *Women and Literature in Britain, 1700–1800* (Cambridge, UK: Cambridge University Press, 2000), 272.

4. Nancy Egloff, Historian, Jamestown-Yorktown Foundation, e-mail correspondence with author, May 21, 2012.

5. Gail Collins, *America's Women: Four Hundred Years of Dolls, Drudges, Helpmates, and Heroines* (New York: William Morrow/HarperCollins, 2003), 49–50.

6. Marylynn Salmon, *Women and the Law of Property in Early America* (Chapel Hill, NC: University of North Carolina Press, 1986), 44.

7. Robert E. Wright, "Women and Finance in the Early National U.S.," *Essays in History*, 42 (2000).

8. Lois Green Carr, "Margaret Brent—A Brief History," *Maryland State Archives*, February 7, 2002, http://www.msa.md.gov/msa/speccol/sc3500/sc3520/002100/002177/html/mbrent2.html.

9. Collins, *America's Women*, 27.

10. Patricia Cleary, *Elizabeth Murray: A Woman's Pursuit of Independence in Eighteenth-Century America* (Amherst, MA: University of Massachusetts Press, 2000), 46.

11. Robert E. Wright, *Hamilton Unbound: Finance and the Creation of the American Republic* (Westport, CT/London: Greenwood Press, 2002), 179.

12. Ibid., 182.

CHAPTER ONE: THE PHILADELPHIA LADIES

1. *The Sentiments of an American Woman* (Philadelphia: John Dunlap, 1780).

2. Melissa A. Marsh, "The Purest Patriotism: The Domestic Sphere and the Ladies Association of Philadelphia," http://www.history1700s.com/articles/article1097.shtml.

3. Ibid.

4. Diane Silcox-Jarrett, *Heroines of the American Revolution: America's Founding Mothers* (Chapel Hill, NC: Green Angel Press, 1988), 17.

5. Richard Carney, "North Carolina History Project: Edenton Tea Party," www.northcarolinahistory.org/encyclopedia/50/entry; Linda Grant De Pauw, *Founding Mothers: Women of America in the Revolutionary Era* (Boston: Houghton Mifflin Company, 1975), 160.

6. Cokie Roberts, *Founding Mothers: The Women Who Raised Our Nation* (New York: William Morrow, 2004), 42.

7. *Sentiments.*

8. Ibid.; Mary Beth Norton, *Liberty's Daughters: The Revolutionary Experience of American Women, 1750–1800* (Boston: Little, Brown & Company, 1980), 178.

9. Norton, *Liberty's Daughters*, 179; Marsh, "The Purest Patriotism."

10. *Sentiments.*

11. Ibid.

12. *Sentiments*; Norton, *Liberty's Daughters*, 179; Marsh, "The Purest Patriotism"; Roberts, *Founding Mothers*, 124–25.

13. Norton, *Liberty's Daughters*, 183–84.

14. *Sentiments.*

15. Ibid.

16. Marsh, "The Purest Patriotism."

17. Roberts, *Founding Mothers*, 125.

18. Marsh, "The Purest Patriotism."

19. Ibid.

20. Ibid.

21. Ibid.

22. Norton, *Liberty's Daughters*, 180–81; Roberts, *Founding Mothers*, 126.

23. Rosemary Fry Plakas, "The Sentiments of an American Woman," *Library of Congress*, http://memory.loc.gov/ammem/awhhtml/awhendp/index.html.

24. De Pauw, *Founding Mothers*, 170–71.

25. Norton, *Liberty's Daughters*, 183–84.

26. Marsh, "The Purest Patriotism"; Roberts, *Founding Mothers*, 126.

27. Miriam Marquez, "Pivotal role at Crucial Time: Cuban Help for Our Freedom," *Orlando Sentinel*, July 4, 2001.

28. Marsh, "The Purest Patriotism."

29. Ibid.

30. Norton, *Liberty's Daughters*, 186; Marsh, "The Purest Patriotism."

31. Roberts, *Founding Mothers*, 128.

32. Marsh, "The Purest Patriotism."

33. Roberts, *Founding Mothers*, 129.

34. Norton, *Liberty's Daughters*, 186.

35. Marsh, "The Purest Patriotism."

36. Roberts, *Founding Mothers*, 130.

37. Keith W. Parker, "The Involvement of 'The Ladies' Economic Support of Women During the American Revolution," *Early America Review*, Summer/Fall 2006, http://www.earlyamerica.com/review/2006_summer_fall/women-revolution.html; Norton, *Liberty's Daughters*, 187.

38. Marsh, "The Purest Patriotism."

39. Norton, *Liberty's Daughters*, 187; Marsh, "The Purest Patriotism."

40. Norton, *Liberty's Daughters*, 187.

41. Ibid.

42. Ibid., 187–88.

43. Ibid., 187.

44. Norton, *Liberty's Daughters*, 187; Marsh, "The Purest Patriotism."

CHAPTER TWO: SHE-MERCHANTS AND DEPUTY HUSBANDS

1. Abigail Adams to Cotton Tufts, May 10, 1785, in Adams Family Correspondence, *Founding Families: Digital Editions of the Papers of the Winthrops and the Adamses*, ed. C. James Taylor (Boston: Massachusetts Historical Society, 2007), http://www.masshist.org/ff/.

2. Abigail Adams to Cotton Tufts, May 10, 1785, in *Founding Families*; Woody Holton, "Abigail Adams, Bond Speculator," *The William and Mary Quarterly*, 64, no. 4 (October 2007): 827.

3. Abigail Adams to John Adams, March 31, 1776, in *Founding Families*; Roberts, *Founding Mothers*, 72; De Pauw, *Founding Mothers*, 202–05; Collins, *America's Women*, 82–83; Norton, *Liberty's Daughters*, 50, 163, 226.

4. John Adams to Abigail Adams, April 14, 1776 in *Founding Families*; Roberts, *Founding Mothers*, 72; De Pauw, *Founding Mothers*, 203–04; Collins, *America's Women*, 83; Norton, *Liberty's Daughters*, 163.

5. Roberts, *Founding Mothers*, 72; De Pauw, *Founding Mothers*, 203–04.

6. Abigail Adams to John Adams, May 7, 1776, in *Founding Families*; Roberts, *Founding Mothers*, 73; De Pauw, *Founding Mothers*, 203.

7. Holton, "Abigail Adams, Bond Speculator," 821.

8. Laura Thatcher Ulrich, *Good Wives: Image and Reality in the Lives of Women in Northern New England, 1650–1750* (New York: Knopf, 1980), 35–50.

9. Abigail Adams to John Adams, September 20, 1776 in *Founding Families*.

10. Abigail Adams to John Adams, April 11, 1776, in *Founding Families*; Woody Holton, *Abigail Adams* (New York: Free Press, 2009), 105.

11. Roberts, *Founding Mothers*, 26–28, 33.

12. Ibid., 33.

13. Landa M. Freeman, Louise V. North, and Janet M. Wedge, eds., *Selected Letters of John Jay and Sarah Livingston Jay* (Jefferson, NC: McFarland & Company, 2005), 13.

14. Norton, *Liberty's Daughters*, 5–7.

15. Ibid., 215.

16. Norton, *Liberty's Daughters*, 6–7, 133; Robert E. Wright, "Women and Finance in the Early National U.S.," University of Virginia, *Essays in History*, Volume 42, 2000.

17. Norton, *Liberty's Daughters*, 214–18.

18. Ibid., 218.

19. Ibid.

20. Ibid., 218–19.

21. Ibid., 219.

22. Ibid.

23. Ibid., 222–24.

24. Ibid., 223.

25. Ibid., 223–24.

26. John Adams to Abigail Adams, May 27, 1776, in *Founding Families*; Roberts, *Founding Mothers*, 74; Holton, *Abigail Adams*, 105.

27. Norton, *Liberty's Daughters*, 50, 116.

28. John Adams to Abigail Adams 2d, April 18, 1776, in *Founding Families*; Roberts, *Founding Mothers*, 74; Holton, "Abigail Adams, Bond Speculator," 830; Holton, *Abigail Adams*, 104.

29. Norton, *Liberty's Daughters*, 116.

30. David McCullough, *John Adams* (New York: Simon & Schuster, 2001), 171.

31. Woody Holton, "On Money, a Founding Mother Knows Best," *Washington Post*, July 5, 2009.

32. Abigail Adams to John Adams, April 25, 1782, in *Founding Families*.

33. Holton, *Abigail Adams*, 177–78.

34. John Adams to Abigail Adams, October 12, 1782, in *Founding Families*.

35. Abigail Adams to John Adams, June 1, 1777, in *Founding Families*.

36. Ibid.

37. Holton, "Abigail Adams, Bond Speculator," 824, 826; Holton, *Abigail Adams*, 133, 189, 276, 310.

38. Holton, "Abigail Adams, Bond Speculator," 824.

39. Abigail Adams to John Adams, January 3, 1784, in *Founding Families*; Holton, "Abigail Adams, Bond Speculator," 821.

40. Abigail Adams to Cotton Tufts, September 8, 1784, in *Founding Families*; Holton, "Abigail Adams, Bond Speculator," 821–22; Holton, *Abigail Adams*, 212.

41. John Adams to Cotton Tufts, April 24, 1785, in *Founding Families*; Holton, "Abigail Adams, Bond Speculator," 821–22; Holton, *Abigail Adams*, 212.

42. Holton, "Abigail Adams, Bond Speculator," 833.

43. Holton, "Abigail Adams, Bond Speculator," 822–23; Holton, *Abigail Adams*, 275.

44. Ibid.

45. Holton, "Abigail Adams, Bond Speculator," 822–34; Holton, *Abigail Adams*, 212, 275.

46. Holton, "Abigail Adams, Bond Speculator," 827, 831.

47. Holton, "Abigail Adams, Bond Speculator," 827–29; Holton, *Abigail Adams*, 189, 213.

48. Ibid.

49. Abigail Adams to John Adams, April 25, 1782, in Founding Families.

50. Holton, "Abigail Adams, Bond Speculator," 830.

51. Abigail Adams to John Adams, December 27, 1783 in *Founding Families*.

52. Abigail Adams to Cotton Tufts, April 26, 1785 in *Founding Families*.

53. Holton, "Abigail Adams, Bond Speculator," 827; Abigail Adams to Cotton Tufts, May 10, 1785, in *Founding Families*; Holton, *Abigail Adams*, 213.

54. Holton, *Abigail Adams*, 273, 340.

55. Freeman, North, and Wedge, *Selected Letters*, 13, 229–41.

56. Ibid., 235–36.

57. Ibid., 237.

58. Wright, "Women and Finance in the Early National U.S."; Wright, *Hamilton Unbound*, 182–85.

59. Marissa Knaak and Megan Soe, "Female Investment in America from the 18th Century to the Great Depression," *Financial History*, Winter 2012, 15.

PART II: PIONEERS

1. Carol R. Berkin and Clara M. Lovett, eds., *Women, War, and Revolution* (New York: Holmes & Meier, 1980), 209.

2. Ibid., 91.

3. Norton, *Liberty's Daughters*, 254.

4. Geisst, *Wall Street*, 64; Gordon, *Great Game*, 181.

5. Gordon, *Great Game*, 181.

6. Catherine Clinton and Christine Lunardini, *The Columbia Guide to American Women in the Nineteenth Century* (New York: Columbia University Press, 2000), 90.

7. U.S. Bureau of the Census, "1870 Census," 832–42, http://www.census.gov/prod/www/abs/decennial/1870.html.

8. U.S. Treasury, "The Treasurer," http://www.treasury.gov/about/organizational-structure/offices/Pages/Office-of-the-Treasurer.aspx (last updated April 27, 2012; accessed May 24, 2012).

9. Ibid.

10. Goldfield Corporation, "History," http://www.goldfieldcorp.com/History-10.asp (accessed June 7, 2012).

11. "The 'Ladies' Deposit" in *The School Herald: A History of 1881* (Chicago: W.I. Chase, 1882), 84; "Arrest of Sarah E. Howe," *New York Times*, December 9, 1888; Mitchell Zuckoff, *Ponzi's Scheme: The True Story of a Financial Legend* (New York: Random House, 2005), 104.

12. Glenda Riley, *Inventing the American Woman: An Inclusive History, Vol. 2: Since 1877* (Wheeling, IL: Harlan Davidson, 2001), 285–301.

13. Ibid., 293.

CHAPTER THREE: TENNESSEE CLAFLIN AND VICTORIA WOODHULL

1. Lois Beachy Underhill, *The Woman Who Ran for President: The Many Lives of Victoria Woodhull* (Bridgehampton, NY: Bridge Works Publishing Co., 1995), 65.

2. Ibid., 69.

3. Ibid., 19–20.

4. Ibid., 30.

5. Ibid., 27.

6. Ibid.

7. Ibid., 29–30.

8. Ibid., 20.

9. T. J. Stiles, *The First Tycoon: The Epic Life of Cornelius Vanderbilt* (New York: Alfred A. Knopf, 2009), 485.

10. Underhill, *The Woman Who Ran for President*, 44.

11. Underhill, *The Woman Who Ran for President*, 44; Edward J. Renehan, Jr., *Commodore: The Life of Cornelius Vanderbilt* (New York: Basic Books, 2007), 268.

12. Underhill, *The Woman Who Ran for President*, 45.

13. Underhill, *The Woman Who Ran for President*, 46; Renehan, *Commodore*, 268.

14. Mary Gabriel, *Notorious Victoria: The Life of Victoria Woodhull, Uncensored* (Chapel Hill, NC: Algonquin Books of Chapel Hill, 1998), 34; Renehan, *Commodore*, 268.

15. Underhill, *The Woman Who Ran for President*, 55–57.

16. Ibid., 57–59.

17. Underhill, *The Woman Who Ran for President*, 57; Barbara Goldsmith, *Other Powers: The Age of Suffrage, Spiritualism, and the Scandalous Victoria Woodhull* (New York: Knopf, 1998), 189–90; Emanie Sachs, *The Terrible Siren: Victoria Woodhull* (New York: Arno Press, 1972), 50.

18. Underhill, *The Woman Who Ran for President*, 59.

19. Ibid.

20. Ibid., 67.

21. Ibid., 63.

22. Gabriel, *Notorious Victoria*, 41.

23. Henry Clews, *Fifty Years in Wall Street* (New York: Arno Press, 1973), 440.

24. Underhill, *The Woman Who Ran for President*, 63.

25. Underhill, *The Woman Who Ran for President*, 64; Stiles, *The First Tycoon*, 501.

26. Underhill, *The Woman Who Ran for President*, 65; Stiles, *The First Tycoon*, 501–03.

27. Underhill, *The Woman Who Ran for President*, 66.

28. Ibid.

29. John Steele Gordon, "The Robber Baronesses," *American Heritage*, 46, no. 8 (December 1995); Johanna Johnston, *Mrs. Satan: The Incredible Saga of Victoria C. Woodhull* (New York: G. P. Putnam's Sons, 1967), 56.

30. Underhill, *The Woman Who Ran for President*, 66–67.

31. Underhill, *The Woman Who Ran for President*, 66–67; Stiles, *The First Tycoon*, 501.

32. Goldsmith, *Other Powers*, 191; Johnston, *Mrs. Satan*, 57; Stiles, *The First Tycoon*, 555–56.

33. Gabriel, *Notorious Victoria*, 1.

34. Clews, *Fifty Years*, 442.

35. Gabriel, *Notorious Victoria*, 1.

36. Underhill, *The Woman Who Ran for President*, 67.

37. "Wall-Street Aroused," *New York Times*, February 6, 1870.

38. Underhill, *The Woman Who Ran for President*, 68.

39. Underhill, *The Woman Who Ran for President*, 69; Gordon, "The Robber Baronesses."

40. "Woman's Right to Speculate," *New York Times*, February 22, 1871; "A Suit Against a Notorious Firm" *New York Times*, January 5, 1875; Underhill, *The Woman Who Ran for President*, 128–29; Stiles, *The First Tycoon*, 555–56.

41. Underhill, *The Woman Who Ran for President*, 69.

42. Ibid., 70.

43. Goldsmith, *Other Powers*, 193–95; Gabriel, *Notorious Victoria*, 43, 72.

44. Underhill, *The Woman Who Ran for President*, 72–74.

45. Ibid.

46. "Lady Cook Dies in London at 77." *New York Times*, January 20, 1923.

47. Stiles, *The First Tycoon*, 501.

48. Underhill, *The Woman Who Ran for President*, 77–78.

49. Underhill, *The Woman Who Ran for President*, 77–78; Ishbel Ross, *Charmers and Cranks: Twelve Famous American Women Who Defied the Conventions* (New York: Harper & Row, 1965), 115.

50. Underhill, *The Woman Who Ran for President*, 81, 85.

51. Ibid., 90, 129–30.

52. Ibid., 130.

53. Ibid., 131–32.

54. Sachs, *The Terrible Siren*, 91.

55. "Principles of Finance," *New York Times*, August 4, 1871; Victoria C. Woodhull, "A Speech on the Principles of Finance," Lecture, Cooper Institute, New York City, August 3, 1871; reprinted in Madeleine B. Stern, ed., *The Victoria Woodhull Reader* (Weston, MA: M&S Press, 1974); Underhill, *The Woman Who Ran for President*, 168.

56. Underhill, *The Woman Who Ran for President*, 194–95.

57. Ibid., 128.

58. "A Suit Against a Notorious Firm"; "Woman's Right to Speculate"; Stiles, *The First Tycoon*, 555–56; Underhill, *The Woman Who Ran for President*, 128.

59. "A Suit Against a Notorious Firm."

60. Underhill, *The Woman Who Ran for President*, 271; Ross, *Charmers and Cranks*, 128.

61. "The Vanderbilt Estate," *New York Times*, May 13, 1877; "The Railroad King's Money," *New York Times*, March 2, 1878; "Mr. Vanderbilt's Will," *New York Times*, October 16, 1878.

62. "Lady Cook Dies in London at 77," *New York Times*, January 20, 1923; Ross, *Charmers and Cranks*, 131–35; Underhill, *The Woman Who Ran for President*, 304.

63. Ross, *Charmers and Cranks*, 123.

64. "Lady Cook Dies in London at 77"; Clews, *Fifty Years*, 437–46.

CHAPTER FOUR: HETTY GREEN

1. "Why Women Don't Get Rich-Mrs. Hetty Green in Success," *New York Times*, April 28, 1901.

2. "Committee Takes Trust Companies," *New York Times*, November 6, 1907.

3. Charles Slack, *Hetty: The Genius and Madness of America's First Female Tycoon* (New York: Harper Perennial, 2004), 168–69.

4. Slack, *Hetty*, 18, 169.

5. Ross, *Charmers and Cranks*, 30; Slack, *Hetty*, 16.

6. Slack, *Hetty*, 1; Boyden Sparkes and Samuel T. Moore, *The Witch of Wall Street: Hetty Green* (Garden City, NY: Doubleday, Doran & Company, 1930), 15.

7. Slack, *Hetty*, 20; Sparkes and Moore, *Witch of Wall Street*, 45.

8. Slack, *Hetty*, 25.

9. Ibid.; 25, "Seventy Years Rest Lightly on Mrs. Hetty Green," *New York Times*, November 5, 1905.

10. Slack, *Hetty*, 41.

11. Gordon, *Great Game*, 154.

12. Slack, *Hetty*, 69–70.

13. Gordon, *Great Game*, 154–55; Sparkes and Moore, *Witch of Wall Street*, 139.

14. Slack, *Hetty*, 96; Sparkes and Moore, *Witch of Wall Street*, 8.

15. Slack, *Hetty*, 99–100; "Mrs. Hetty Green's Defeat," *New York Times*, July 1, 1888.

16. Slack, *Hetty*, 100.

17. Ibid., 121.

18. Ibid., 122.

19. Ibid.

20. Slack, *Hetty*, 122; Ross, *Charmers and Cranks*, 40–41.

21. "Hetty Green Talks Cash and Politics," *New York Times*, February 15, 1908.

22. "Mrs. Hetty Green, Menaced, Arms Herself," *New York Times*, May 9, 1902.

23. "Hetty Green Dies, Worth $100,000,000," *New York Times*, July 4, 1916; Ross, *Charmers and Cranks*, 56; Slack, *Hetty*, ix.

24. "Busy Women of the Idle Rich," *New York Times*, October 15, 1911.

25. "Women Seeking 'Points'," *New York Times*, September 24, 1882; "Women in Wall Street," *New York Times*, December 12, 1909.

26. "Women Seeking 'Points.'"

27. Clews, *Fifty Years*, 445.

28. "Women Seeking 'Points'"; "Women in Wall Street."

29. Slack, *Hetty*, xi.

30. "Hetty Green Talks Cash and Politics."

31. Slack, *Hetty*, 191–92.

32. "Hetty Green Taking Beauty Treatments," *New York Times*, May 28, 1908.

33. "When Wall Street Goes to Its Noonday Luncheon," *New York Times*, May 12, 1907.

34. Ross, *Charmers and Cranks*, 42; Sparkes and Moore, *Witch of Wall Street*, 182.

35. "Hetty Green Dies."

36. Slack, *Hetty*, 190–91.

37. Slack, *Hetty*, 190; Ross, *Charmers and Cranks*, 52–53.

38. Slack, *Hetty*, 190.

39. Ibid., 155.

40. "Hetty Green at 80 Rests on Birthday," *New York Times*, November 21, 1915; Hetty Green, "Why Women Don't Get Rich," *New York Times*, April 28, 1901.

41. Slack, *Hetty*, 111.
42. Green, "Why Women Don't Get Rich."
43. "Hetty Green at 80."
44. Green, "Why Women Don't Get Rich."
45. Ross, *Charmers and Cranks*, 50.
46. Slack, *Hetty*, 112.
47. "Seventy Years Rest Lightly."
48. Ibid.
49. "A Prodigy Because a Woman," *New York Times*, July 15, 1916.

CHAPTER FIVE: MAGGIE WALKER

1. Maggie Walker, "An Address to the 34th Annual Session of the Right Worthy Grand Council of Virginia, Independent Order of St. Luke," Richmond, VA, August 20, 1901.

2. *Encyclopedia Virginia*, "Maggie Lena Walker (1864–1934)" (by Muriel Miller Branch), http://www.encyclopediavirginia.org/Maggie_Lena_Walker_1864–1934 (accessed October 24, 2011).

3. Muriel Miller Branch and Dorothy Marie Rice, *Pennies to Dollars: The Story of Maggie Lena Walker* (North Haven, CT: Linnet Books, 1997), 8.

4. Elsa Barkley Brown, "Constructing a Life and a Community: A Partial Story of Maggie Lena Walker," *OAH Magazine of History*, 7, no. 4 (Summer 1993): 28; Gertrude Woodruff Marlowe, *A Right Worthy Grand Mission: Maggie Lena Walker and the Quest for Black Economic Empowerment* (Washington, DC: Howard University Press, 2003), 5; Branch and Rice, *Pennies*, 16.

5. Rita G. Koman, "Servitude to Service: African-American Women as Wage Earners," *OAH Magazine of History*, 11, no. 2, Labor History (Winter 1997): 1; Brown, "Constructing a Life," 29; Marlowe, *Grand Mission*, 4.

6. Marlowe, *Grand Mission*, 11–12; Branch and Rice, *Pennies*, 25–29; Anthony J. Mayo and Shandi O. Smith, "Maggie Lena Walker and the Independent Order of St. Luke," HBS No. 9–409–057 (Boston: Harvard Business School Publishing, 2008; revised 2011), 3.

7. Marlowe, *Grand Mission*, 18–19; Branch and Rice, *Pennies*, 32–34; Mayo and Smith, "Maggie Lena Walker," 4; Brown, "Constructing a Life," 29.

8. Marlowe, *Grand Mission*, 30–31; Branch and Rice, *Pennies*, 44.

9. Koman, "Servitude," 1–2; Marlowe, *Grand Mission*, 64, 82.

10. Brown, "Constructing a Life," 30.

11. Elsa Barkely Brown, "Womanist Consciousness: Maggie Lena Walker and the Independent Order of Saint Luke," *Signs*, 14, no. 3 (Spring 1989): 617; Branch and Rice, *Pennies*, 53; Mayo and Smith, "Maggie Lena Walker," 6.

12. Brown, "Constructing a Life," 29.

13. Brown, "Constructing a Life," 29; Mayo and Smith, "Maggie Lena Walker," 7.

14. Walker, 1901 Address.

15. Marlowe, *Grand Mission*, 44–45, 79–85; Gray Madison, "Maggie Walker, Bank On It," *Time*, January 12, 2007; Branch and Rice, *Pennies*, 66; Jeremy Quittner, "Maggie Walker: A Rich Legacy for the Black Woman Entrepreneur," *BusinessWeek*, July 6, 1999; Mayo and Smith, "Maggie Lena Walker," 6.

16. Marlowe, *Grand Mission*, 90–91; "Colored Woman's Appeal," *New York Times*, August 10, 1903.

17. Wells Fargo Bank, "Women Making Financial History," http://www.wells fargomedia.com/wmfh/womenBankers.html; "General Notes," *New York Times*, April 20, 1883; Federal Reserve Bank of Richmond, *Walker Leaves Lasting Legacy*, 6, http://www.richmondfed.org/publications/education/maggie_walker/pdf/mwalker.pdf; *The Handbook of Texas Online*, "Martin, Anna Henriette Mebus," http://www.tshaonline.org/handbook/online/articles/fmaax.

18. Brown, "Constructing a Life," 29–30; Marlowe, *Grand Mission*, 91–92.

19. Marlowe, *Grand Mission*, 104.

20. "Colored Woman's Appeal," *New York Times*, August 10, 1903; Marlowe, *Grand Mission*, 90–91.

21. "Colored Woman's Appeal."

22. Branch and Rice, *Pennies*, 68.

23. Marlowe, *Grand Mission*, 92; Branch and Rice, *Pennies*, 69.

24. Marlowe, *Grand Mission*, 99; Madison, "Maggie Walker."

25. Marlowe, *Grand Mission*, 99.

26. Ibid., 108.

27. Booker T. Washington, *The Negro in Business* (Boston: Hertel, Jenkins & Co., 1907), 124; National Park Service, "Maggie L. Walker National Historic Site," http://www.nps.gov/mawa/index.htm.

28. Marlowe, *Grand Mission*, 116–18; Mayo and Smith, "Maggie Lena Walker," 7–8; Branch and Rice, *Pennies*, 71–72.

29. Marlowe, *Grand Mission*, 210; Branch and Rice, *Pennies*, 72–73.

30. Brown, "Constructing a Life," 29; Brown, "Womanist Consciousness," 624–25; Marlowe, *Grand Mission*, 97; Mayo and Smith, "Maggie Lena Walker," 8–9.

31. Marlowe, *Grand Mission*, 119, 153–54; Mayo and Smith, "Maggie Lena Walker," 8–10; Branch and Rice, *Pennies*, 81.

32. Marlowe, *Grand Mission*, 242–47; Mayo and Smith, "Maggie Lena Walker," 11–12; Branch and Rice, *Pennies*, 73–74.

33. Marlowe, *Grand Mission*, 247.

34. Branch and Rice, *Pennies*, 96; Marlowe, *Grand Mission*, 129, 255; Brown, "Womanist Consciousness," 612, 618.

35. Brown, "Constructing a Life," 30; Marlowe, *Grand Mission*, 141.

36. Marlowe, *Grand Mission*, 142–43.

37. Brown, "Constructing a Life," 30.

38. Marlowe, *Grand Mission*, 251; Branch and Rice, *Pennies*, 97.

39. Marlowe, *Grand Mission*, 80.

40. Carol Hazard, "Consolidated Bank to Become a Branch of Adams National," *Richmond Times-Dispatch*, August 18, 2009; Carol Hazard, "Consolidated Bank to Become Premier Bank," *Richmond Times-Dispatch*, March 4, 2011.

41. Marlowe, *Grand Mission*, 56.

PART III: PATRIOTS AND BANKERS

1. Riley, *Inventing the American Woman*, 341; Nancy F. Cott, ed., *No Small Courage: A History of Women in the United States* (Oxford: Oxford University Press, 2000), 364, 393.

2. Geisst, *Wall Street*, 124–29; Gordon, *Great Game*, 193–94.

3. "Our War Expense Is 30 Billions," *New York Times*, July 10, 1919; Geisst, *Wall Street*, 149–50; "Oct. 5 to Be Women's Day," *New York Times*, September 21, 1918; "Wilson Backs Amendment for Woman Suffrage," *New York Times*, January 10, 1918; Cott, *No Small Courage*, 405–12.

4. Gordon, *Great Game*, 202.

5. Ibid., 203, 208–12, 226–28.

6. Riley, *Inventing the American Woman*, 346.

7. Riley, *Inventing the American Woman*, 348; Cott, *No Small Courage*, 408; Tom Shachtman, *The Day America Crashed: A Narrative Account of the Great Stock Market Crash of October 24, 1929* (New York: G. P. Putnam's, 1979), 81, 108–09.

8. Cott, *No Small Courage*, 413.

9. Gordon, *Great Game*, 229.

10. Gordon Thomas and Max Morgan-Witts, *The Day the Bubble Burst: A Social History of the Wall Street Crash of 1929* (Garden City, NY: Doubleday, 1979), 72–74.

11. Ibid., 71–73.

12. Ibid., 73.

13. Ibid., 191.

14. Ibid., 194.

15. Ibid., 74.

16. Ibid.

17. Ibid., 195, 304.

18. Ibid., 70.

19. Geisst, *Wall Street*, 187; Thomas and Morgan-Witts, *The Day the Bubble Burst*, 70.

20. Gordon, *Great Game*, 231–33; Thomas and Morgan-Witts, *The Day the Bubble Burst*, 369–70.

21. Gordon, *Great Game*, 233–34.

22. Ibid., 235–36.

23. Riley, "Inventing the American Woman," 392–400, 418.

24. Gordon, *Great Game*, 236–37.

25. Ibid.

26. Ibid., 238–42.

27. Ibid., 249–50.

28. Geisst, *Wall Street*, 189, 267; Gordon, *Great Game*, 250.

29. "Women Traders Going Back to Bridge Games."

CHAPTER SIX: THE WOMEN'S LIBERTY LOAN COMMITTEE

1. Report of the Secretary of the Treasury on the State of the Finances for the fiscal year ended June 30, 1918 with appendices, Washington, DC: U.S. Government Printing Office, 1919.

2. Ida Clyde Clarke, *American Women and the World War* (New York: D. Appleton and Company, 1918), Chapter I, http://net.lib.byu.edu/estu/wwi/comment/Clarke/Clarke00TC.htm; "Colorado's First Female Senator," *Denver Post*, February 23, 2007.

3. Nancy Woloch, *Women and the American Experience* (New York: Alfred A. Knopf, 1984), 276.

4. J.C. Croly, *The History of the Woman's Club Movement in America* (New York: H.G. Allen, c. 1898), 15–18, 85; General Federation of Women's Clubs, "History and Mission," http://www.gfwc.org/gfwc/History_and_Mission.asp?SnID=1093694035; "Woman's Club 40 Years Old," *New York Times*, January 2, 1909; Mary I. Wood, *The History of the General Federation of Women's Clubs for the First Twenty-Two Years of Its Organization* (New York: History Department, General Federation of Women's Clubs, c. 1912), 47–48; National Council of Jewish Women, "History," http://www.ncjw.org/content_85.cfm?navID=27; National Association of Colored Women's Clubs, "Our History," http://www.nacwc.org/aboutus/index.html.

5. Cott, *No Small Courage*, 377, 384–85; Anne Kessler-Harris, *Out to Work: The History of Wage-Earning Women in the United States* (Oxford: Oxford University Press, 1983), 149.

6. "The Feeding of New York's Down Town Women Workers—A New Social Phenomenon," *New York Times*, October 15, 1905.

7. Dana L. Thomas, *The Plungers and the Peacocks: 150 Years of Wall Street* (New York: G.P. Putnam's Sons, 1967), 97.

8. Joshua S. Goldstein, *War and Gender: How Gender Shapes the War System and Vice Versa* (Cambridge, UK: Cambridge University Press, 2001), 318.

9. Woodrow Wilson, *Request for Declaration of War, Address Delivered at a Joint Session of the Two Houses of Congress, April 2, 1917* (Washington, DC: Government Printing Office, 1917).

10. "President Ignores Suffrage Pickets," *New York Times*, January 11, 1917; "Suffragists Again Attack President," *New York Times*, August 7, 1918; "Arrest 41 Pickets for Suffrage at the White House," *New York Times*, November 11, 1917; Cott, *No Small Courage*, 409–10.

11. Emily Newell Blair, *The Woman's Committee, United States Council of National Defense: An Interpretative Report, April 21, 1917 to February 27, 1919* (Washington, DC: Government Printing Office, 1920), 7, 15.

12. Blair, *The Woman's Committee*, 8, 19–20; Lynn Dumenil, "American Women and the Great War," *OAH Magazine of History*, 17, no. 1 (October 2002): 35–37.

13. "Mobilizing Women for Unity in Work," *New York Times*, May 10, 1917.

14. Blair, *The Woman's Committee*, 18, 56; "Mobilizing Women for Unity in Work"; "Our War Expense Is 30 Billions," *New York Times*, July 10, 1919; Geisst, *Wall Street*, 149–50; The Historical Society of Pennsylvania, "Background Note," in *South Philadelphia Women's Liberty Loan Committee Records (Collection 217)* (Philadelphia: The Historical Society of Pennsylvania, 2004), 1.

15. "Mobilize to Sell Liberty Bonds," *New York Times*, May 20, 1917.

16. "M'Adoo Offers $2,000,000,000 of Liberty Loan," *New York Times*, May 3, 1917.

17. Blair, *The Woman's Committee*, 30; "Partial Payment Plan to Sell Liberty Bonds," *New York Times*, May 19, 1917; Clark, *American Women and the World War*, Ch. IX.

18. "Women to Aid Bond Sale," *New York Times*, September 20, 1917.

19. The Historical Society of Pennsylvania, "Background Note," 2.

20. Blair, *The Woman's Committee*, 31–32.

21. Ibid., 32.

22. Ibid., 21–22.

23. Blair, *The Women's Committee,* 32; "Women Open 'Bank' for Loan Subscribers," *New York Times*, October 9, 1917; The Historical Society of Pennsylvania, "Background Note," 2; U.S. Treasury Department, *Report of National Women's Liberty Loan Committee, Fourth Liberty Loan Campaign*, September 28 to October 19, 1918 (Washington, DC: Government Printing Office, 1918), 5–28.

24. "Women's War Work Chief Forum Topic," *New York Times*, November 17, 1917.

25. Ibid.

26. "Women and the Victory Loan," *New York Times*, April 6, 1919; "Women Open 'Bank' for Loan Subscribers"; Clark, *American Women and the World War*, Ch. IX.

27. "Women Urge More Thrift," *New York Times*, July 16, 1918.

28. The Historical Society of Pennsylvania, "Background Note," 4.

29. Ibid.

30. Rchibald Henderson, *North Carolina Women in the World War* (Chapel Hill, NC: University of North Carolina at Chapel Hill, 2002), 5. Original edition, Raleigh, NC: North Carolina Literary and Historical Association, 1920, http://docsouth.unc.edu/wwi/henderson/henderson.html.

31. Ibid., 6.

32. Trail End State Historic Site, "Domestic Duties," http://www.trailend.org/keep-domestic.htm.

33. WLLC Report, 5.

34. "Women Open 'Bank' for Loan Subscribers," *New York Times*, October 9, 1917.

35. Clark, *American Women and the World War*, Ch. IX; Treasury Report, 67; "Women Urge More Thrift."

36. "Women Prepare for Loan," *New York Times*, July 18, 1918; WLLC Report, 4; The Historical Society of Pennsylvania, "Background Note"; WLLC Report, 2.

37. "Liberty Bond Medals to Girls," *New York Times*, June 23, 1918.

38. "Oct. 5 to Be Women's Day"; Treasury Report, 67.

39. "Wilson Backs Amendment for Woman Suffrage," *New York Times*, January 10, 1918; Cott, *No Small Courage*, 410.

40. *Address of the President of the United States, Sept. 30, 1918* (Washington, DC: U.S. Government Printing Office, 1918).

41. "Oct. 5 to Be Women's Day."

42. Treasury Report, 67.

43. Blair, *The Woman's Committee*, 36.

44. Kessler-Harris, *Out to Work*, 219, 224; "War Calls Many Men from Banks," *New York Times*, August 7, 1917.

45. The Historical Society of Pennsylvania, "Background Note," 4.

46. "More Women in Banks," *New York Times*, August 14, 1918; "How Draft Hits Big Banks," *New York Times*, September 1, 1918; "War Calls Many Men from Banks."

47. Treasury Report, 802–03.

48. Treasury Report, 802; "Wall St. Women Organize," *New York Times*, September 19, 1918; "Business Women's War Service," *New York Times*, September 10, 1918.

49. "How Draft Hits Big Banks."

50. "More Women in Banks"; "War Calls Many Men from Banks."

51. "Fit Women for War Work," *New York Times*, July 1, 1917.

52. Kessler-Harris, *Out to Work*, 219.

53. Rochester Institute of Technology, "About Kate Gleason (1865–1933)," http://www.rit.edu/kgcoe/about/aboutkategleason.htm.

CHAPTER SEVEN: WOMEN BANKERS

1. Anne Seward, "Woman's Place in Banking Not a New Social 'Peril' as Hinted in English Novel," *New York Times*, October 15, 1922.

2. Genieve N. Gildersleeve, *Women in Banking: A History of the National Association of Bank Women* (Washington, DC: Public Affairs Press, 1959), 1.

3. Ibid.

4. Ibid.

5. "Woman Gets Bank Office." *New York Times*, July 18, 1919; Gildersleeve, *Women in Banking*, 1–2.

6. Nancy Marie Robertson, " 'The Principles of Sound Banking and Financial Noblesse Oblige': Women's Departments in U.S. Banks at the Turn of the

Twentieth Century," in *Women and Their Money 1700–1950*, eds. Anne Laurence, Josephine Maltby, and Janette Rutterford (London/New York: Routledge, 2009), 243–44.

7. Robertson, "Principles of Sound Banking," 243–44; "A Bank for Women All to Themselves," *New York Times*, September 23, 1906; "Has a 'Stocking' Room," *The Telegraph*, August 28, 1903; "The 'Stocking Room'," *Meriden Morning Record*, September 28, 1903; "Women as Customers," Wells Fargo Bank, http://www.wellsfargomedia.com/wmfh/womenAsCustomers.html (accessed January 27, 2012).

8. "Women's Bank Accounts," *New York Times*, October 7, 1894.

9. "A Bank for Women All to Themselves."

10. Ibid.

11. Robertson, "Women's Departments," 243–44.

12. "Women as Bank Depositors," *New York Times*, December 5, 1897.

13. Ibid.

14. Robertson, "Women's Departments," 243–44.

15. "Women as Bank Depositors."

16. H. G. Robison, "Women Learn How to Invest on Big Scale," *New York Times*, July 25, 1926.

17. Helen Bullitt Lowry, "Only a Woman to Wall Street," *New York Times*, December 4, 1921; Eunice Fuller Barnard, "Women in Wall Street Wielding a New Power," *New York Times*, June 23, 1929.

18. Eunice Fuller Barnard, "Ladies of the Ticker," *The North American Review*, 227, no. 4 (April 1929): 406.

19. "Bankers Addressed by Woman Banker," *New York Times*, September 19, 1918.

20. Ibid.

21. Elizabeth Ellsworth Cook, "Opportunities for Women in Finance," *Journal of the Association of Collegiate Alumnae*, XI, no. 5 (January 1918): 294.

22. Robertson, "Women's Departments," 244.

23. Texas Bankers Association, "Proceedings of Women's Convention," *Texas Bankers Record*, 6 (June 1917): 73.

24. "Women Establish a Bank," *New York Times*, September 5, 1920; "First Woman's Bank," *New York Times*, September 12, 1920; Margaret D. Binnicker, "First Woman's Bank," *The Tennessee Encyclopedia of History and Culture*, Version 2.0, http://tennesseeencyclopedia.net/entry.php?rec=465 last updated January 1, 2010; accessed December 23, 2011).

25. Gildersleeve, *Women in Banking*, 1–2; "Woman Gets Bank Office."

26. Key Cammack, "High Finance," appearing in *Cosmopolitan*, Volume L, December 1910–May 1911 (New York: International Magazine Company, 1911).

27. *Bankers Magazine*, "Another Woman Bank Officer," Vol. C, January–June 1920, 258; "Bard of the Budget Is Abroad in the Land." *New York Times*, July 1, 1923; Gildersleeve, *Women in Banking*, 2.

28. "Mrs. Laimbeer Penniless," *New York Times*, May 5, 1914; "Mrs. N.S. Laimbeer, Noted Banker, Dies," *New York Times*, October 26, 1929; "Woman Wins Place as Bank Executive," *New York Times*, February 13, 1925; Gildersleeve, *Women in Banking*, 11–12.

29. Gildersleeve, *Women in Banking*, 9–10.

30. Ibid., 7–8.

31. Gildersleeve, *Women in Banking*, 2; "Bank Has Woman Officer," *New York Times*, May 1, 1920; "Clara F. Porter, Ex-Bank Officer," *New York Times*, June 27, 1956.

32. Gildersleeve, *Women in Banking*, 2.

33. Ibid.

34. Ibid., 2–3.

35. Ibid., 3–4.

36. Ibid., 4.

37. Ibid., 14–15.

38. Ibid.

39. Robertson, "Women's Departments," 247, 251.

40. Gildersleeve, *Women in Banking*, 17–23, 43.

41. Robertson, "Women's Departments," 244; Gildersleeve, *Women in Banking*, 42–43.

42. Robertson, "Women's Departments," 244.

43. Seward, "Woman's Place in Banking Not a New Social 'Peril' as Hinted in English Novel."

44. Ibid.

45. "Women Bankers Here as Delegates," *New York Times*, October 3, 1922.

46. Robertson, "Women's Departments," 246.

47. "Mrs. N.S. Laimbeer, Noted Banker, Dies."

48. Barnard, "Women in Wall Street Wielding a New Power."

49. Robertson, "Women's Departments," 247; Gildersleeve, *Women in Banking*, 45.

50. Geisst, *Wall Street*, 197.

51. Gildersleeve, *Women in Banking*, 48, 110.

52. Ibid., 47.

53. Eva v. B. Hansl, "Leaders Discuss Women in Finance," *New York Times*, March 15, 1936.

54. "Women Investors of Nation Organize," *New York Times*, May 14, 1935.

55. Bernard A. Cook, ed., *Women and War: A Historical Encyclopedia from Antiquity to the Present*, Volume 1 (Santa Barbara, CA: ABC-CLIO, 2006), 138.

56. Hansl, "Leaders Discuss Women in Finance."

57. Ibid.

58. Gildersleeve, *Women in Banking*, 49.

59. Ibid., 52–53.

60. Ibid., 53.

61. Ibid., 46–55.

62. Ibid., 110.

63. Kathleen McLaughlin, "Women's Progress as Bankers Symbolized by Brilliant Career of Mary Vail Andress," *New York Times*, February 5, 1939; Gildersleeve, *Women in Banking*, 110.

64. Gildersleeve, *Women in Banking*, 3.

65. Ibid., 110.

CHAPTER EIGHT: ROSIE THE WALL STREETER

1. Lucy Greenbaum, "Wall Street: Man's World," *New York Times*, May 13, 1945.

2. "Din Like Dodger Ball Game Sounds as Girl Takes Up Job on Exchange," *New York Times*, April 29, 1943.

3. "Exchange Tradition to Go as Woman Gets Floor Job." *New York Times*, April 28, 1943.

4. "Flurry in the Stock Exchange," *Time*, May 10, 1943; "Exchange Tradition to Go"; "Din Like Dodger Ball Game."

5. "Helen 2d at Exchange," *New York Times*, June 2, 1943.

6. "Din Like Dodger Ball Game."

7. "Helen 2d at Exchange."

8. "Stock Exchange to Make 36 Young Women 'Quote Girls' and 'Carrier Pages' on Floor," *New York Times*, July 11, 1943; "More Girls on Job at Stock Exchange," *New York Times*, July 13, 1943.

9. "Topics of Interest in Wall Street," *New York Times*, August 6, 1943.

10. Ibid.

11. "Women Seek a Seat on Stock Exchange; Would Upset Male-Membership Tradition," *New York Times*, January 14, 1927; Muriel Siebert with Aimee Lee Ball, *Changing the Rules: Adventures of a Wall Street Maverick* (New York: The Free Press, 2002), 36.

12. "Topics of Interest in Wall Street."

13. Charles A. Selden, "Changing Wall Street: A Vivid Decade," *New York Times*, April 15, 1928; John Brooks, *Once in Golconda: A True Drama of Wall Street 1920–1938* (New York: Harper & Row, 1969), 5.

14. Tracy L. Lucht, "Sylvia Porter: Gender, Ambition, and Personal Finance Journalism, 1935–1975" (PhD diss., University of Maryland, 2007), 67.

15. " 'Mrs. E' Has Set a Bond Record," *New York Times*, April 17, 1927.

16. "30 Billions in Bonds Handled by Woman"; " 'Mrs. E' Has Set a Bond Record."

17. " 'Mrs. E' Has Set a Bond Record."

18. Ibid.

19. Barnard, "Women in Wall Street Wielding a New Power."

20. Gildersleeve, *Women in Banking*, 110; Barnard, "Women in Wall Street Wielding a New Power."

21. Barnard, "Women in Wall Street Wielding a New Power."

22. Maury Klein, *Rainbow's End: The Crash of 1929* (Oxford: Oxford University Press, 2003), 148.

23. Barnard, "Women in Wall Street Wielding a New Power."

24. Ibid.

25. Ibid.

26. Lucht, "Sylvia Porter," 58.

27. Ibid., 66–70.

28. Ibid., 69.

29. Ibid., 66.

30. Pat Ellebracht, "Riding the Rails with Madam Railroad," *Financial History*, no. 67 (1999): III, 23.

31. *Bryn Mawr Alumnae Bulletin*, "A Career in Motion," http://www.brynmawr.edu/alumnae/bulletin/benham.htm (accessed January 4, 2012).

32. Ibid.

33. Elizabeth M. Fowler, "Personality: Rail Analyst Started as Clerk," *New York Times*, August 2, 1964.

34. Grace Hendrick Eustis, "Women Investors Ferret Out Facts," *New York Times*, November 1, 1936; Hansl, "Leaders Discuss Women in Finance."

35. McLaughlin, "Women's Progress as Bankers Symbolized by Brilliant Career of Mary Vail Andress."

36. Nona Baldwins, "Women's War Work May Enlist 6,000,000," *New York Times*, March 5, 1942.

37. "6,500,000 Women Took Jobs Since War Began," *New York Times*, September 25, 1944.

38. Lucht, "Sylvia Porter," 72–74.

39. U.S. Treasury Department, *Women's Work in War Finance 1941–1945* (Washington, DC: Government Printing Office, 1946), 1–2.

40. "Women over Country Spur War Bond Drive," *New York Times*, August 7, 1943.

41. Beatrice Meyers, "Out to Sell the Bonds," *New York Times*, September 5, 1943.

42. "Women over Country Spur War Bond Drive."

43. Ibid.

44. Lucht, "Sylvia Porter," 86.

45. Ibid., 78–84, 90.

46. Ibid., 59–60.

47. Gildersleeve, *Women in Banking*, 56–58.

48. "Unparalleled Chances Are Seen for Women in the Fields of Finance and Banking," *New York Times*, September 27, 1942.

49. Gildersleeve, *Women in Banking*, 58–59.

50. Ibid., 61.

51. Ibid.

52. Ibid., 65.

53. Ibid., 61–62.

54. Gildersleeve, *Women in Banking*, 110; "Unparalleled Chances."

55. Lucht, "Sylvia Porter," 1.

56. Ibid.

57. Greenbaum, "Wall Street: Man's World."

PART IV: MAVERICKS

1. Riley, *Inventing the American Woman*, 467–68; Cott, *No Small Courage*, 534.

2. Riley, *Inventing the American Woman*, 473; Cott, *No Small Courage*, 501–05.

3. Riley, *Inventing the American Woman*, 478–80; Cott, *No Small Courage*, 491.

4. Riley, *Inventing the American Woman*, 479–81; Cott, *No Small Courage*, 496–98, 503, 519; Melissa S. Fisher, *Wall Street Women* (Durham/London: Duke University Press, 2012), 51–52.

5. Riley, *Inventing the American Woman*, 500–03, 518; Cott, *No Small Courage*, 531, 545.

6. Riley, *Inventing the American Woman*, 519–24, 537; Cott, *No Small Courage*, 565; Ms. Magazine, "HerStory: 1971—Present," http://www.msmagazine.com/about.asp.

7. Riley, *Inventing the American Woman*, 537–38; Cott, *No Small Courage*, 513.

8. Gordon, *Great Game*, 258.

9. Gordon, *Great Game*, 251–58; Geisst, *Wall Street*, 281.

10. Gordon, *Great Game*, 251–58.

11. Gordon, *Great Game*, 259–60; Geisst, *Wall Street*, 274.

12. Gordon, *Great Game*, 258–60; Geisst, *Wall Street*, 280, 290.

13. Gordon, *Great Game*, 260–63; Geisst, *Wall Street*, 282, 296; John Brooks, *The Go-Go Years* (New York: Weybright and Talley, 1973), 97.

14. Gordon, *Great Game*, 264–69; Geisst, *Wall Street*, 283, 296.

15. Gordon, *Great Game*, 269–72; Geisst, *Wall Street*, 296–97.

16. Gordon, *Great Game*, 272–74; Geisst, *Wall Street*, 304, 315.

17. Gordon, *Great Game*, 277–78; Geisst, *Wall Street*, 305–06.

18. Gordon, *Great Game*, 277–80; Geisst, *Wall Street*, 308.

19. Robert A. Bennett, "No Longer a Wasp Preserve," *New York Times*, June 29, 1986; Geisst, *Wall Street*, 306; Gordon, *Great Game*, 267; Brooks, *Go-Go Years*, 114–18.

20. Christine Gillis, "Memoir of the Women's Stockbrokers' Association," *New York Stock Exchange Archives*, Manuscript Collections, 2000.

21. "Amply Gifted Female Attracts Mob of 6,000 Outside of Big Board," *Wall Street Journal,* September 20, 1968; "Girl on Wall St. Turns Bull and Bear into Wolf," *New York Times*, September 20, 1968.

22. Marilyn Bender, "Women's Lib Bearish in Wall St.," *New York Times*, October 11, 1970.

CHAPTER NINE: MARY ROEBLING

1. Jon Blackwell, "She Banked on Trenton," *The Capital Century 1900–1999* (reprinted from *The Trentonian*), http://www.capitalcentury.com/1937.html.

2. "Symbol of Enterprise," *New York Times*, May 22, 1963; Blackwell, "She Banked on Trenton."

3. Blackwell, "She Banked on Trenton."

4. Faulk, "Gender and Power," 4–5, 29, 34–35; Blackwell, "She Banked on Trenton"; Susan Ware and Stacy Braukman, eds., *Notable American Women: A Biographical Dictionary Completing the Twentieth Century* (Cambridge, MA: Harvard University Press, 2004), 550; Joan N. Burstyn, ed., *Past and Promise: Lives of New Jersey Women* (Syracuse, NY: First Syracuse University Press, 1997), 386.

5. Faulk, "Gender and Power," 20–21, 80; Burstyn, *Past and Promise*, 385.

6. Faulk, "Gender and Power," 24–26; Ware and Braukman, *Notable American Women*, 550; Carmen Godwin and Fernanda Perrone, "Woman in a Man's World: The Career of Mary G. Roebling," *The Rutgers Scholar*, 1999, http://rutgersscholar.rutgers.edu/volume01/perrgodw/perrgodw.htm; "Symbol of Enterprise"; Blackwell, "She Banked on Trenton."

7. Faulk, "Gender and Power," 16, 29, 209–10.

8. Ibid., 31, 33.

9. Faulk, "Gender and Power," 33–35; "Symbol of Enterprise."

10. Blackwell, "She Banked on Trenton."

11. "Personnel," *Time*, February 15, 1937.

12. Ibid.

13. Blackwell, "She Banked on Trenton"; Faulk, "Gender and Power," 118.

14. Blackwell, "She Banked on Trenton."

15. Ibid.

16. "Symbol of Enterprise."

17. Godwin and Perrone, "Woman in a Man's World"; Faulk, "Gender and Power," 2–3, 46–52.

18. Blackwell, "She Banked on Trenton."

19. Ware and Braukman, *Notable American Women*, 550.

20. Blackwell, "She Banked on Trenton"; Faulk, "Gender and Power," 116–17; Godwin and Perrone, "Woman in a Man's World."

21. "Women's Talents in Industry Hailed," *New York Times*, June 22, 1938.

22. Ibid.

23. Ibid.

24. Gildersleeve, *Women in Banking*, 73.

25. Ibid., 72–74, 110.

26. "Woman Carves Place for Self in Banking as Head of $70,000,000 Trenton Trust," *New York Times*, September 7, 1952; Blackwell, "She Banked on Trenton"; Faulk, "Gender and Power," 63.

27. "Woman Carves Place for Self"; "Banker in High Heels," *Greater Philadelphia Magazine*, July 1952.

28. "Symbol of Enterprise"; Faulk, "Gender and Power," 114.

29. Ware and Braukman, *Notable American Women*, 550.

30. Faulk, "Gender and Power," 69; Jon Blackwell, "The Governor Was a Thief," The Capital Century 1900–1999 (reprinted from *The Trentonian*) http://www.capitalcentury.com/1954; "Joker's Heritage," *Time*, June 28, 1954.

31. Faulk, "Gender and Power," 65; "Banker in High Heels."

32. "Woman Carves Place for Self."

33. Ibid.

34. Ibid.

35. Lillian Ruiz and Rupali Arora, "100 Years of Power: Mary Gindhart Roeblin (1905–1944)," *Fortune*, 2007, http://money.cnn.com/galleries/2007/fortune/0709/gallery.MPW_100_years.fortune/5.html.

36. Faulk, "Gender and Power," 47, 71, 95, 207; Craig Claiborne, "Plan in Advance Is Wise Counsel of Busy Hostess," *New York Times*, July 16, 1958; Godwin and Perrone, "Woman in a Man's World"; George Cable Wright, "Woman Banker Builds a Luxurious Home," *New York Times*, July 6, 1959; "Symbol of Enterprise"; Blackwell, "She Banked on Trenton."

37. Faulk, "Gender and Power," 4.

38. "Business Women," *The New York Times*, April 23, 1953.

39. Ibid.

40. Faulk, "Gender and Power," v.

41. Claiborne, "Plan in Advance."

42. "American Board Opens Ranks," *New York Times*, October 29, 1958.

43. Ibid.

44. Ibid.

45. Ibid.

46. Godwin and Perrone, "Woman in a Man's World."

47. Robert E. Bedingfield, "American Board Studying Report," *New York Times*, January 9, 1962.

48. Bedingfield, "American Board Studying Report"; "American Exchange Nominates Posner to Be Its Chairman," *New York Times*, January 9, 1962.

49. Faulk, "Gender and Power," 74.

50. Godwin and Perrone, "Woman in a Man's World"; Faulk, "Gender and Power," 182–83.

51. Godwin and Perrone, "Woman in a Man's World."

52. "Distaff Banker Sees Automation Ending Most Jobs for Women," *New York Times*, October 16, 1964.

53. Ibid.

54. Ware and Braukman, *Notable American Women*, 551; Faulk, "Gender and Power," 188–90.

55. Blackwell, "She Banked on Trenton."

56. Faulk, "Gender and Power," 136.

57. "Women Move Toward Credit Equality," *Time*, October 27, 1975; Faulk, "Gender and Power," 140.

58. Jeanne Varnell, *Women of Consequence: The Colorado Women's Hall of Fame* (Boulder, CO: Johnson Books, 1999), 232; Faulk, "Gender and Power," 136–37, 169.

59. Eric Pace, "Mary Roebling," 89, First Woman to Head Major U.S. Bank, Dies," *New York Times*, October 27, 1994.

60. Faulk, "Gender and Power," 147.

61. Ibid., 141.

62. Faulk, "Gender and Power," 143–69, 202–04; N.R. Kleinfield, "A Bank of His Own," *New York Times*, February 8, 1987; Ware and Braukman, *Notable American Women*, 550; Godwin and Perrone, "Woman in a Man's World"; Varnell, *Women of Consequence*, 232–33.

63. Ware and Braukman, *Notable American Women*, 551; Faulk, "Gender and Power," 182.

64. Faulk, "Gender and Power," 107, 182–87, 204, 214; Godwin and Perrone, "Woman in a Man's World"; Ware and Braukman, *Notable American Women*, 550–51.

65. Pace, "Mary Roebling"; Faulk, "Gender and Power," 199.

66. Blackwell, "She Banked on Trenton."

67. Faulk, "Gender and Power," 184.

68. Pace, "Mary Roebling."

69. Faulk, "Gender and Power," 36.

70. Ibid., 46, 65–67, 81.

71. Blackwell, "She Banked on Trenton."

72. Faulk, "Gender and Power," 2, 11, 207.

73. Ibid., 212.

CHAPTER TEN: JULIA MONTGOMERY WALSH

1. Vartanig G. Vartan, "Wall Street Can Be a Girl's Best Friend," *New York Times*, March 27, 1972.

2. Julia Montgomery Walsh with Anne Conover Carson, *Risks and Rewards: A Memoir* (McLean, VA: EPM Publications, Inc., 1996), 77.

3. Chantal Mompoullan, *Voice of America Interviews with Eight Women of Achievement* (Washington, DC: United States Information Agency, 1985), 51.

4. Ibid., 50.

5. Walsh with Carson, *Risks and Rewards*, 15–16.

6. Ibid., 17.

7. Ibid., 18.

8. Ibid., 22.

9. Ibid., 16–23.

10. Ibid., 26.

11. Ibid.

12. Ibid., 30.

13. Ibid., 39.

14. Mompoullan, *Voice of America Interviews*, 51, 56.

15. Walsh with Carson, *Risks and Rewards*, 49.

16. Ibid.

17. Ibid., 64.

18. Ibid., 64–68, 77.

19. Ibid., 78.

20. Ibid.

21. Ibid.

22. Ibid., 78–79.

23. Ibid., 79–80.

24. Ibid., 80–81.

25. Ibid., 81–82.

26. Ibid., 85.

27. Ibid.

28. Ibid., 87.

29. Walsh with Carson, *Risks and Rewards*, 86–88; Vartan, "Wall Street Can Be a Girl's Best Friend."

30. Walsh with Carson, *Risks and Rewards*, 89.

31. Ibid., 90.

32. Walsh with Carson, *Risks and Rewards*, 94; Mompoullan, *Voice of America Interviews*, 51–52.

33. Walsh with Carson, *Risks and Rewards*, 96.

34. Ibid., 97.

35. Ibid., 98.

36. Ibid., 99.

37. Ibid.

38. Ibid., 103–06.

39. Ibid., 115.

40. Sylvia Porter, "Major Exchange Due to Admit Women," *St. Petersburg Times*, November 11, 1965.

41. "Caution: Women at Work," *Time*, May 24, 1968.

42. Marilyn Bender, "Business Discovers Women," *New York Times*, January 9, 1972; Sean Madigan, "A Long Journey: Julia Montgomery Walsh," *Washington Business Journal*, February 1, 2002; Walsh with Carson, *Risks and Rewards*, 130.

43. Walsh with Carson, *Risks and Rewards*, 122; Mompoullan, *Voice of America Interviews*, 52.

44. Walsh with Carson, *Risks and Rewards*, 123; Alexander B. Hammer, "Amex Nominates Woman as a Member of Its Board," *New York Times*, February 17, 1972.

45. Walsh with Carson, *Risks and Rewards*, 123.

46. Ibid., 134–35.

47. Ibid., 6.

48. Ibid., 150.

49. Ibid., 133.

50. Mompoullan, *Voice of America Interviews*, 53.

51. Walsh with Carson, *Risks and Rewards*, 123.

52. Ibid., 140.

53. Ibid.

54. Ibid., 143.

55. Ibid., 144.

56. Ibid., 145–49.

57. "A Good Woman Is Easier to Find," *Time*, March 19, 1979; Walsh with Carson, *Risks and Rewards*, 149–50, 154–55.

58. Walsh with Carson, *Risks and Rewards*, 160–61.

59. Pamela B. Hollie, "Julia Walsh to Sell Firm to Tucker, Anthony," *New York Times*, July 8, 1983; Madigan, "A Long Journey"; Walsh with Carson, *Risks and Rewards*, 163.

60. Walsh with Carson, *Risks and Rewards*, 171.

61. Walsh with Carson, *Risks and Rewards*, 164–65, 171, 181; Madigan, "A Long Journey."

62. Walsh with Carson, *Risks and Rewards*, 150.

63. Bender, "Business Discovers Women."

64. Ibid.

65. Walsh with Carson, *Risks and Rewards*, 10.

66. Vartan, "Wall Street Can Be a Girl's Best Friend."

67. Walsh with Carson, *Risks and Rewards*, 187.

68. Ibid., 185.

69. Ibid., 188.

70. Ibid., 185–88.

71. Walsh with Carson, *Risks and Rewards*, 85, 90–97.

72. Mompoullan, *Voice of America Interviews*, 55.

73. Walsh with Carson, *Risks and Rewards*, 185.

74. Ibid., 163.

CHAPTER ELEVEN: MURIEL SIEBERT

1. Siebert with Ball, *Changing the Rules*, 28–29.

2. Siebert with Ball, *Changing the Rules*, 1–2, 25–28; Lynn Gilbert and Gaylen Moore, *Particular Passions: Talks with Women Who Have Shaped Our Lives* (New York: Clarkson N. Potter, 1981), 234–35.

3. Siebert with Ball, *Changing the Rules*, 5–6; Gilbert and Moore, *Particular Passions*, 235.

4. Siebert with Ball, *Changing the Rules*, 7–8; Muriel Siebert, "Investing in Women and Girls" (address, United Nations, New York City, March 6, 2008).

5. Siebert with Ball, *Changing the Rules*, 7–9; Siebert, "Investing in Women and Girls"; Sue Herera, *Women of the Street: Making It on Wall Street—The World's Toughest Business* (New York: John Wiley & Sons, 1997), 86.

6. Siebert with Ball, *Changing the Rules*, 8–10; Herera, *Women of the Street*, 87.

7. Siebert with Ball, *Changing the Rules*, 10–11; Siebert, "Investing in Women and Girls"; Susan Chira, "Ginsburg's Spirit Is Echoed by Other Pioneers," *New York Times*, August 2, 1993; *BusinessWeek*, "Q&A with Wall Street Veteran Muriel Siebert," July 16, 2001; Herera, *Women of the Street*, 92–93.

8. Siebert with Ball, *Changing the Rules*, 12–16; Herera, *Women of the Street*, 87.

9. Siebert with Ball, *Changing the Rules*, 24.

10. Siebert with Ball, *Changing the Rules*, 17–26; Herera, *Women of the Street*, 87; Gilbert and Moore, *Particular Passions*, 26–27; Gordon, *Great Game*, 257–59.

11. Siebert with Ball, *Changing the Rules*, 28.

12. Bender, "Women's Lib Bearish in Wall Street"; Gordon, *Great Game*, 267; Geisst, *Wall Street*, 306; Bennett, "No Longer a Wasp Preserve."

13. Siebert with Ball, *Changing the Rules*, 28; Herera, *Women of the Street*, 87; Siebert, "Investing in Women and Girls."

14. Siebert with Ball, *Changing the Rules*, 29; Herera, *Women of the Street*, 91.

15. Siebert with Ball, *Changing the Rules*, 29.

16. Ibid.

17. Siebert, *Changing the Rules*, 36; "Woman Seeks a Seat on Stock Exchange," *New York Times*, January 14, 1927.

18. Joan Hanauer, "Distaff Broker Calmly Copes with Wizards of Wall Street," *St. Petersburg Times*, February 27, 1955.

19. "Robert J. O'Brien, Sr. Inducted into Futures Hall of Fame," R.J. O'Brien and Associates, Inc. News Release, Chicago, IL, May 2, 2007.

20. Siebert with Ball, *Changing the Rules*, 31; "First New York Exchange Seat for Woman Sought by Analyst," *New York Times*, December 9, 1967.

21. Siebert with Ball, *Changing the Rules*, 31.

22. Ibid.

23. Ibid., 32–34.

24. Gilbert and Moore, *Particular Passions*, 234.

25. Siebert with Ball, *Changing the Rules*, 34–35; Siebert, "Investing in Women and Girls."

26. Vartanig G. Vartan, "Miss Siebert's Memorable Day," *New York Times*, January 1, 1968; Siebert, *Changing the Rules*, 37.

27. Siebert with Ball, *Changing the Rules*, 37.

28. Siebert with Ball, *Changing the Rules*, 36, 52; Siebert, "Investing in Women and Girls"; "Big Board Accepts Woman as Member," *New York Times*, December 29, 1967; Anne B. Fisher, *Wall Street Women: Women in Power on Wall Street Today* (New York: Knopf, 1990), 8.

29. Siebert with Ball, *Changing the Rules*, 38; Vartan, "Miss Siebert's Memorable Day."

30. Siebert with Ball, *Changing the Rules*, 38.

31. Ibid., 40–41.

32. Siebert with Ball, *Changing the Rules*, 38–40; Susan Antilla, "Muriel Siebert's Declaration of War," *New York Times*, November 6, 1994; Gilbert and Moore, *Particular Passions*, 234; Siebert, "Investing in Women and Girls."

33. Manuel F. Cohen, "Address of Chairman" (speech, Securities and Exchange Commission, Women's Bond Club of New York, NY, December 13, 1968).

34. Siebert with Ball, *Changing the Rules*, 41–42; Fisher, *Wall Street Women*, 8.

35. Siebert with Ball, *Changing the Rules*, 76.

36. Terry Robards, "Women's Strike: Big Board View," *New York Times*, August 27, 1970.

37. Gilbert and Moore, *Particular Passions*, 234.

38. Siebert with Ball, *Changing the Rules*, 43–45.

39. Siebert with Ball, *Changing the Rules*, 62–64; Gordon, *Great Game*, 276–78; Geisst, *Wall Street*, 305–06.

40. Gilbert and Moore, *Particular Passions*, 236.

41. Siebert with Ball, *Changing the Rules*, 67.

42. Ibid., 73.

43. Siebert with Ball, *Changing the Rules*, 74–75, 111, 117–18, 127; Robert A. Bennett, "Muriel Siebert: Bank 'Pioneer,'" *New York Times*, June 10, 1982; Herera, *Women of the Street*, 93, Siebert, "Investing in Women and Girls"; "New York State's Banking Overseer," *New York Times*, January 8, 1978.

44. Siebert with Ball, *Changing the Rules*, 133.

45. Ibid., 145.

46. Ibid., 144–58.

47. Ibid., 163.

48. Ibid., 162–65.

49. Ibid., 192.

50. Bloomberg Business News, "Siebert Goes Public by an Unusual Route," *New York Times*, February 3, 1996; Edward Wyatt, "Wall St.'s Top Woman Slips in the Back Door," *New York Times*, February 11, 1996; Siebert, *Changing the Rules*, 186–87, 196–97; Siebert Financial Corp., December 31, 2011, 10-K Annual Report, 3.

51. Julie Flaherty, "Finding a Woman's Place on the Web and in the Market," *New York Times*, October 22, 2000.

52. Ibid.

53. Siebert Financial Corp., Dec. 31, 2011 Form 10-K, 16.

54. Bennett, "Muriel Siebert."

55. Siebert with Ball, *Changing the Rules*, 212.

56. Ibid., 210.

57. Diana B. Henriques, "Ms. Siebert Still on the Barricades," *New York Times*, July 5, 1992; William J. Holstein, "An Insider's Advice on Corporate Ethics," *New York Times*, November 24, 2002.

58. Gilbert and Moore, *Particular Passions*, 235.

59. Ibid., 237.

60. "Muriel Siebert-First Woman of Finance," Muriel Siebert & Co., Inc., https://www.siebertnet.com/index.aspx.

61. Robin Finn, "In She Rushed, Where Men Feared She'd Tread," *New York Times*, November 8, 2002.

PART V: ICONS

1. Cott, *No Small Courage*, 562.

2. Cott, *No Small Courage*, 576; Riley, *Inventing the American Woman*, 549, 561, 571.

3. Riley, *Inventing the American Woman*, 525–61; Cott, *No Small Courage*, 563, 584.

4. Riley, *Inventing the American Woman*, 538–60; Cott, *No Small Courage*, 577–79.

5. U.S. Equal Employment Commission, Notice N-915–050, March 19, 1990, http://www.eeoc.gov/policy/docs/currentissues.html (last modified June 21, 1999).

6. Riley, *Inventing the American Woman*, 553.

7. Bender, "Business Discovers Women."

8. Ibid.

9. Gordon, *Great Game*, 279–80; Geisst, *Wall Street*, 308.

10. Gordon, *Great Game*, 280–83; Geisst, *Wall Street*, 325.

11. Geisst, *Wall Street*, 318–20, 325; Gordon, *Great Game*, 287.

12. Geisst, *Wall Street*, 325–42; Gordon, *Great Game*, 287.

13. Geisst, *Wall Street*, 349.

14. Gordon, *Great Game*, 288–90; Geisst, *Wall Street*, 350; "New York Stock Exchange Ends Member Seat Sales Today," New York Stock Exchange Press Release, New York, December 30, 2005.

15. Geisst, *Wall Street*, 328.

16. Gordon, *Great Game*, 288; Geisst, *Wall Street*, 339–41.

17. Geisst, *Wall Street*, 328–60; Gordon, *Great Game*, 290–93; see James B. Stewart, *Den of Thieves* (New York: Simon & Schuster, 1991).

18. Geisst, *Wall Street*, 345–48, 361–67; Gordon, *Great Game*, 293.

19. Geisst, *Wall Street*, 367.

20. Peter Truell, "The Wall Street Soothsayer Who Never Blinked," *New York Times*, July 27, 1997; Gordon, *Great Game*, 294–95; Geisst, *Wall Street*, 367.

21. Gordon, *Great Game*, 286.

22. See Susan Antilla, *Tales from the Boom-Boom Room: Women vs. Wall Street* (Princeton, NJ: Bloomberg Press, 2002).

CHAPTER TWELVE: ELAINE GARZARELLI

1. Fisher, *Wall Street Women*, 41.

2. Greg Anrig, Jr., "The Newest Seer Now Predicts a Bear Market Rally (What a Relief!)," *Money*, December 1, 1987.

3. Christopher Knowlton, "Elaine Garzarelli Wall Street Finds a Million Dollar Oracle at Shearson," *Fortune*, January 4, 1988.

4. Susan Antilla, "The Hottest Woman on Wall Street," *Working Woman*, August 1991.

5. Susan Antilla, "Garzarelli Driven to Excel," *USA Today*, April 10, 1991.

6. Fisher, *Wall Street Women*, 112–13; Knowlton, "Elaine Garzarelli"; Herera, *Women of the Street*, 150,160–61; Antilla, "Garzarelli"; Haitham Haddadin, "Guru Garzarelli Back as Market Timer," *Reuters*, February 27, 2003; Haitham Haddadin, "Stock Prophet Finds Fit in Market Timing Garzarelli's Back Crunching Numbers," *Reuters*, 2003.

7. Antilla, "Hottest Woman."

8. Ibid.

9. Knowlton, "Elaine Garzarelli"; Antilla, "Garzarelli"; "Hottest Woman."

10. Antilla, "Garzarelli."

11. Knowlton, "Elaine Garzarelli"; Haddadin, "Guru Garzarelli"; "Stock Prophet"; Fisher, *Wall Street Women*, 113; Antilla, "Garzarelli"; Herera, *Women of the Street*, 151.

12. Fisher, *Wall Street Women*, 40; Knowlton, "Elaine Garzarelli"; Fisher, *Wall Street Women*, 40; Herera, *Women of the Street*, 151; Antilla, "Hottest Woman"; Elaine Garzarelli, e-mail correspondence with author, April 12, 2011.

13. Fisher, *Wall Street Women*, 40.

14. Ibid., 41.

15. Knowlton, "Elaine Garzarelli"; Antilla, "Garzarelli"; Stewart, "Calling the Crash"; Antilla, "Hottest Woman."

16. Knowlton, "Elaine Garzarelli."

17. Fisher, *Wall Street Women*, 94.

18. Garzarelli, e-mail correspondence with author, April 12, 2011.

19. Antilla, "Hottest Woman"; Herera, *Women of the Street*, 160.

20. Antilla, "Hottest Woman."

21. Garzarelli, e-mail correspondence with author, October 5, 2012; Antilla, "Hottest Woman."

22. Fisher, *Wall Street Women*, 41.

23. Wayne Leslie, "What the Bears of Summer Sensed," *New York Times*, November 8, 1987; Stewart, "Calling the Crash."

24. Leslie, "Bears of Summer."

25. Karyn McCormack, "Memories and Lessons of the '87 Crash: Elaine Garzarelli," *BusinessWeek*, October 12, 2007, http://images.businessweek.com/ss/07/10/1012_crash/index_01.html; Herera, *Women of the Street*, 154.

26. Stewart, "Calling the Crash"; Leslie, "Bears of Summer"; Herera, *Women of the Street*, 154; McCormack, "Elaine Garzarelli."

27. Garzarelli, e-mail correspondence with author, April 12, 2011; David Gaffen, "Black Monday Reflections: Garzarelli Looks Back," *Wall Street Journal*, October 19, 2007; Corey Hajim, and Jia Lynn Yang, "Remembering Black Monday: Elaine Garzarelli," *Fortune*, October 2007, http://money.cnn.com/galleries/2007/fortune/0709/gallery.black_monday.fortune/2.html; McCormack, "Elaine Garzarelli"; Herera, *Women of the Street*, 154; Stewart, "Calling the Crash."

28. Gaffen, "Garzarelli Looks Back."

29. Knowlton, "Elaine Garzarelli"; Hajim and Yang, "Elaine Garzarelli."

30. Knowlton, "Elaine Garzarelli."

31. Stewart, "Calling the Crash."

32. Ibid.

33. Ibid.

34. Hajim and Yang, "Elaine Garzarelli."

35. Garzarelli, e-mail correspondence with author, October 5, 2012.

36. Antilla, "Garzarelli"; Knowlton, "Elaine Garzarelli."

37. Antilla, "Hottest Woman."

38. Antilla, "Hottest Woman"; Floyd Norris, "Garzarelli Is Ousted By Lehman," *New York Times*, October 27, 1994.

39. Antilla, "Hottest Woman."

40. Ibid.

41. Andrew Leckey, "For Garzarelli, Wall St. Star System Raises Scrutiny," *Chicago Tribune*, October 9, 1994.

42. Antilla, "Garzarelli"; Norris, "Garzarelli Is Ousted"; Haddadin, "Guru Garzarelli"; Haddadin, "Stock prophet."

43. Norris, "Garzarelli Is Ousted"; Herera, *Women of the Street*, 159; Haddadin, "Guru Garzarelli"; Haddadin, "Stock prophet"; Elizabeth Judd, "What's Sex Got to Do with It?" *IR Magazine*, April 1, 1998; Garzarelli, e-mail correspondence with author, April 12, 2011.

44. Judd, "What's Sex Got to Do with It?"

45. Ibid.

46. Ibid.

47. Ibid.

48. Garzarelli, e-mail correspondence with author, April 12, 2011.

49. Knowlton, "Elaine Garzarelli."

50. Wayne, "Bears of Summer."

CHAPTER THIRTEEN: ABBY JOSEPH COHEN

1. Abby Joseph Cohen, "Women of Wall Street," Museum of American Finance, New York, June 2009–March 2010.

2. Truell, "Wall Street Soothsayer."

3. Anthony Bianco, "The Profit of Wall Street," *BusinessWeek*, June 1, 1998.

4. Bianco, "Profit of Wall Street"; Truell, "Wall Street Soothsayer."

5. Bianco, "Profit of Wall Street."

6. Truell, "Wall Street Soothsayer."

7. Bianco, "Profit of Wall Street"; Ashish Nanda and Kristin Lieb, "Abby Joseph Cohen: A Career Retrospective," HBS No. 9–903–118 (Boston: Harvard Business School Publishing, 2003; revised June 9, 2003), Harvard Business Online, 2, http://harvardbusinessonline.hbsp.harvard.edu/; Truell, "Wall Street Soothsayer."

8. Nanda and Lieb, "Abby Joseph Cohen," 2; Bianco, "Profit of Wall Street"; Truell, "Wall Street Soothsayer."

9. Bianco, "Profit of Wall Street"; Nanda and Lieb, "Abby Joseph Cohen," 2–4; Truell, "Wall Street Soothsayer."

10. Bianco, "Profit of Wall Street."

11. Herera, *Women of the Street*, 61.

12. Nanda and Lieb, "Abby Joseph Cohen," 4.

13. Nanda and Lieb, "Abby Joseph Cohen," 5; Abby Joseph Cohen, interview with author, September 20, 2012.

14. Nanda and Lieb, "Abby Joseph Cohen," 5.

15. Bianco, "Profit of Wall Street"; Truell, "Wall Street Soothsayer."

16. Nanda and Lieb, "Abby Joseph Cohen," 6.

17. Bianco, "Profit of Wall Street."

18. Bianco, "Profit of Wall Street"; Truell, "Wall Street Soothsayer."

19. Comments related to author per Abby Joseph Cohen, October 4, 2012; Bianco, "Profit of Wall Street."

20. Herera, *Women of the Street*, 67.

21. Bianco, "Profit of Wall Street."

22. Nanda and Lieb, "Abby Joseph Cohen," 7.

23. Bianco, "Profit of Wall Street"; Nanda and Lieb, "Abby Joseph Cohen," 7; Herera, *Women of the Street*, 63.

24. Truell, "Wall Street Soothsayer."

25. Ibid.

26. Bianco, "Profit of Wall Street."

27. Ibid.

28. Nanda and Lieb, "Abby Joseph Cohen," 8; Bianco, "Profit of Wall Street"; Truell, "Wall Street Soothsayer."

29. Nanda and Lieb, "Abby Joseph Cohen," 9.

30. Bianco, "Profit of Wall Street"; Truell, "Wall Street Soothsayer."

31. Truell, "Wall Street Soothsayer."

32. Bianco, "Profit of Wall Street."

33. Nanda and Lieb, "Abby Joseph Cohen," 8; Truell, "Wall Street Soothsayer."

34. Bianco, "Profit of Wall Street."

35. Truell, "Wall Street Soothsayer"; Joseph Kahn, "With Stock Issue Ahead, Goldman Sachs Names 57 as Partners," *New York Times*, October 21, 1998; Patricia Sellers and Cora Daniels, "The 50 Most Powerful Women in American Business," *Fortune*, October 12, 1998.

36. Cohen, interview with author.

37. Sellers and Daniels, "50 Most Powerful Women"; Lisa Endlich, *Goldman Sachs: The Culture of Success* (New York: Alfred A. Knopf, 1999), 4, 26; Fisher, *Wall Street Women*, 7–8, 11; Antilla, *Tales from the Boom-Boom Room*, 40; Nanda and Lieb, "Abby Joseph Cohen," 7; "Taking On the Great White Way," *Newsweek*, July 18, 1993; Kenneth N. Gilpin, "A Sex-Bias Case Is Lost by Goldman," *New York Times*, October 29, 1993.

38. Nanda and Lieb, "Abby Joseph Cohen," 10.

39. Kahn, "Goldman Sachs Names 57 as Partners."

40. Nanda and Lieb, "Abby Joseph Cohen," 10.

41. Ibid.

42. Nanda and Lieb, "Abby Joseph Cohen," 10; Alex Berenson, "Wall Street Conquered. And Next, the World," *New York Times*, April 2, 2000.

43. Berenson, "Wall Street Conquered."

44. Nanda and Lieb, "Abby Joseph Cohen," 12–13.

45. Abby Joseph Cohen, interview by Karen Gibbs, *Wall Street Week with Fortune*, PBS, October 4, 2002.

46. Eric Martin and Alexis Xydias, "Goldman's Cohen Sees S&P 500 Rising 14% by 2008's End (Update 6)," Bloomberg LP, December 4, 2007.

47. Nanda and Lieb, "Abby Joseph Cohen," 14.

48. Ibid.

49. Leslie Wayne, "Celebrating Women's Success," *New York Times*, May 23, 1999.

50. Herera, *Women of the Street*, 66–67; Nanda and Lieb, "Abby Joseph Cohen," 10–14; Bianco, "Profit of Wall Street."

51. Nanda and Lieb, "Abby Joseph Cohen," 11.

52. Ibid.

53. "Women of Wall Street", Museum of American Finance; Cohen, interview with author.

54. Bianco, "Profit of Wall Street."

55. Nanda and Lieb, "Abby Joseph Cohen," 15–16.

56. U.S. Treasury, Women in Finance Symposium, March 29, 2010; Stephen Foley, "Would Women Have Averted the Bubble on Wall Street?" *The Independent*, March 30, 2010.

57. Deborah Solomon, "Questions for Abby Joseph Cohen: A Steady Hand," *New York Times Magazine*, January 28, 2011.

58. Ibid.

59. Comments related to author per Abby Joseph Cohen, October 9, 2012.

60. Cohen, interview with author.

CHAPTER FOURTEEN: AMY DOMINI

1. Amy Domini, "Sustainability Investing, Green Investing, Socially Responsible Investing, What's Going on Here?" (Speech, FRA Family Offices Conference, Aventura, FL, May 21, 2008).

2. Amy Domini, "Praxis Award Acceptance," Villanova University, Villanova, PA, March 31, 2009; Marc Gunther, *Faith and Fortune: How Compassionate Capitalism Is Transforming American Business* (New York: Crown Business, 2004), 221.

3. Gunther, *Faith and Fortune*, 221; "Amy Domini: In Good Conscience," *Boston Business Journal*, May 14, 2007.

4. Amy Domini and Alisa Tang, "A Son with a Conscience" (reprinted from *New York Times*, 2009), http://www.amydomini.com/ason (accessed March 13, 2012).

5. Domini, "Praxis Award"; Amy Domini, "Commencement Speech," Northfield Mount Hermon School, Mount Hermon, MA, May 28, 2008.

6. Domini, "Praxis Award."

7. Domini and Tang, "A Son with a Conscience"; "Amy Domini: In Good Conscience"; Domini, "Praxis Award."

8. Domini, "Praxis Award."

9. Amy Domini, interview with author, October 24, 2011.

10. Gunther, *Faith and Fortune*, 222; Domini, "Praxis Award."

11. Gunther, *Faith and Fortune*, 222.

12. Domini, "Praxis Award"; Domini, "Commencement Speech."

13. Amy Domini, *Socially Responsible Investing: Making a Difference and Making Money* (Chicago: Dearborn Trade, 2001), 14–15; Gunther, *Faith and Fortune*, 217.

14. Amy Domini, interview by Tavis Smiley, *Tavis Smiley Show*, PBS, May 24, 2005.

15. Gunther, *Faith and Fortune*, 222.

16. Gunther, *Faith and Fortune*, 42, 218; Peter D. Kinder, Steven D. Lydenberg, and Amy L. Domini, *Investing for Good: Making Money While Being Socially Responsible* (New York: HarperBusiness, 1993), 18, 83; Kirk Kazanjian, *Wizards of Wall Street* (New York: New York Institute of Finance, 2000), 125; "Calvert & SRI: History and Leadership," Calvert Investments, Inc., http://www.calvert.com/sri-history.html.

17. Gunther, *Faith and Fortune*, 218.

18. Robert A. G. Monks, and Nell Minow, *Corporate Governance* (Fourth Edition) (West Sussex, UK: John Wiley & Sons, 2008), 184.

19. Ibid.

20. Richard Marens, "Inventing Corporate Governance: The Mid-Century Emergence of Shareholder Activism," *Journal of Business and Management*, 8, no. 4 (Fall 2002): 365+.

21. Ibid.

22. Ibid.

23. Gary Strauss, " 'Queen of the Corporate Jungle' Stalks Annual Meetings," *USA Today*, April 27, 2003.

24. Amy L. Domini with Peter D. Kinder, *Ethical Investing* (Reading, MA: Addison-Wesley Publishing Company, 1984).

25. Domini, "Praxis Award."

26. Mari Kane, "The Domini Effect," *Buyside*, Winter 2000, http://www.amydomini.com/sites/default/files/buyside.pdf.

27. Domini, "Praxis Award"; "The Domini Story," Domini Social Investments, http://www.domini.com; Domini, interview with author; Domini and Kinder, *Ethical Investing*, xii; Gunther, *Faith and Fortune*, 224.

28. "Milestones," Domini Social Investments, http://www.domini.com (accessed November 18, 2011).

29. Gunther, *Faith and Fortune*, 226.

30. Gunther, *Faith and Fortune*, 226; "Milestones"; Domini, interview with author.

31. "Milestones"; Gunther, *Faith and Fortune*, 232.

32. Kazanjian, *Wizards of Wall Street*, 136; Domini Social Investments LLC, "Domini Social Equity Fund Investor Shares: Fund Fact Sheet Fourth Quarter 2011," http://www.domini.com/sites/default/files/pdf/DSEFX_FFS_4Q11.pdf; Gunther, *Faith and Fortune*, 228–29.

33. Paul Hawken and Amy Domini, "Letter to the Editor and Response," *GreenMoneyJournal.com*, February/March 2003, http://www.organicconsumers. org/organic/hawken032403.cfm ; Gunther, *Faith and Fortune*, 230–31.

34. Kane, "The Domini Effect"; "Milestones."

35. Kane, "The Domini Effect."

36. "Milestones"; Gunther, *Faith and Fortune*, 232–33; Domini, interview with author.

37. "Milestones"; "Amy Domini: In Good Conscience."

38. Domini, *Socially Responsible Investing*, 47; Kinder et al., *Investing for Good*, 192.

39. Domini, *Ethical Investing*, 235–40; Anita Saville, "Investing in Women," http://www.feminist.com/resources/artspeech/work/sri.htm; Kinder et al., *Investing for Good*, 192–94; Alicia Epstein Korten, *Change Philanthropy: Candid Stories of Foundations Maximizing Results through Social Justice* (San Francisco: Jossey-Bass, 2009), 55–56.

40. Sean Silverthorne, "Profits and Prophets: The Role of Values in Investment," Harvard Business School Working Knowledge blog, April 22, 2002, http:// hbswk.hbs.edu/item/2900.html.

41. Domini, interview with author. [In 1976, Merrill Lynch entered into consent decrees in two cases that included directing the firm to increase the number of female executives. See EEOC v. Merrill Lynch, Civ. No. 76–754 (W.D.Pa. June 4, 1976); O'Bannon v. Merrill Lynch, Civ. No. 73–905 (W.D.Pa. June 4, 1976).]

42. Ibid.

43. Ibid.

44. Spencer Stuart, "Women in Asset Management," March 2005, http://content. spencerstuart.com/sswebsite/pdf/lib/Women_in_Asset_Mgmt_Mar05.pdf, 5.

45. Ibid., 9.

46. Domini and Kinder, *Ethical Investing*, dedication.

47. Domini, *Socially Responsible Investing*, iii.

48. "Amy Domini: In Good Conscience."

49. Domini and Tang, "A Son with a Conscience."

50. Ibid.

51. "Investing with Your Values: Making Money, Making a Difference and Managing Abundance," *GreenMoney Journal*, Spring 2012, http://www.green moneyjournal.com/article.mpl?newsletterid=18&articleid=151.

52. Social Investment Forum Foundation, 2010 Report on Socially Responsible Investing Trends in the United States, http://www.socialinvest.org/resources/research/documents/2010TrendsES.pdf.

53. Domini, "Praxis Award."

54. Domini, interview with author.

55. "Amy Domini: In Good Conscience."

56. Domini, interview by Tavis Smiley.

57. "The Starfish Story," Domini Social Investments, http://www.domini.com; Domini, *Socially Responsible Investing*, iv.

58. Domini, "Praxis Award."

CONCLUSION

1. United States Department of Labor, Women's Bureau, "Women in the Labor Force in 2010," http://www.dol.gov/wb/factsheets/Qf-laborforce-10.htm.

2. Liza Mundy, "Women, Money and Power," *Time*, March 26, 2012.

3. U.S. Census Bureau, "Income, Poverty and Health Insurance Coverage in the United States: 2011," September 12, 2012 News Release, http://www.census.gov/newsroom/releases/archives/income_wealth/cb12–172.html; Chrystia Freeland, "Why Are There So Few Female Plutocrats?" *The Daily Beast*, October 16, 2012, http://www.thedailybeast.com/articles/2012/10/16/why-are-there-so-few-female-plutocrats.html.

4. Mundy, "Women, Money and Power."

5. "The Female Financial Paradox," March 19, 2012, dailyworth.com; http://dailyworth.com/posts/1168-The-Female-Financial-Paradox.

6. Patrick McGeehan, "The Women of Wall Street Get Their Day in Court," *New York Times*, July 11, 2004; Louise Marie Roth, *Selling Women Short: Gender and Money on Wall Street* (Princeton: Princeton University Press, 2006), 5.

7. Patrick McGeehan, "Morgan Stanley Settles Bias Suit with $54 Million," *New York Times*, July 13, 2004; Dan Ackman, "Morgan Stanley: Big Bucks for Bias," *Forbes*, July 13, 2004; Roth, *Selling Women Short*, 1–2.

8. McGeehan, "Morgan Stanley Settles Bias Suit."

9. Ibid.

10. Susan Antilla, "Money Talks, Women Don't," *New York Times*, July 21, 2004; Roth, *Selling Women Short*, 2.

11. Antilla, "Money Talks."

12. Anita Raghavan, "Terminated: Why the Women of Wall Street Are Disappearing," *Forbes*, February 25, 2009.

13. Frank Bass, "Shining Shoes Best Way Wall Street Women Outearn Men," Bloomberg LP, March 16, 2012, http://www.bloomberg.com/news/2012–03–16/shining-shoes-best-way-wall-street-women-outearn-men.html.

14. Dawn Kopecki, "Wall Street Says Women Worth Less as Disparity over Pay Widens," Bloomberg LP, October 6, 2010, http://www.bloomberg.com/

news/2010–10–06/wall-street-says-women-worth-less-as-pay-disparity-widens-in-finance-ranks.html.

15. U.S. Government Accountability Office, "Financial Services Industry: Overall Trends in Management-Level Diversity and Diversity Initiatives, 1993–2008," Released May 12, 2010, 3, GAO-10–736T, http://www.gao.gov/new.items/d10736t.pdf.

16. "Women in U.S. Finance," Catalyst, December 2011, http://www.catalyst.org/publication/504/women-in-us-finance.

17. Carol Hymowitz, "Wall Street's Women Problem," *Wall Street Journal*, June 27, 2008.

18. Karey Wutkowski, "If Women Ran Wall Street? Geithner Likes the Idea," *Reuters*, March 29, 2010, http://www.reuters.com/article/2010/03/29/financial-regulation-women-idUSN2922195520100329 (accessed April 5, 2012).

19. Heather Foust-Cummings, Sarah Dinolfo, and Jennifer Kohler, "Sponsoring Women to Success." Catalyst, 2011, http://www.catalyst.org/file/497/sponsoring_women_to_success.pdf.

20. David Leonhardt, "Financial Careers Come at a Cost to Families," *New York Times*, May 26, 2009.

21. Emily Thornton, Mara Der Hovanesian, and Jennifer Merritt, "Fed Up—And Fighting Back," *Bloomberg BusinessWeek*, September 18, 2004, http://www.businessweek.com/stories/2004–09–19/fed-up-and-fighting-back.

Bibliography

Adams Family Correspondence. In *Founding Families: Digital Editions of the Papers of the Winthrops and the Adamses*, ed. C. James Taylor. Boston: Massachusetts Historical Society, 2007. http://www.masshist.org/ff/.

Address of the President of the United States, September 30, 1918. Washington, DC: U.S. Government Printing Office, 1918.

Antilla, Susan. *Tales from the Boom-Boom Room: Women vs. Wall Street.* Princeton: Bloomberg Press, 2002.

Barkley Brown, Elsa. "Constructing a Life and a Community: A Partial Story of Maggie Lena Walker," *OAH Magazine of History*, Vol. 7, No. 4 (Summer 1993): 28–31.

Barkley Brown, Elsa. "Womanist Consciousness: Maggie Lena Walker and the Independent Order of Saint Luke." *Signs*, Vol. 14, No. 3 (Spring 1989): 610–33.Bell, Gregory S. *In the Black: A History of African Americans on Wall Street.* New York: John Wiley & Sons, 2002.

Berkin, Carol R. and Clara M. Lovett, eds. *Women, War and Revolution.* New York: Holmes & Meier, 1980.

Blackwell, Jon. "She Banked on Trenton." *The Capital Century 1900–1999* (reprinted from *The Trentonian*). http://www.capitalcentury.com/1937.html.

Blackwell, Jon. "The Governor Was a Thief." *The Capital Century 1900–1999* (reprinted from *The Trentonian*). http://www.capitalcentury.com/1954.html.

Blair, Emily Newell. *The Woman's Committee, United States Council of National Defense: An Interpretative Report, April 21, 1917 to February 27, 1919.* Washington, DC: Government Printing Office, 1920.

Blair, Karen J. *The Clubwoman as Feminist: True Womanhood Redefined, 1868–1914.* New York: Holmes & Meier Publishers, Inc., 1980.

Branch, Muriel Miller Branch and Dorothy Marie Rice. *Pennies to Dollars: The Story of Maggie Lena Walker*. North Haven, CT: Linnet Books, 1997.

Brooks, John. *Once in Golconda: A True Drama of Wall Street 1920–1938*. New York: Harper & Row, 1969.

Brooks, John. *The Go-Go Years*. New York: Weybright and Talley, 1973.

Buck, James E., ed. *The New York Stock Exchange: Another Century*. Lyme, CT: Greenwich Publishing Group, Inc., 1999.

Burstyn, Joan N., ed. *Past and Promise: Lives of New Jersey Women*. Syracuse: First Syracuse University Press, 1997.

Calvert Investments, Inc. "Calvert & SRI: History and Leadership." http://www. calvert.com/sri-history.html.

Cammack, Key. "High Finance." *Cosmopolitan*, Volume L, December 1910–May 1911. New York: International Magazine Company, 1911.

Carr, Lois Green. *Margaret Brent—A Brief History*. Maryland State Archives, February 7, 2002. http://www.msa.md.gov/msa/speccol/sc3500/sc3520/002100/002177/html/mbrent2.html.

Clarke, Ida Clyde. *American Women and the World War*. New York: D. Appleton and Company, 1918. http://net.lib.byu.edu/estu/wwi/comment/Clarke/Clarke00TC.htm.

Cleary, Patricia. *Elizabeth Murray: A Woman's Pursuit of Independence in Eighteenth-Century America*. Amherst, MA: University of Massachusetts Press, 2000.

Clews, Henry. *Fifty Years in Wall Street*. New York: Arno Press, 1973. First published 1908 by Irving Publishing Company.

Clinton, Catherine and Christine Lunardini. *The Columbia Guide to American Women in the Nineteenth Century*. New York: Columbia University Press, 2000.

Cohen, Abby Joseph. Interview by Karen Gibbs. *Wall Street Week with Fortune*, PBS, October 4, 2002.

Cohen, Manuel F. "Address of Chairman." Speech, Securities and Exchange Commission, Women's Bond Club of New York, NY, December 13, 1968.

Collins, Gail. *America's Women: Four Hundred Years of Dolls, Drudges, Helpmates, and Heroines*. New York: William Morrow/HarperCollins, 2003.

Cook, Bernard A., ed. *Women and War: A Historical Encyclopedia from Antiquity to the Present*, Vol. 1. Santa Barbara: ABC-CLIO, 2006.

Cook, Elizabeth Ellsworth. "Opportunities for Women in Finance." *Journal of the Association of Collegiate Alumnae*, Vol. XI, No. 5 (January 1918): 289–94.

Cott, Nancy F., ed. *No Small Courage: A History of Women in the United States*. Oxford: Oxford University Press, 2000.

Croly, J.C. *The History of the Woman's Club Movement in America*. New York: H.G. Allen, c. 1898.

De Pauw, Linda Grant. *Founding Mothers: Women of America in the Revolutionary Era*. Boston: Houghton Mifflin Company, 1975.

Domini, Amy. Commencement Speech, Northfield Mount Hermon School, Mount Hermon, MA, May 28, 2008.

Domini, Amy. Interview by Tavis Smiley. *Tavis Smiley Show*, PBS, May 24, 2005.

Domini, Amy. Praxis Award Acceptance, Villanova University, Villanova, PA, March 31, 2009.

Domini, Amy. *Socially Responsible Investing: Making a Difference and Making Money*. Chicago: Dearborn Trade, 2001.

Domini, Amy. "Sustainability Investing, Green Investing, Socially Responsible Investing, What's Going On Here?" Speech, FRA Family Offices Conference, Aventura, FL, May 21, 2008.

Domini, Amy and Alisa Tang. "A Son with a Conscience." reprinted from *New York Times*, 2009. Accessed March 13, 2012. http://www.amydomini.com/ason.

Domini, Amy L. with Peter D. Kinder. *Ethical Investing*. Reading, MA: Addison-Wesley Publishing Company, 1984.

Dumenil, Lynn. "American Women and the Great War." *OAH Magazine of History*, Vol. 17, No. 1 (October 2002): 35–7.

Ehrlich, Judith Ramsey and Barry J. Rehfeld. *The New Crowd: The Changing of the Jewish Guard on Wall Street*. Boston: Little, Brown and Company, 1989.

Ellebracht, Pat. "Riding the Rails with Madam Railroad." *Financial History*, Issue 67–1999 III, 20–25, 34.

Endlich, Lisa. *Goldman Sachs: The Culture of Success*. New York: Alfred A. Knopf, 1999.

Faulk, Patricia. "Gender and Power in the 20th Century: Mary G. Roebling, Pioneer Banker." PhD diss., University of Pennsylvania, 1992.

Federal Reserve Bank of Richmond. *Walker Leaves Lasting Legacy*. http://www.richmondfed.org/publications/education/maggie_walker/pdf/mwalker.pdf.

Fisher, Anne B. *Wall Street Women: Women in Power on Wall Street Today*. New York: Knopf, 1990.

Fisher, Melissa S. *Wall Street Women*. Durham and London: Duke University Press, 2012.

Foust-Cummings, Heather, Sarah Dinolfo, and Jennifer Kohler. "Sponsoring Women to Success." Catalyst, 2011. http://www.catalyst.org/file/497/sponsoring_women_to_success.pdf.

Freeman, Landa M., Louise V. North, and Janet M. Wedge, eds. *Selected Letters of John Jay and Sarah Livingston Jay*. Jefferson, NC: McFarland & Company, 2005.

Frisken, Amanda. *Victoria Woodhull's Sexual Revolution: Political Theater and the Popular Press in Nineteenth-Century America*. Philadelphia: University of Pennsylvania Press, 2004.

Gabriel, Mary. *Notorious Victoria: The Life of Victoria Woodhull, Uncensored*. Chapel Hill: Algonquin Books of Chapel Hill, 1998.

Geisst, Charles R. *Wall Street: A History*. New York: Oxford University Press, 1977.

Gilbert, Lynn and Gaylen Moore. *Particular Passions: Talks with Women Who Have Shaped Our Lives*. New York: Clarkson N. Potter, 1981.

Gildersleeve, Genieve N. *Women in Banking: A History of the National Association of Bank Women*. Washington, DC: Public Affairs Press, 1959.

Gillis, Christine. "Memoir of the Women Stockbrokers' Association." New York Stock Exchange Archives, Manuscript Collections, 2000.

Goldsmith, Barbara. *Other Powers: The Age of Suffrage, Spiritualism, and the Scandalous Victoria Woodhull*. New York: Knopf, 1998.

Goldstein, Joshua S. *War and Gender: How Gender Shapes the War System and Vice Versa*. Cambridge, UK: Cambridge University Press, 2001.

Gordon, John Steele. *The Great Game: The Emergence of Wall Street as a World Power 1653–2000*. New York: Scribner, 1999.

Gunther, Marc. *Faith and Fortune: How Compassionate Capitalism Is Transforming American Business*. New York: Crown Business, 2004.

Hegewisch, Ariane, Cynthia Deitch, and Evelyn Murphy. *Ending Sex and Race Discrimination in the Workplace: Legal Interventions that Push the Envelope*. Washington, DC: Institute for Women's Policy Research, 2011.

Henderson, Archibald. *North Carolina Women in the World War*. Chapel Hill: University of North Carolina at Chapel Hill, 2002. Original edition Raleigh North Carolina: North Carolina Literary and Historical Association, 1920. http://docsouth.unc.edu/wwi/henderson/henderson.html

Herera, Sue. *Women of the Street: Making It on Wall Street—The World's Toughest Business*. New York: John Wiley & Sons, 1997.

The Historical Society of Pennsylvania. *South Philadelphia Women's Liberty Loan Committee Records 1917–1919 (Collection 217)*. Philadelphia: The Historical Society of Pennsylvania, 2004.

Holton, Woody. *Abigail Adams*. New York: Free Press, 2009.

Holton, Woody. "Abigail Adams, Bond Speculator." *The William and Mary Quarterly*, Vol. 64, No. 4 (October 2007): 821–38.

Johnston, Johanna. *Mrs. Satan: The Incredible Saga of Victoria C. Woodhull*. New York: G. P. Putnam's Sons, 1967.

Jones, Vivien, ed. *Women and Literature in Britain, 1700–1800*. Cambridge, UK: Cambridge University Press, 2000.

Kessler-Harris, Anne. *Out to Work: The History of Wage-Earning Women in the United States*. Oxford: Oxford University Press, 1983.

Kinder, Peter D., Steven D. Lydenberg, and Amy L. Domini. *Investing for Good: Making Money While Being Socially Responsible*. New York: HarperBusiness, 1993.

Klein, Maury. *Rainbow's End: The Crash of 1929*. Oxford: Oxford University Press, 2003.

Knaak, Marissa and Megan Soe. "Female Investment in America from the 18th Century to the Great Depression." *Financial History* (Winter 2012): 14–16, 38.

Koman, Rita G. "Servitude to Service: African-American Women as Wage Earners." *OAH Magazine of History*, Vol. 11, No. 2, Labor History (Winter 1997): 42–9.

Korten, Alicia Epstein. *Change Philanthropy: Candid Stories of Foundations Maximizing Results through Social Justice.* San Francisco: Jossey-Bass, 2009.

"The Ladies' Deposit" in *The School Herald: A History of 1881.* Chicago: W.I. Chase, 1882.

Lewis, Arthur H. *The Day They Shook the Plum Tree.* New York: Harcourt, Brace, 1963.

Lucht, Tracy L. "Sylvia Porter: Gender, Ambition, and Personal Finance Journalism, 1935–1975." PhD diss., University of Maryland, 2007.

Mackay, Charles. *Memoirs of Extraordinary Popular Delusions and the Madness of Crowds.* 1852. Project Gutenberg, 2008. http://www.gutenberg.org/files/24518/24518-h/24518-h.htm.

Marens, Richard. "Inventing Corporate Governance: The Mid-Century Emergence of Shareholder Activism." *Journal of Business and Management*, Vol. 8, No. 4 (Fall 2002): 365–89.

Marlowe, Gertrude Woodruff. *A Right Worthy Grand Mission: Maggie Lena Walker and the Quest for Black Economic Empowerment.* Washington, DC: Howard University Press, 2003.

Marsh, Melissa A. "The Purest Patriotism: The Domestic Sphere and the Ladies Association of Philadelphia." http://www.history1700s.com/articles/article 1097.shtml.

Mayo, Anthony J. and Shandi O. Smith, "Maggie Lena Walker and the Independent Order of St. Luke." HBS No. 9–409–057 (Boston: Harvard Business School Publishing, 2008; revised 2011). *Harvard Business Online.* http://harvardbusinessonline.hbsp.harvard.edu/.

McCullough, David. *John Adams.* New York: Simon & Schuster, 2001.

Mompoullan, Chantal. *Voice of America Interviews with Eight Women of Achievement.* Washington, DC: United States Information Agency, 1985.

Monks, Robert A. G. and Nell Minow. *Corporate Governance* (Fourth Edition). West Sussex, UK: John Wiley & Sons, 2008.

Nanda, Ashish and Kristin Lieb. "Abby Joseph Cohen: A Career Retrospective." HBS No. 9–903–118 (Boston: Harvard Business School Publishing, 2003; revised June 9, 2003). *Harvard Business Online.* http://harvardbusinessonline.hbsp.harvard.edu/.

Newell, Margaret Ellen. *From Dependency to Independence: Economic Revolution in Colonial New England.* Ithaca, NY: Cornell University Press, 1998.

New York Stock Exchange Archives. "Early Minority Women NYSE Members"; "Women's Milestones at the NYSE," "Women's Milestones at the Amex." Historical Notes; Women in Wall Street Press Relations/Public Information Files.

Norton, Mary Beth. *Liberty's Daughters: The Revolutionary Experience of American Women, 1750–1800*. Boston: Little, Brown & Company, 1980.

Office of History and Preservation, Office of the Clerk. *Women in Congress, 1917–2006*. Washington, DC: U.S. Government Printing Office, 2007.

Parker, Keith W. "The Involvement of 'The Ladies' Economic Support of Women During the American Revolution." *Early America Review* (Summer/Fall 2006). http://www.earlyamerica.com/review/2006_summer_fall/women-revolution.html.

Plakas, Rosemary Fry. "The Sentiments of an American Woman." *Library of Congress*. http://memory.loc.gov/ammem/awhhtml/awhendp/index.html.

[Reed, Esther deBerdt]. *The Sentiments of an American Woman*. Philadelphia: John Dunlap, 1780.

Renehan, Jr., Edward J. *Commodore: The Life of Cornelius Vanderbilt*. New York: Basic Books, 2007.

Report of the Secretary of the Treasury on the State of the Finances for the fiscal year ended June 30, 1918 with appendices. Washington, DC: U.S. Government Printing Office, 1919.

Riley, Glenda. *Inventing the American Woman: An Inclusive History, Vol. 2: Since 1877*. Wheeling, IL: Harlan Davidson, 2001.

Roberts, Cokie. *Founding Mothers: The Women Who Raised Our Nation*. New York: William Morrow, 2004.

Robertson, Nancy Marie. "'The Principles of Sound Banking and Financial Noblesse Oblige': Women's Departments in U.S. Banks at the Turn of the Twentieth Century." In *Women and Their Money 1700–1950*, edited by Anne Laurence, Josephine Maltby, and Janette Rutterford. London and New York: Routledge, 2009.

Ross, Ishbel. *Charmers & Cranks: Twelve Famous American Women Who Defied the Conventions*. New York: Harper & Row, 1965.

Roth, Louise Marie. *Selling Women Short: Gender and Money on Wall Street*. Princeton: Princeton University Press, 2006.

Sachs, Emanie. *The Terrible Siren: Victoria Woodhull*. New York: Arno Press, 1972. First published 1928 by Harper & Brothers.

Salmon, Marylynn. *Women and the Law of Property in Early America*. Chapel Hill: University of North Carolina Press, 1986.

SEC Women Commissioners Roundtable. SEC Headquarters, Washington, DC, May 31, 2006. http://bit.ly/NXlHwV.

Selmi, Michael L. "Sex Discrimination in the Nineties, Seventies Style: Case Studies in the Preservation of Male Workplace Norms." *Bepress Legal Series*, 2003. http://law.bepress.com/expresso/eps/53.

Shachtman, Tom. *The Day America Crashed: A Narrative Account of the Great Stock Market Crash of October 24, 1929*. New York: G.P. Putnam's, 1979.

Siebert, Muriel. "Investing in Women and Girls." Address, United Nations, New York City, March 6, 2008. http://www.un.org/events/women/iwd/2008/docs/siebert.pdf.

Siebert, Muriel with Aimee Lee Ball. *Changing the Rules: Adventures of a Wall Street Maverick*. New York: The Free Press, 2002.

Siebert Financial Corp. Dec. 31, 2011 Form 10-K. Filed March 30, 2012. EDGAR Online. http://www.sec.gov/Archives/edgar/data/65596/00013544 8812001532/n12381_10-k.htm.

Silcox-Jarrett, Diane. *Heroines of the American Revolution: America's Founding Mothers*. Chapel Hill: Green Angel Press, 1988.

Slack, Charles. *Hetty: The Genius and Madness of America's First Female Tycoon*. New York: Harper Perennial, 2004.

Sobel, Robert. *The Great Bull Market: Wall Street in the 1920s*. New York: W. W. Norton & Company, 1968.

Social Investment Forum Foundation. 2010 Report on Socially Responsible Investing Trends in the United States. http://www.socialinvest.org/resources/research/documents/2010TrendsES.pdf.

Sparkes, Boyden and Samuel T. Moore. *The Witch of Wall Street: Hetty Green*. Garden City, NY: Doubleday, Doran & Company, 1930.

Spencer Stuart. "Women in Asset Management." March 2005. http://content.spencerstuart.com/sswebsite/pdf/lib/Women_in_Asset_Mgmt_Mar05.pdf.

Stewart, James B. *Den of Thieves*. New York: Simon & Schuster, 1991.

Stiles, T. J. *The First Tycoon: The Epic Life of Cornelius Vanderbilt*. New York: Alfred A. Knopf, 2009.

Texas Bankers Association. "Proceedings of Women's Convention." *Texas Bankers Record*, Volume 6, June 1917.

Texas State Historical Association. "Martin, Anna Henriette Mebus." *The Handbook of Texas Online*. http://www.tshaonline.org/handbook/online/articles/fmaax.

Thomas, Dana L. *The Plungers and the Peacocks: 150 Years of Wall Street*. New York: G. P. Putnam's Sons, 1967.

Thomas, Gordon and Max Morgan-Witts. *The Day the Bubble Burst: A Social History of the Wall Street Crash of 1929*. Garden City, NY: Doubleday, 1979.

Ulrich, Laura Thatcher. *Good Wives: Image and Reality in the Lives of Women in Northern New England, 1650–1750*. New York: Knopf, 1980.

Underhill, Lois Beachy. *The Woman Who Ran for President: The Many Lives of Victoria Woodhull*. Bridgehampton, NY: Bridge Works Publishing Co., 1995.

U.S. Bureau of the Census. "1870 Census." http://www.census.gov/prod/www/abs/decennial/1870.html.

U.S. Department of Labor, Women's Bureau. "Women in the Labor Force in 2010." http://www.dol.gov/wb/factsheets/Qf-laborforce-10.htm.

U.S. Department of the Treasury, Bureau of the Public Debt. "The Volunteer Program and Series E Savings Bonds." Last updated October 16, 2007. http://www.treasurydirect.gov/indiv/research/history/history_ebond.hm.

U.S. Equal Employment Commission. Notice N-915–050, March 19, 1990. Last modified June 21, 1999. http://www.eeoc.gov/policy/docs/currentissues.html.

U.S. Government Accountability Office. "Financial Services Industry: Overall Trends in Management-Level Diversity and Diversity Initiatives, 1993–2008." GAO-10–736T. Released May 12, 2010. Accessed April 5, 2012. http://www.gao.gov/new.items/d10736t.pdf.

U.S. Treasury Department. "Report of National Women's Liberty Loan Committee, Fourth Liberty Loan Campaign." September 28 to October 19, 1918. Washington, DC: Government Printing Office, 1918.

U.S. Treasury Department. "Women in Finance Symposium." March 29, 2010. http://www.treasury.gov/press-center/Video-Audio-Webcasts/Pages/Webcasts.aspx.

U.S. Treasury Department. *Women's Work in War Finance 1941–1945*. Washington, DC: Government Printing Office, 1946.

Varnell, Jeanne. *Women of Consequence: The Colorado Women's Hall of Fame*. Boulder, CO: Johnson Books, 1999.

Wachtel, Howard M. *Street of Dreams-Boulevard of Broken Hearts: Wall Street's First Century*. London and Sterling, VA: Pluto Press, 2003.

Walker, Maggie. "An address to the 34th Annual Session of the Right Worthy Grand Council of Virginia, Independent Order of St. Luke." Richmond, VA, August 20, 1901.

Walsh, Julia Montgomery with Anne Conover Carson. *Risks and Rewards: A Memoir*. McLean, VA: EPM Publications, Inc., 1996.

Ware, Susan and Stacy Braukman, eds. *Notable American Women: A Biographical Dictionary Completing the Twentieth Century*. Cambridge, MA: Harvard University Press, 2004.

Washington, Booker T. *The Negro in Business*. Boston: Hertel, Jenkins & Co., 1907.

Wilson, Woodrow. *Request for Declaration of War, Address Delivered at a Joint Session of the Two Houses of Congress, April 2, 1917*. Washington, DC: Government Printing Office, 1917.

Woloch, Nancy. *Women and the American Experience*. New York: Alfred A. Knopf, 1984.

"Women in U.S. Finance." Catalyst, December 2011. http://www.catalyst.org/publication/504/women-in-us-finance.

"Women of Wall Street." Museum of American Finance. New York, June 2009–March 2010.

Wood, Mary I. *The History of the General Federation of Women's Clubs for the First Twenty-Two Years of Its Organization*. New York: History Department, General Federation of Women's Clubs, c.1912.

Woodhull, Victoria C. "A Speech on the Principles of Finance." Lecture, Cooper Institute, New York City, August 3, 1871; reprinted in Madeleine Stern, B., ed. *The Victoria Woodhull Reader*. Weston, MA: M&S Press, 1974.

Wright, Robert E. *Hamilton Unbound: Finance and the Creation of the American Republic*. Westport, CT and London: Greenwood Press, 2002.

Wright, Robert E. "Women and Finance in the Early National U.S." *Essays in History*, Vol. 42 (2000).

Wulf, Karin. *Not All Wives: Women of Colonial Philadelphia*. Ithaca, NY: Cornell University Press, 2000.

Zuckoff, Mitchell. *Ponzi's Scheme: The True Story of a Financial Legend*. New York: Random House, 2005.

Index

An expansive list of Leading Ladies starts on page 187.

About the Author

Sheri J. Caplan earned her B.A. in history from Yale, where she was co-publisher of the *Yale Daily News*, and her J.D. from the University of Virginia School of Law, where she was Executive Editor of the *Virginia Journal of International Law* and a Dillard Fellow, a faculty-appointed legal writing teaching assistant. She served as Vice President, Derivative Finance, for Lehman Brothers Inc. and subsequently as Vice President and Assistant General Counsel at Goldman Sachs. She presently serves as a securities arbitrator for the Financial Industry Regulatory Authority and is a member of 85 Broads, a women's networking organization originally comprised of Goldman Sachs alumnae.